RISE AND DEFEND

A HISTORY OF THE UNITED STATES AIR FORCE
AT MANSTON
1950–1958

DUNCAN CURTIS

FLIGHT
RECORDER
PUBLICATIONS

A passion for accuracy

First published in Great Britain in 2006 by
Flight Recorder Publications Ltd
Ashtree House, Station Road, Ottringham,
East Yorkshire, HU12 0BJ
Tel: 01964 624223
E-mail: beketley@btinternet.com
Website: www.flight-recorder.com
© 2006 Flight Recorder Publications Ltd

ISBN 0 9545605 5 8

Edited by Barry Ketley
Artwork by David Howley
Design by Flight Recorder Publications Ltd
Printed in EEC

ALSO AVAILABLE

AIR WAR OVER EAST YORKSHIRE IN WORLD WAR II
by
Paul Bright
ISBN 0 9545605 7 4

AUSTER
A Brief History of the Auster Aircraft in British Military Service
by
Barry Ketley
ISBN 0 9545605 6 6

THE LONG DRAG
A Short History of British Target Towing
by
Don Evans BEM
ISBN 0 9545605 4 X

KURT TANK'S PHOTO ALBUM 1940-1943
by
Roy Powell & Barry Ketley
ISBN 0 9545605 3 1

THE WARLORDS
US Eighth Air Force Fighter Colours of World War II
Volume 1
The 4th, 20th & 55th Fighter Groups
by
Barry & Ann Money
ISBN 0 9545605 1 5

A CIVILIAN AFFAIR
A Brief History of the Civilian Aircraft Company of Hedon
by
Eduard F. Winkler
ISBN 0 9545605 0 7

FORTHCOMING

WEKUSTA
Luftwaffe Weather Reconnaissance Units & Operations 1938-1945
by
John Kington & Franz Selinger
ISBN 0 9545605 8 2

CHECKERBOARD HUNTERS
The Croatian Volunteers of 15./JG 52 on the Eastern Front
by
Marko Jeras, Dragisa Brasnovic & Zdenko Kinjerovac
ISBN 0 9545605 2 3

Caption to title page: One of a number of 406th FIW Sabres displayed at airshows in 1957, 52-10061 of 514th FIS was shown at Prestwick in May. (Author's collection).

FOR TANYA

CONTENTS

3: A formal portrait of Major-General Hugh B. Manson. His medal ribbons denote the award of, from left to right, top to bottom: Purple Heart with oak leaf cluster; Air Medal; Air Force Presidential Unit Citation; American Defense Service Medal; American Campaign Medal with star; Asiatic-Pacific Campaign Medal with two stars; World War II Victory Medal; Army of Occupation Medal; National Defense Service Medal and the Longevity Service Award Ribbon with oak leaf cluster.

FOREWORD
Major-General Hugh B. Manson

The author has done a remarkable job of tracing the USAF history at Manston. He has depicted the American military in a warm and honest manner that brought to sudden life memories that I would not have recalled. The buildings, the people, the runways, the aircraft, the Channel, all suddenly became real again. And the deafening roar of the jets in afterburner climbing after take-off. It is no wonder the local population finally decided that enough noise was too much.

The author of this history has my utmost respect for telling it like it was, at least while I was there; July 1955 to July 1958, including Napoleon Green,

Rees-Davies, the Mayors of Ramsgate and Margate and the pilots. I saw a different side to Manston; problems inherent in 3,000 foreigners locked up in a foreign country—but that takes nothing away from the book.

Hugh Manson
Major-General, Retired
406th FIW
Commanding Officer
Manston, 1955-58

ACKNOWLEDGEMENTS

This book would not have come about without the great assistance of the following: First and foremost, my good friend the late Pete Hutting, ex-512th FIS, who was always willing to spend time listening to my questions, and kept me supplied with all sorts of information. Secondly to Mike Fox, who gave me the inspiration to 'do it right'. Milt Torres, leader of the Manston Reunion organisation and ex-514th FIS Sabre pilot also helped a great deal. Frank J. Brehm, formerly of 156th FBS and 512th FBS did much research into the USAF records at Maxwell AFB, Alabama. Finally, Dave McLaren, my Stateside contact, also provided a wealth of information in the early stages of this book.

In addition, over the years, the following people have taken the time to sit down and write to me, in answer to my thousands of questions, and their help has been beyond measure: Mrs. Ethel Abbott (wife of Hardy Abbott, 512th FIS), Sam Adams (92nd FBS), Alyce Ankney (wife of Darrell Ankney, 66th ARS), Gene Armstrong (31st FMS and GE Tech. Rep.), Jack Austin (92nd FBS), Jerome R. Barnes (513th FIS), Max Beasley (514th FIS), Col. Bernard B. Berklund (USAF Safety Agency), Dick Bingaman (512th FBS), Duane E. 'Bud' Biteman (514th FIS), Tom Blakey (513th FIS), Jay Blanco (514th FBS/FIS), Elliot F. Bouck (561st FEW), Cal Bricker (79th FBS), Bob Brinker (92nd FBS), H. Cowles Bristol, Jr. (406th FIW), Larry Brooks (Lear Tech Rep), Paul B. Byrum (514th/513th FIS), Drury Callahan (514th FIS), Roy Cantey (79th FBS), David G. Collyer, W. Richard Craig (514th FIS), Charles M. Crawford (165th FBS), Chris Dadds (Culham/Harwell Press Officer), Col. George Daughtry (513th FBS/FIS), Alex Davis (123rd FBW/406th FBW), Judy Duignan (66th ARS), Albert Farnes (31st FEW), Aldon P. Ferguson (Burtonwood Association), Dick Forsgren (514th FBS), Paul R. Fry (123rd FBW and 513th FBS), Richard T. Grace (156th FBS and 512th FBS/FDS), Walter G. Gutman (513th FIS), Rodger Hatfield (513th FIS), Conrad J. Herlick (406th FIW CO), William H. Holt (406th FIW), Robert Hoover (North American Aviation), Roy E. Jacobsen (USAF Air Rescue Association), Robert Jacobson (12th FEW), John M. Jennings (123rd MS), Roy E. Jennings, Jr. (512th FBS), Alan Johnson of Air Britain, Bill R. Jones (79th FBS), Michael J. Kelly, Jr. (66th ARS), Alfred F. Kemnitz (514th FS WWII), Gregory I. Kirkwood (123rd FBW/406th FBW), Rob Lautzenhiser (Hughes Tech. Rep.), Scottie H. McHenry (9th ARS Flight 'A'), George McNally (559th FES and 3917th ABG), Hugh B. Manson (406th FIW CO), Milt Markowitz (167th FBS/514th FBS), Glenn W. Mayer (406th FIW), John H. 'Hank' Meierdierck (31st FEW),

Dave Menard (USAF Museum), Chuck Metz (87th and 512th FIS), Larry Milberry (Author of 'Canadair Sabre'), Richard J. Montgomery (513th FIS), Bill Moss (512th FIS), G. J. Naber (513th FIS), Clifford W. Nelson (513th FIS), Gale Nelson (3917th ABG), Jack H. Owen (123rd FBW/406th FBW), Bob Page (12th FEW), George W. Pennick (USAFE Historian), Gordon F. Peters (513th FIS), Jack Phelps (123rd FBW), Bill Plunk (513th FIS), Dave Roberson (514th FBS/FIS), Richard B. Saich (9th ARS), Ken Schanke (406th FG WWII historian), John G. Schmidl (406th TFTW Historian), Jim Shankles (92nd FBS), Donald C. Sidak (167th FBS and 514th FBS/FIS), Max E. Skirvin (156th FBS/512th FBS), Forrest E. Smith (156th FBS/512th FBS), Jack H. Smith (167th Squadron WV ANG Historian), Ed Spencer (406th FIW), Herbert H. Stone (92nd FBS), David B. Tharp (3917th Ops Sqn), Bill Thomasson, Bob Thomasson (513th FIS), Robert G. Trentman (3917th ABG), Bob Van Arsdall (66th ARS), Jay W. Vandertoll (514th FIS), Frederick L. Vess (9th ARS, 66th ARS), Col. Al Vette (66th ARS), Wayne R. Viets (513th FIS), William Vogel (156th FBS/512th FBS), Bob & Pauline Wagner (513th FIS), Lt Col. Noble L. Webster, Jr. (9th ARG), Lt Col Richard T. White (513th FIS), Wayne & Deirdre Wick (406th MVS), Bob Williams (31st FEW), Mrs Betty Wright and Robert 'Zeb' Zbornak (513th FIS).

4 Above: *Reconditioned Bristol Fighter F4500 of No. II Squadron served with the unit when it was based at Manston between late 1927 and November 1929 when it began to re-equip with the Armstrong-Whitworth Atlas. The triangle on the fin may indicate the second flight as the squadron traditionally writes its number as 'II' not '2'. F4500 ended its days with No. 3 Squadron.*

INTRODUCTION
Manston and the RAF

The vast airfield at Manston, which is nowadays grandly titled 'Kent International Airport' grew from humble beginnings during the First World War. The Royal Naval Air Service (RNAS) spotted the large flat area of land outside Ramsgate in 1915, and began to use it as a landing field for their aircraft. Initially manned by just two naval airmen, operating from a solitary wooden hut, Manston Landing Ground was further built up in early 1916, with the addition of two sheds and one temporary hangar. At this point, aircraft on anti-Zeppelin raids from the airfields at Westgate and Detling were using Manston as a forward operating base.

In March 1916, as a result of gale damage and its dangerous location, the cliff-top aerodrome at Westgate, 1½ miles (2.4km) west of Margate, was abandoned. The aircraft were transferred to Manston, with the Avro 504Bs and Curtiss JN3s from 'A' Flight, No. 2 Squadron, RNAS moving in straight away, followed a few months later by the War Flight. In addition, the Sopwith 1½ Strutter biplanes of No. 3 (Aeroplane) Wing used Manston for its Zeppelin-hunting patrols. These arrivals marked the start of a great build-up of personnel, machinery and buildings at Manston, which became a Permanent Station in 1917. The training of Air Mechanics also commenced on the airfield and workshops and training buildings soon took shape to support the influx.

The Royal Air Force (RAF) officially came into being on April 1 1918, and the nascent RAF quickly established a three-squadron day bomber-training wing at Manston. By September 1918 there were 2,500 personnel stationed on the airfield, which now covered an area of 680 acres. Additionally, over 100 aircraft were permanently based there, including De Havilland DH 9s and Sopwith Camels. The cessation of hostilities in the First World War inevitably saw a decrease in activity at Manston, but this was offset with the arrival during the winter of 1919-1920 of the School of Technical Training from Halton in Buckinghamshire. May 1921 saw the arrival of No. 6 Flying Training School from Spitalgate, and it immediately set about the task of training pilots prior to their dispatch overseas. This unit was, however, disbanded less than a year later.

No. 2 Squadron's Bristol Fighters arrived from RAF Andover early in 1924 and would remain for the next six years alongside the Vickers Virginias of No. 9 Squadron. The School of Technical Training (SoTT) became No. 3 SoTT in July 1935, and was increased in size to reflect the expansion of the RAF. During the inter-war period, RAF and Fleet Air Arm (FAA) aircraft used Manston, and on the outbreak of the Second World War in September 1939, there were two squadrons of FAA Fairey Swordfish torpedo bombers operating from the base. Manston was soon recognised to be an ideal location for short-legged fighter aircraft, and as a result, on 15 November 1939 the airfield was transferred to RAF Fighter Command, and became home to the Hurricanes of No. 79 Squadron. The squadron later returned to its former base at Biggin Hill, though a detachment remained at Manston. The Blenheim 1Fs of No. 600 Sqn, based at Hornchurch were detached to the airfield from October 1939, and the squadron became permanently-based before the end of the year, by which time it was flying the Blenheim IV.

During the early part of the War, detachments of Hurricanes and Spitfires from Nos. 32, 54, 65 and 79 Squadrons utilised Manston as a forward operating base. 12 August 1940 saw the first major German attack when Messerschmitt 110s and Dornier 17s bombed the airfield. Damage was fairly serious, but operational flying resumed within 24 hours. It should be remembered that aircraft were still operating from two grass runways at Manston during the early war years; one of 4,800 feet (1,463m) in length, and the other slightly longer at 5,700 feet (1,737m). When damaged Allied bombers began to divert to Manston in large numbers from 1942 onwards, the case for laying a permanent runway was further strengthened.

On 15 June 1943, work finally commenced on constructing a proper runway. To cater for the many expected diversions, the paved area would be 750 feet (228m) wide, and 9,000 feet (2,743m) long — one of the longest in the country. In total, 370,000 cubic yards of soil had to be removed, and was replaced by 379,000 square yards of concrete, which was laid seven inches thick. Almost one year after work commenced, on 5 April 1944, Manston's newly completed runway was used for the first time. Emergency landings began almost immediately, with 56 logged by the end of April. Another feature installed into the runway was Fog Investigation and Dispersal Operation (FIDO) equipment. This consisted of a system of pipework, running either side of the runway, through which petrol was pumped, which could be ignited at intervals to 'burn off' fog. FIDO enabled numerous aircraft, short on fuel or badly shot-up to reach terra firma safely, and had saved 122 Allied aircraft by the War's end.

The latter stages of the War saw Typhoons and Mosquitos flying from the base, and the RAF's first jet-equipped fighter unit, No. 616 Sqn with Meteors, began operations from Manston in July 1944. In September of that year nearly a hundred Horsa gliders arrived at Manston, towed in by Armstrong-Whitworth Albemarle bombers. They departed, fully laden with soldiers, for the Arnhem landings on 17 September. By now, the tide was turning in the Allies' favour, and the War would soon be over. Manston became the short-term host to numerous squadrons during this period, which were either on their way to bases in Europe, or were returning to the UK as their services were no longer required. At the beginning of 1945, there were six squadrons based at Manston, flying Spitfires, Mosquitos and Meteors. Considerable upheaval occurred as the War ended, and on VE Day there were two squadrons of Mosquitos, a Czech/RAF Wing with Spitfires and an FAA Barracuda squadron using the airfield. By the end of the year, this had shrunk to only one flying unit, the RAF's No. 567 Squadron, which flew a mixture of Oxfords, Spitfires and Vultee Vengeances for anti-aircraft gunnery practice.

In peacetime, Manston became an RAF and Civil Customs Aerodrome on 1 April 1946, and was given the title of No. 91 Staging Post. Transfer to 46 Group, RAF Transport Command, was approved on 15 July 1946 and for the next few years the airfield became temporary home to many RAF aircraft being delivered overseas by No. 1 Overseas Ferry Unit (OFU), which finally departed the Station in July 1950. So ended the large-scale RAF use of Manston — for a few years at least — but the United States Air Force (USAF) would take over where the RAF had left off, and the next nine years would see the base's busiest period.

5: *Sopwith Camel B6230 served with the War School at Manston in early 1918 until early in May, by which time the unit had become a Pilot Pool. Earlier, the aircraft had had a distinguished career with Naval 9 Squadron, with whom it had been used to shoot down five enemy aircraft.*

6: *This 55th FBS Thunderjet was pictured visiting an RAF base during the squadron's first deployment to England. Colours consisted of blue nose scallop, blue band around tail and the group badge on the vertical fin. (Paul Cooper)*

[1] The USAF came into being as an independent force on 18 September 1947, replacing the United States Army Air Force (USAAF). At the same time, the Army Air Field (AAF) title was changed to Air Force Base (AFB).

THE 20TH FIGHTER-BOMBER GROUP
'Victory by Valor'

The United States Air Force (USAF)[1] had retained many aircraft in the European Theatre since the end of World War Two, but regular tours of Temporary Duty (TDY) for Stateside-based units began only in late 1946, as a result of two incidents which underlined the growing rift between East and West. On 9 August 1946, fighter aircraft shot down a USAAF C-47 transport on the run from Vienna to Udine in Italy, when it crossed unintentionally into Yugoslavia. Although no one was seriously hurt on this occasion, ten days later the crew of another C-47 were killed under similar circumstances. As a show of force, the USAAF immediately deployed six B-29 Superfortress bombers of the 43rd Bomb Group (BG) from Davis Monthan Army Air Field (AAF) in Arizona, to Rhein-Main Field in West Germany.

B-29 detachments to the UK began in June of 1947, when nine aircraft from the 340th Bomber Squadron (BS), based at Smoky Hill AAF, Kansas arrived at RAF Marham. The visit was largely a goodwill gesture and the bombers only remained for a week. By this time, however, the Soviet Union was well advanced in the production of its own long-range bomber, the Tupolev Tu-4, later codenamed 'Bull' by NATO. The Tu-4 was a direct, reverse-engineered copy of the B-29, based upon three USAAF aircraft that had force-landed in Soviet territory in July and November 1944. Its introduction into Soviet Air Force service justified the deployment of USAAF/USAF B-29s to Europe. In addition to their deterrent capabil-

ity, the B-29 deployments gave RAF and USAAF/USAF fighter pilots experience in intercepting the visually-similar Tu-4 bomber.

Early in 1948, the USAF began a concerted effort to permanently station a Bomb Group of B-29s in the UK. Manston, with 9,000 feet (2743m) of runway, was viewed as an ideal base for the bombers, having been prepared by the RAF for B-29 deployments since 1946. Indeed, as a demonstration of its suitability, two Superfortresses from the 301st BG landed at the Kent airfield on 16 February 1948 after completing their first practice mission with RAF fighters. The lack of facilities at Manston did, however preclude its permanent use by the USAF for the moment at least, and better-equipped bases in East Anglia were brought into use after upgrading, while Oxfordshire was viewed as providing an ideal location for four other airfields.

By June of 1948, an outline agreement had been made to station ten B-29s in the UK for training exercises, and these aircraft would be based at Marham from July 1948. However, the blockade of Berlin by the Soviets on 24 June made these plans largely irrelevant, and to emphasise their resolve, the American and British governments agreed on the immediate deployment to the UK of two B-29 bomb groups, with a total of sixty aircraft, to be followed by another bomber group soon after. On 17 July 1948, aircraft from the three squadrons of the 28th BG, Rapid City AFB began arriving at RAF Scampton in Lincolnshire.

The 307th BG from MacDill AFB in Florida took up station at Marham, with some aircraft based at Waddington. Finally, at the beginning of August, the 2nd Bomb Group moved into Lakenheath from its base at Davis Monthan AFB. In November 1948, three fresh Bomb Groups arrived to relieve the three resident B-29 units, and throughout 1949 and into the early part of 1950, Superfortress deployments continued, and those from B-50-equipped Wings were initiated.

By the end of 1949, £350,000 had been spent on modernising UK airfields for use by the USAF. Further to this, three major Anglo-American agreements were signed to ensure that any cost of further development to USAF bases in the UK was jointly shared. First off, on 15 April 1950 an 'Ambassador's Agreement' was signed by US Ambassador Lewis Douglas and UK Under-Secretary for Air, Aidan Crowley. This paved the way for the construction of bomber bases for the USAF at Brize Norton, Fairford, Greenham Common and Upper Heyford. Secondly, a settlement on special constructions, signed in February and April 1951 revised the programme for works services, and allowed a £35 million budget to be shared between the two governments. Gen. Johnson of Third AF and Air Chief Marshal Dickson for the Air Ministry signed this declaration. Finally, a Cost-Sharing Agreement was signed on 9 September 1953, which stated that costs up to a value of £45 million would be shared evenly, but any further development costs over this figure would be paid in full by the US government. By 28 February 1956, the British Government had already committed £21.56 million of its £22.5 million 'share'.

At the start of 1950, no USAF fighters had yet been deployed to the UK, but events across the globe would soon change that. At 0400 hours on Sunday 25 June 1950, the communist North Korean People's Army streamed south into the Republic of Korea. The invasion — though instigated by the North Koreans under Kim Il Sung — was fully approved by Joseph Stalin, albeit after many months of consideration. Within hours, in-theatre USAF combat squadrons were on the move to counter the North Koreans, but the Korean War would prove to be a drawn-out affair, and resulted in the need for further USAF deployments across the World to counter other anticipated communist aggression elsewhere. Part of that requirement was for the stationing of an F-84 Thunderjet Wing on TDY at RAF Manston.

The notion of deploying a USAF Fighter Wing to the UK had been formulated as early as 15 May 1950, when the RAF Chief of Air Staff was informed by memo that twenty-five F-84s could be based at Manston from 1 July for a period of 60 days, to be replaced by a similar USAF unit after that time. On 9 July 1950, Lord Tedder in Washington cabled the Defence Committee in London to inform them of the USAF desire to base a Fighter Wing and two Medium

Bomb Wings in the UK. As the British Government had by all accounts anticipated this, they were ready to make a fast decision. Less than 24 hours after receiving Tedder's message, the Committee announced that bombers would go to Mildenhall in Suffolk, and fighters to Manston. On 14 July 1950, Manston was transferred to the control of No.11 Group, RAF Fighter Command and within a day, the first B-50D bombers from the 93rd BW arrived at Mildenhall. On 15th July the advance detachment of men from the USAF Strategic Air Command's 7512th Air Base Squadron (ABS) arrived at Manston to prepare the base for the arrival of the F-84 fighter wing. 7512th ABS, formed on 11 July, would undertake day-to-day administrative running of the station and ensure a modicum of continuity despite the prospect of many rotational Fighter Wings passing through the base. On 25 October 1950, the unit was upgraded to Air Base Group (ABG) status, and remained at Manston until 16 May 1951 when it was inactivated. On the same day, 3917th ABG was activated at Manston to take over the duties of the outgoing Group. The 3917th, under Base Commander Col. F.J. Schuck, would keep overall control of Manston until its departure in 1954.

Though envisaged as a stop-gap measure, the USAF presence at Manston would be maintained for nearly eight years. Initial deployments to the base would be temporary, but the British Government was in favour of the permanent stationing of USAF aircraft in the UK. In a memo to the Cabinet dated 23 February 1950, the Defence Minister had urged the Labour government under Clement Attlee to accept the permanent deployment of USAF aircraft to the UK. In the event, the first permanently based combat Wing (as distinct from the TDY units) was not assigned until September 1951. In the build-up of USAF Europe forces during the early 'fifties, personnel in-theatre grew from 35,120 at the end of 1950 to 136,475 in only five years. During the same period, numbers of USAF aircraft based in Europe rose from 371 to 2,096. Manston played a key role in these critical years of what would become known as The Cold War.

In order to provide some sort of command structure for the control of USAF units in Great Britain, the USAF 3rd Air Division (Provisional) had been activated at RAF Marham in July 1948. Initially this organisation exercised operational control over the B-29 TDY units which generally stayed in the UK for periods of 30 to 60 days. However, the Berlin Crisis brought home to military planners the fact that this situation was unlikely to be temporary, and on 23 August 1948, the 'Provisional' tag was dropped from the 3rd AD's title. Further to this, the Division moved its headquarters temporarily to Bushey Park in Middlesex during the following month, before relocating to more spacious and permanent facilities at South Ruislip in Middlesex on 15 April 1949. In March 1951, Strategic Air Command activated the 7th Air

Division at South Ruislip, and this organisation took over control of deployed bomber units. By this time, 3rd AD had begun to receive fighter squadron attachments, and the prospect of increasing numbers of permanently based USAF Wings in the UK following a large airfield construction programme led to the upgrading to 'Air Force' status. Thus, on 1 May 1951, the 3rd AD title was inactivated and replaced by that of the Third Air Force. The Third AF was assigned to Headquarters USAF Europe, and charged with the control of tactical and logistical activities in Britain.

On 1 July 1950, the 20th Fighter Bomber Wing (FBW) based at Shaw Air Force Base in South Carolina, received notice of a move to Great Britain as part of Project 'Ready' — the dispatch of a Fighter Group to the UK to back up Strategic Air Command (SAC) bomber units based there on TDY. The move would involve flying all of the 20th Fighter Bomber Group (FBG) Republic F-84D Thunderjet aircraft to the UK, whilst the ground personnel would be moved by C-54 and C-74 aircraft of the Military Air Transport Service (MATS). The TDY was scheduled to last 90 days, with the Group returning in mid October, and this generally fell in with the RAF plans outlined in May 1950. The 20th would be based — as expected — at Manston, and it was planned that another F-84 unit would replace the Group after its 90-day TDY.

Republic Aviation, the manufacturer of the F-84, was put on overtime working to cope with spares shortfalls prior to the move. Not only were they now producing spares to support the 20th FBG on an overseas deployment, but the USAF would soon also be required to resupply two F-84 groups in Germany from September 1950, with a further Thunderjet group deploying to the Korean Theatre in November. During the following months, the F-84 spares situation would be seriously stretched. Fortunately, 20th FBG had been flying various models of the F-84 since February 1948, and had enough experienced personnel to reduce the effects of these shortages.

From a maintenance standpoint, these supply problems made preparations much more difficult. One of the main tasks performed on the Thunderjets was the fitting of 230-gallon F-84E-type wing-tip fuel tanks to the Group's older F-84Ds. This later style of tank incorporated a small fin on its outer rear edge, which enabled the Thunderjet to reach maximum speed without danger of twisting loads stressing the wing. The modification, which was initially carried out only as a stop-gap measure proved so successful that these fuel tanks were retained on all 20th FBG F-84Ds. Many aircraft had their Allison J35 engines replaced prior to the move, and the task of fitting modified A1B gunsights and inverters to aircraft was begun. Alas, the lack of spares was again a problem and resulted in the shipping of twenty-seven gunsights by sea, direct from the manufacturer to the UK for fitment there. In addition, two technical representatives were sent to Manston to assist in their

fitting, and would also set up training sessions and help 20th Maintenance Squadron personnel in building gunsight test stands. All F-84Ds were put through a 100-hour inspection before departure for Manston.

The pilots from the 20th FBG's three Fighter Bomber Squadrons (FBS): the 55th, 77th and 79th, had been training for deployment for some time, and earlier in 1950 had undertaken a long-range overwater navigation exercise in preparation. Nonetheless, the flight to Manston would test their skills to the fullest. As a rescue aid during the ferry flight, 20th FBW Headquarters had requested that Air Material Command supply AN/URC emergency radio sets for the F-84 pilots during the deployment. The 20th was informed that the allocation of these pocketsize sets had been prioritised by HQ USAF, (Korea again) and none could be issued until early 1951! This would not be an easy deployment.

The F-84D Thunderjet

The Republic F-84 resulted from a USAAF request, placed in 1944, for a jet-powered development of the famous P-47 Thunderbolt fighter. This idea eventually proved impractical, but from the same request, Republic Aircraft Corporation came up with the P-84[2]. Designed by the talented Chief Engineer Dr. Alexander Kartveli, with assistance from aerodynamicist C. E. 'Gus' Pappas, the prototype XP-84 took to the air for the first time on 28 February 1946. This first flight from Republic's Farmingdale, New York facility, was flown by Major Wallace A. Lien, who, in February 1944, as a Captain in the USAAF, had become the first military pilot to fly the XP-80 Shooting Star.

Of fairly conventional layout, the P-84 had tricycle landing gear, a nose intake for its Allison J35 engine and short, straight wings. 16 pre-production YP-84As were followed by 226 P-84Bs, which had more powerful, 4,000 lb.(1778kg)-thrust engines, six .50-calibre machine guns and an ejection seat. However, due to their unreliability, use of the ejection seat was prohibited! First deliveries of the P-84, by now officially named 'Thunderjet' began in mid-1947. The P-84B was followed on the production line, logically by the P-84C. This aircraft brought numerous improvements, including electrical and hydraulic system modifications, and inner-wing pylons to enable bombs to be carried. 191 P-84Cs were produced.

The F-84D that followed into production was a far more effective aircraft. The previous models of Thunderjet were, by 1948, being phased out as a result of their unreliability and lack of engine power. This was a problem throughout the F-84's career, USAF personnel joking that; "If a runway was built around the World, Republic would build an airplane to use all of it". The -D model was designed to overcome these failings, and introduced a 5,000 lb. (2224kg)-thrust version of the J35 engine, which ena-

7: *48-753 was the personal F-84D of group commander Col John A. Dunning, seen here in the cockpit during an engine start en route to Manston. Coloured nose bands were blue, red and yellow, signifying the three squadrons within the group. S/Sgt Ken Dunton looks on. (Bill R Jones)*

8: *The start of it all. 20th FBG Thunderjets line up at Goose Bay, Labrador on 22 July 1950 during the group's deployment to Manston. Third aircraft in line, 48-770, later served in Korea and was lost in action there on 10 May 1952. Nearest aircraft are from 55th FBS. (Bill R Jones)*

9: *Basic conditions on the 'loop' dispersal at Manston, summer 1950; aircraft are parked on bare earth. Aircraft at right is 48-723, which was lost in the English Channel along with pilot Lewis R. Striegle on 5 August 1950. (Bill R Jones)*

10: *World War II-era nissen huts abounded at Manston and were heavily utilised by the USAF units there. This group were located on the 'loop' dispersal. Nearest hut is Building 336; the line of huts on the right in the background were situated along the western edge of Hangar 4. (Cal Bricker)*

11: *Radio repair men pose in front of the 79th FBS communications shack, L-R: J. Baird, S. White, J. Murrell and J. J. Labuda. Sheepskin jackets are noteworthy. (Bill R Jones)*

12: *Sqn Ldr Cal Bricker was the only non-USAF pilot to fly with the 20th FBG at Manston. He is seen here in standard working dress on Manston's 'loop' dispersal during the summer of 1950. Coincidentally, Cal had flown Spitfire XIVs into Manston with 79 Sqn during the War. Nissen hut at rear is one of a row (Buildings 336, 337, 338 and 800) located to the southwest end of Hangar 4. (Cal Bricker)*

bled wing skins to be thickened for increased structural strength. At this time, a fully equipped F-84D cost $250,000, and with full tanks, had a range of 1,485 miles. This made it an ideal bomber escort, and it was with this model that the 20th Fighter Bomber Group would deploy to England in 1950. Upon their return from England in late 1950/early 1951, the majority of the 20th FBG's F-84Ds were sent back to Republic for strengthened wing leading edges to be fitted. Eventually, it was decided to upgrade these F-84s by fitting the J-35A-17B engine, along with the addition of AN/APX-6 IFF equipment. Thus modified, these aircraft began to roll out of Republic's modification line in July 1951, under the designation F-84D-11.

On Thursday 20 July 1950, the seventy-five F-84Ds took to the skies over South Carolina, and flew north en route to Manston. Their mission, code-named 'Fox Able 2' took them initially to Otis AFB in Maine, where the Group arrived 2 hours and 10 minutes later. A further day was spent in Maine, the aircraft travelling on to Goose Bay in Labrador on 22 July — 2 hours 20 minutes flying time away. Following a nightstop at Goose Bay, it was on to Bluie West One in Greenland, where the majority of the Group arrived on 23 July. This leg took 1 hour and 50 minutes. After a two-day delay due to weather, the aircraft flew on to Keflavik in Iceland (2 hours and 15 minutes), and to UK landfall at RAF Kinloss on 26 July (2 hours and 5 minutes). The final leg of 1 hour and 20 minutes took the F-84s into Manston, where the first group of 54 aircraft arrived on 26 July 1950. Throughout the whole deployment, the meteorological forecasting for each leg had been particularly accurate, with only 1 hour and 25 minutes flown in 'weather'. One pilot was killed on 26 July during the deployment phase, when he had to bail out of his F-84D (48-726) over the iceberg-strewn waters of the Davis Strait on the leg into Bluie West One. Despite the fact that he was wearing his immersion suit, and was only in the water a matter of minutes before being picked up by the Weather Ship, he sadly died of hypothermia.

A small number of maintenance personnel had flown in transport aircraft ahead of the Thunderjets along the route to render technical assistance at each fuel stop. The remainder of the 20th FBG personnel travelled to England by boat, ahead of the flying echelon, 80 lorry loads of personnel and equipment arriving at Manston on 18 July alone.

One unusual member of the USAF detachment was Squadron Leader Cal Bricker, on loan to the 20th FBG from the Royal Canadian Air Force. As Cal relates, the early days at Manston often relied upon the resourcefulness of the personnel on base to overcome problems that would be considered trivial elsewhere:

"I was a Royal Canadian Air Force [RCAF] exchange pilot — the RCAF, RAF and USAF had an aircrew exchange programme. I was not a liaison of-ficer or 'observer', I was for all intents and purposes a USAF pilot in the 79th Squadron, 20th Fighter Bomber Group, flying the F-84 Thunderjet. Where they went, I went. They went from Shaw AFB, South Carolina, via the North Atlantic in July 1950, so did I. I landed at Manston on the 26 July 1950 and departed Manston 4 December 1950, the same days as the Group".

"On arrival at Manston, I didn't remember much of it from the times I had been in and out (never stationed) during wartime in a Spitfire XIV. On my arrival with 79th Squadron the allocation of my quarters led to an argument with the chap responsible in the Officers' Mess. He insisted on a room [for me] in the Mess proper, by reason of my exalted (to him) rank. I won the discussion and joined 79th Squadron pilots in a temporary, low wooden, officers for the use of, building near the Mess".

"On arrival, the Group was confronted with aircraft dispersals around the airfield and a shortage of ground transport, [with] a long walk from one part of the 'field to another. So, the Captain in charge of ground transport went into town and contracted civilian buses. They were almost immediately running a scheduled route and times around the Station".

The three squadrons were located such that the 55th and 77th occupied the main airfield area, whilst the 79th FBS were dispatched to the 'loop' dispersal on the north east side of the airfield. As the aircraft parking areas consisted of pierced steel plate (PSP) standings laid directly onto the bare earth, the thick Kentish mud was ever present, and working conditions were basic at best. The squadron aircraft wore fairly simple markings comprising of a curved noseband, which swept aft under the fuselage, and upwards and slightly rear of the machine-gun muzzles. Each noseband was coloured for the particular squadron that the aircraft belonged to: blue for the 55th FBS, red for the 77th FBS and yellow for the 79th FBS. Col. Dunning's aircraft was painted with three stripes on the nose to reflect all three squadron colours on the Group commander's aircraft.

Flying began immediately, and with it the loss of aircraft and crews. At the beginning of August, two of the Group's Thunderjets were lost in accidents. 48-723 crashed into the sea three miles south-east of Deal on the 5th, killing the pilot, Lewis R. Striegle. Three days later, aircraft 48-787 landed short at Manston and was also destroyed; pilot John J. Walsh escaped this time.

By late August of 1950, the civilian population around Manston was already complaining of the noise caused by low-flying Thunderjets. The RAF Station Commander, Group Captain Rankin, told the local Town Clerks that the situation was unavoidable, but the complaints persisted, and some years later, the sheer weight of protest against aircraft from Manston would force its abandonment by the USAF.

The USAF personnel of the 20th FBG had a busy time during their tenure at Manston. Cal Bricker again:

"After we had been there a while, there was an official welcome Ceremony. A stage was adorned by RAF Marshals and USAF Generals of various ranks. The Guest of Honour was Mr. Douglas, United States Ambassador to the Court of St. James, Mrs. Douglas and their daughter. The 'troops' were gathered on the floor in front of the stage — not a parade".

"The Squadron pilots visited an RAF aircraft control centre (GCI) [Ground Controlled Intercept] for a tour of the facility, and to meet the controllers who we only knew as voices in the earphones. We were very impressed with the operation. Our official tour was followed by an RAF/USAF game of softball — we had brought the bats and balls. Partway through the game cricket balls were allowed — players and spectators had a ball. Possibly the supply of beer near home plate added to the hilarity".

"We also went by bus to an RAF Station for a day of familiarization with the Martin-Baker ejection seat. It was like a day at the fair with rides free. After the briefings on the principle and operation of the seat we headed for the outdoor demonstrator. A pilot was strapped in a seat, as in a cockpit, [and] pulled down a blind over his face. This activated the propulsion explosives, and the seat and pilot were blown up vertical rails, duplicating — as much as possible — the real thing. A Lieutenant known for his insistence on always being first in everything bet one and all that he would go higher than anyone else. Bets were made and money entrusted to a stake holder".

"His turn arrived and he was strapped in and pulled down the blind. The charge went off and up the rails he went — to the 3-foot level, short by about 15 feet of the average. Pulling up the blind, he was

13: *Cal Bricker shows off his rubberised 'poopy suit' just prior to return to Shaw AFB, December 1950. These suits were worn by all 20th FBG pilots en route to and from Manston and were designed to give vital minutes of survival in the freezing Atlantic waters. Note C-54 transport in background. (Cal Bricker)*

eye to eye with an appreciative and somewhat richer audience, busily pocketing pound notes. With the co-operation of the RAF NCO in charge, the explosives had been reduced!"

On 5 September, 77th FBS F-84D, 48-710, overshot the runway at Waterbeach and was damaged beyond economical repair; it was officially written off four days later. Pilot Charles A. King escaped without injury. At the time of 48-710's accident, the Group had been based at Waterbeach for a short period to perform intercepts with B-29s, and again used the airfield for a few days at the end of September. Another 20th FBG F-84D (48-754, Charles E. Wilson) was lost in a head-on collision with an RAF Meteor (VW431) near Marham on 14 September; both pilots were killed.

In the first three months of its detachment to Manston, 20th FBG concentrated on the training syllabus. 1,338 hours were flown in July, rising to a peak of 2,612 in August, and reducing to 1,602 hours in September. On 16 September, F-84Ds from Manston flew a display for RAF West Malling's 'At Home' day, in front of 10,000 spectators. This was possibly the first public display of a USAF aircraft in this country. At about this time it was learnt that the ninety-day TDY, originally due to end in October, had been extended and 20th FBG would not return home until at least 1 December. But, despite the obvious decrease in morale, the Group would be ready for the annual UK air defence exercise in October.

One notable event which occurred during September was the arrival at Manston of two EF-84E Thunderjets, piloted by Lt. Col. Dave Schilling and his close friend Lt. Col. William Ritchie. The two pilots were attempting an east-west Atlantic crossing record by using in-flight refuelling. Departure date of the mission that became known as *Fox Able Four* was initially set at 20 September 1950, but the flight was aborted after Schilling's in-flight refuelling probe was damaged during the first tanker fill-up, near Scotland. Following repair, on Friday 22 September the two aircraft left Manston at 2.01 in the afternoon to start the first non-stop crossing of the Atlantic by jet aircraft. After departing the Kent airfield, the pair flew their aircraft up to the west coast of Scotland, reporting overhead Prestwick at 3.08 PM, then continuing north to intercept 'Camelback 1', the first refuelling link-up. With a full fuel load, the F-84s then set course for Iceland. Problems in refuelling the aircraft in flight led Lt. Col. Ritchie to bail out over Newfoundland, but Schilling managed to make landfall at Limestone, Maine (rather than his planned destination in Long Island). The total time for the epic flight was ten hours and two minutes — a record for the crossing. Dave Schilling would return to Manston in late May of 1951 as the commander of the 31st Fighter Escort Wing.

Exercise *Emperor* started on 7 October, and lasted just over a week. A 'warm-up' period from 2-7 October preceded the exercise, which was designed to test the UK's air defence system under central control. Much of the exercise consisted of UK-based B-29s and B-50s attempting to 'attack' mainland targets. As bomber escorts, the Thunderjets of 20th FBG were in the thick of it, the Group committing one squadron of 16 fighters to the exercise. The RAF also provided bombers and escorts, in the shape of Lincoln, Wellington, Valetta, Mosquito, Spitfire and Vampire aircraft. On 11 October, B-50 bombers flew a mission to Millwall docks in London. F-84s from the 20th escorted the raiders, but were separated when RAF fighters attacked the formation. The next night, Millwall was again targeted, and their escorts were again in action. In general, the RAF attacks were unsuccessful in getting through the escorts to attack the bombers — so long as the latter had a height advantage. If, however, the RAF fighters had the height advantage, they had little trouble in separating the escorts from the bombers and pressing home their attacks.

At 4.50PM on 13 October, B-29 42-63750 from the 718th Bomb Squadron diverted into Manston en route from Wiesbaden Air Base in Germany to the supply depot at Burtonwood. This was the first time that bomber and escort had met on the ground at Manston. The B-29 departed next day. On missions carried out on the 14 October, the Thunderjets from the 20th FBG came up against many RAF Meteors again. During the course of Exercise *Emperor*, which ended on 15 October, the 20th FBG F-84Ds had flown 52 bomber escort missions, and learnt a few lessons during their realistic sorties against the RAF. 79th FBS, as an example, flew missions on 5, 7, 8, 10, 11, 14 (two), and 15 October, each intercept sortie lasting between 50 minutes and 1 hour 10. Sadly, the exercise was marked by the tragic loss of six lives after a mid-air collision near the Thanet coast. An RAF Wellington bomber with four on board slammed into a Belgian Air Force Mosquito, killing its crew. The Wellington came down near the Reculver Towers; the Mosquito crashed into the sea four miles off Margate.

Exercise *Emperor* was considered to have been of dubious value, owing to a number of factors. It was thought that because of the small number of escorts available, any conclusions drawn from the many interceptions were of little relevance. In any case, it was recognised that the UK air defence system was at no time over-stretched, though the post-exercise report did suggest more training on interception techniques, for both pilots and fighter controllers. Finally, and significantly, the exercise had highlighted the inadequacy of the RAF's all-weather fighter force. The effects of this shortfall would soon be felt at Manston.

It was on one mission during October 1950 that Cal Bricker had a rather unusual — and alarming — experience:

"In October, I was detailed to lead a night flying formation. After briefing we headed to our aircraft.

I climbed the ladder into the cockpit and was getting strapped in with the help of the crew chief. I turned to say something to him, but he was gone, replaced by a very large individual holding a .45 automatic, pointed at my head. The holder of the weapon ordered me out of the aircraft. As discussion under the circumstances was futile, I climbed out".

"On the tarmac I was met by more armed service police. I found myself in a vehicle between two heavily armed men of very large size. On arrival at the guardroom, I was ordered into a room that held two chairs — one for me and the other for yet another armed gentleman. By this time I was really worried, as no one would tell me anything. After what seemed like hours of silence (it was only minutes), the door opened and in came a Lt Colonel. He looked at me and said, 'Take him to his aircraft', and left. I never saw him before or after. The delayed flight went off, albeit a little late. I never did find out why I was detained".

This frightening episode does not cloud Cal's memories of Manston, or of the 20th. As he says,

"The 20th FBG, 79th Squadron pilots and other trades were a professional, highly motivated enthusiastic organization — a privilege and pleasure to be a part of. The Group had Esprit de Corps".

Throughout his time at Manston, Cal Bricker flew one aircraft, 48-711, in all but two of his 57 missions from the base, and this was not unusual. These missions were generally less than two hours in duration, and were evenly spread between formation navigation, instrument flying, fighter sweeps, QGH, interceptions and night flying.

To support the spares consumption of the 75-aircraft 20th Fighter Bomber Group, the maintenance personnel had made up 30-Day Kits prior to departure from Shaw AFB, containing all spare parts required to supply the aircraft for an average 30 day period. With the critical supply problems in the UK, it was now realised that without these kits, the mission of the 20th FBG would have been severely curtailed. In addition to these problems, as a result of insufficient cargo flights during the initial deployment, the majority of the 20th's target tow equipment was left Stateside, and air-to-air gunnery training was affected as a result. The spares situation resulted in lower in-commission rates for the aircraft, and from 1,712 hours flown in October (a large portion on missions supporting Exercise *Emperor*), only 602 hours were flown in November. Another major cause of the decrease in flying hours was that severe cracking had been found in the wing skins of many of the Group's F-84s. Repairs took a long time to effect, and temporary 'fixes' were made, generally by 'stop-drilling' small holes at the extremities of each crack to prevent further propagation. It was arranged to have all aircraft pass through Republic's factory at Farmingdale upon return to the US, for full rectification to be carried out. In the event, around 34 of the Group's Thunderjets were returned to the manufacturer.

The situation in Eastern Europe was highlighted by an event that was played out at Manston on the afternoon of Saturday 7 October 1950. Earlier that day, a Czechoslovakian civil Dakota aircraft had taken off from Prague's Ruzyne Airport, supposedly for a test flight. Those on the Dakota had only one thought, however — to escape the effects of Stalin's grip on Czechoslovakia and flee to the West. Aboard were not only the airline's chief test pilot, Capt. Jan Kaucky, an ex-RAF WWII flyer, but also two other pilots — Captains Prchal and Rechka. Others aboard included Kaucky's two year-old son Josef and daughter Eda, Prchal's British-born daughter, two other pilots, their wives and a civilian. Turning for the West after take-off, Capt. Kaucky had soon found himself flying over occupied Germany, and also discovered that fighter planes had intercepted his aircraft. Fortunately, these aircraft proved to be from the American Occupation force, and after a five minute look over the Dakota, peeled away to land. Kaucky then turned for the safety of England and brought his Dakota in to land at Manston. The RAF Station Commander, Group Captain Rankin, was on the tarmac to meet the aircraft, which had by now been declared missing by the Czech authorities. Rankin was surprised to see a familiar face among the crew of the Dakota — that of Captain Prchal. The two officers had been wartime colleagues at the same airfield. After spending four days in secrecy at Manston, all those aboard the Czech Dakota were taken to London to contact the Free Czech Organisation and seek asylum.

Meanwhile, the 20th FBG's detachment to the UK did not proceed without further serious accidents. On 20 November an F-84D from the 55th FBS (48-762) was on a QGH letdown into Manston after a routine mission, when transmissions from the aircraft suddenly stopped. The pilot simply went off the air and was not heard from again. Immediately, a large air and sea search was put into effect, which included aircraft from the RAF's 19 Group and the USAF 9th Air Rescue detachment at Manston, along with the Walmer and Ramsgate lifeboats, but no trace of man or machine was ever found. It was thought that the pilot had become unconscious and lost control of his aircraft, sending it into the icy depths of the English Channel. A similar crash had occurred on 5 August, when 48-723 was lost in the Channel along with the pilot. Ironically in July, the 55th FBS had received mention in the *Air Force Times* for their 5,301 flying hours of accident-free flying. Two other pilots and their aircraft were lost over Germany during an exercise on 7 September; one of the F-84Ds crashed near Fürstenfeldbruck, the other 22 miles west of Stuttgart. Photos of these accidents adorned the Operations Hut flying safety notice board, alongside such sobering phrases as; "You'll get more than a sneer when you fail to lower your gear" and "When flying low, don't fly slow".

By late 1950, the personnel of the 20th FBG were getting thoroughly fed up with the constant changes to their TDY expiry dates. Cal Bricker relates that:

"At this time it looked like we'd be spending Christmas in Olde England. So, in the spirit of Yuletide, a deciduous tree outside the billet was adorned with the only decorations available — empty beer cans".

The 1 December deadline for return to the USA came and went, and it was not until 4 December that the first personnel and aircraft left Manston by air for Prestwick, Scotland and home to Shaw AFB. The last of the Group's F-84Ds departed on the 10 December, retracing the route they had flown nearly six months earlier. The first three Thunderjets arrived back at Shaw AFB on 18th December, routing from Goose Bay to Dow AFB, Maine and through Andrews AFB in Maryland. Cal Bricker was one of that trio, and was met by a throng of Air Force personnel and families on the tarmac at Shaw. One wife, eager to greet her husband, declared upon seeing the first arrivees step from their aircraft, "Wouldn't you know, they're all bachelors"! As with the departure to the UK, maintenance crews were on hand at each stop to service the aircraft.

Almost immediately, Manston became home to another F-84 unit, the 31st Fighter Escort Wing, whose aircraft arrived in the first week of 1951. The 20th FBW would continue flying its F-84s in the United States, and in May 1952, returned to the UK — this time equipped with the vastly improved F-84G model. The 20th would initially be based at RAF Wethersfield in Essex, and would remain in the UK for over 40 years — the longest-serving USAF unit in Great Britain.

20th FBW Commanders - Manston era

20th FBW (USA):
Col. Phineas K. Morrill, Jr.

20th FBG TDY (Manston):
Col. John A. Dunning

55th FBS (Manston):
Lt. Col. William A. Mitchell, Jr.

77th FBS (Manston):
Lt. Col. Dean Davenport

79th FBS (Manston):
Capt. Richard F. Jones

14: First three pilots to return to Shaw AFB are greeted by Col Phineas K Morrill, 18 December 1950. Pilot with 'bone dome' is thought to be Capt. Bean, and next to him Cal Bricker. Aircraft is 48-794, a 79th FBS machine (Cal Bricker)

15: An element of 307th FES Thunderjets depart on another sortie. Aircraft at left is 49-2053, which was lost in Luxembourg during December 1951. (via Dave McLaren)

16: 49-2121 was an 'A' Flight aircraft, probably with blue-trimmed 309th FES. Aircraft is taxiing through standing water on bare earth. (Al Farnes)

THE 31ST FIGHTER ESCORT WING

The boys from Georgia

On 8 December 1950, the 31st Fighter Escort Wing (FEW) and its three squadrons, the 307th, 308th and 309th Fighter Escort Squadrons (FES), based at Turner AFB in Georgia, received a telex which gave warning notice that the Wing would deploy to RAF Manston in England for an indefinite period of temporary duty (TDY). This kind of TDY invariably lasted one day less than six months, as families could legally accompany USAF personnel on TDY for longer, 'definite' periods. The 31st FEW was equipped with the F-84E Thunderjet.

More detailed movement orders arrived at Wing Headquarters on 9 December. The 2nd AF Operations Order detailed how the unit would be required to be ready to deploy from 'X' day, 14 December 1950. A core of personnel (later known as the 31st FEW (Rear), and comprising around 35 officers and 220 airmen) would remain at Turner AFB for the duration of the period of TDY, along with the Wing's TF-51D Mustangs, some C-47s, T-33s, T-6Ds and two F-84Es. During March of 1951, the 108th Fighter Wing (ANG), with their F-47D/Ns would arrive at Turner, requiring specialist assistance and training from the men of the 31st FEW (Rear). Additionally, these personnel assisted in bringing facilities up to scratch in preparation for the TDY party's return.

The Wing Mobility Plan, which had been drawn up for just this kind of contingency, was found to be lacking in several areas. The most notable was that the Plan provided for airlift by ten C-54 aircraft, whereas the 2nd AF Operations Order allowed for only seven. In addition to this, the Plan was originally drawn up for movement of 625 personnel and 275,000 lbs. (122,330kg) of cargo, but, in practice 740 personnel and 295,000 lbs. (131,227kg) of cargo would need to be moved. Some juggling of personnel and equipment was made, and the deployment was carried out in accordance with revised Mobility Plan 2-50.

The route to be flown by the Wing's assigned aircraft, comprising seventy-four F-84Es and a C-47 was as follows: from Turner, the Wing would route to Otis AFB in Massachusetts — Goose Bay, Labrador; — Bluie West One, Greenland; — Keflavik, Iceland, and finally on to Manston. The T-33 trainers, as a result of their shorter range, would fly from Turner to McGuire AFB, New Jersey; — Dow AFB, Maine; — Goose Bay; — Bluie West One; — Keflavik; — Prestwick, Scotland, to Manston. Minimum weather for all legs was 2,000 feet (609m) ceiling and 3 miles (4.9km) visibility, while the leg to Bluie West One (the difficult leg) required a 5,000 feet (2224m) ceiling. Lakenheath and Waterbeach were designated as alternate airfields within UK, but not surprisingly, there were no alternatives between the Canadian and Icelandic coasts.

Prior to the move, there was much maintenance activity required to bring the aircraft to a safe condition for overseas deployment. The first problem to be resolved concerned the F-84E's powerplant, the Allison J35A-17, which was proving to be unsuitable for use in a long-range escort fighter. The J35 lubrication system was originally designed to dump used engine oil overboard during flight, and this was a system which worked fine for short-duration flights, but longer missions would undoubtedly lead to the engine oil supply simply running out, followed swiftly by engine failure. F-84s had previously been grounded in early July 1950 until a solution could be reached.

Fortunately, Allison had devised a modified Oil Mist Lubrication System to bring consumption down to an acceptable limit. In order to pass these engine modifications as fit for use, 31st FEW assisted in one of the fastest Accelerated Service Test programs achieved up to that point by flying five of its F-84Es fitted with the modified engine, by now designated the J35A-17A. Two other Air Force units also took part in the tests; Air Material Command (AMC) at Wright-Patterson AFB, Ohio and 27th FEW at Bergstrom AFB, Texas.

In addition to the engine problems, it had been known for some time that the bubble-type cockpit canopy of the F-84 was prone to explode when the aircraft was flying at altitude. In an effort to discover how bad the problem would affect 31st FEW, the entire Wing flew a test sortie on 21 December 1950. During this test flight, four canopies exploded. Sadly, during the same sortie, Lt Col. Bascom A. Brooks, 31st Fighter Escort Group commander, was killed when his aircraft crashed. Col. E.H. Dunham was therefore recalled from the Air War College to lead the 31st's Thunderjets across the Atlantic. As a result of the disastrous canopy test, on 22 December an emergency telex was sent to Air Material Command in an attempt to rectify the situation. The result was a recommendation that canopies on all seventy-four F-84Es possessed by the Wing would be replaced with a strengthened version, which outwardly resembled the earlier type.

On 23 December, the process of changing the canopies was begun. 20 civilian personnel from Warner Robins Air Material Area (WRAMA) in Georgia were assigned to Turner AFB, and augmented the personnel of the maintenance section, as well as many of the Wing pilots, who turned out to assist. They were tasked with setting up a production line to modify canopy bubbles, and the reinforced items were brought in by air to fulfil this requirement. The Maintenance Section began a 24-hour work schedule to bring all aircraft up to standard, and in only 3 days, all seventy-six F-84Es had been fitted with the modified canopy. The Engine Build-Up Section built and installed approximately fifteen J35A-17A engines during the month, whilst a further eighteen were assembled for dispatch to the UK as spares. In addition, the Electrical and Instrument section carried out a gunsight inverter modification to all 74 of the aircraft being deployed. Lack of aircraft spares added to the problems faced by the Wing, to such an extent that one F-84 was put aside for cannibalization. The remains of this aircraft (49-2104) were eventually transported to the Mobile Air Material Area during February 1951 for repair and rebuild.

Several F-84Es, newly assigned to the Wing had to be painted in the squadron colours, and this took up much of the time for the paint shop, who were keenly assisted by the Thunderjet crews themselves. 31st FEW Thunderjets had a very distinctive colour scheme, which consisted of a painted ring around the air intake in the squadron colour, to the rear of which was an area of black-on-natural metal checks, bordered by a thin curved band in the squadron colour. This colour was also echoed on the tip of the vertical stabiliser, and on the tip tanks, where an arrow shape was painted. The squadron colours were red for the 307th, yellow for the 308th, and blue for the 309th. Most of the maintenance personnel had departed for Manston on 15 December, and this repainting was made more difficult, along with all the other maintenance tasks, such as winterization of the F-84s, as a result of the limited manpower available. It was a great credit to those who remained at Turner AFB that the aircraft were ready for deployment on time. Many of these men worked an 18-hour day. Then, as now, the spanner men were the unsung heroes of such achievements. Their Christmas would be one to forget!

The F-84E Thunderjet

The 31st FEW and subsequent Thunderjet wings at Manston utilised the F-84E Thunderjet, which followed the F-84D down the production lines after only 154 of the former model had been completed. The F-84E was extended 12 inches (33cm) in the cockpit area to provide more room for taller pilots, making the more spacious aircraft easier to fly on long missions. Powerplant for the E model was the J35A-17 engine, the -17B being retrofitted later in the Thunderjet's career. An improved Sperry radar-ranging gunsight and the ability to carry thirty-two 5-inch unguided rockets upgraded the weapons capability. Retractable racks for Jet Assisted Take Off (JATO) rockets rounded off the major additions. In all, 843 F-84Es were made, and after use by USAF and the Air National Guard, many were flown by NATO countries, such as Belgium and Holland. Aircrews had mixed feelings about the E-model. Frank Brehm of the 156th FBS:

"...the F-84E was underpowered and slow. It was very heavy and was supposed to perform a double duty: fighter-bomber. At best, it could only carry 500-lb [222kg] bombs, needed at least three miles of runway to take off, and would come out second best in a dogfight. I can remember some of your [RAF] boys used to get at high altitude, and we would have mock dogfights over Manston. The Canberra would whip it [the F-84E] every time. I can remember one day one of the Canberras had to land on the grass strip adjacent to the taxi strip. I said to my partner; 'Well, we finally got one!' The Canberra had gear trouble".

Another problem with the Thunderjet was its rather poor ejection seat. Many pilots were injured

18 Above: *Fine in-flight view of an F-84E prior to delivery. Clear bubble canopy is noteworthy; 31st FEW had to modify their canopies a number of times to prevent explosion at altitude. All aircraft at Manston were fitted with externally-braced F-84G-style canopies by the time 12th FEW arrived in mid-1951. (via Bruce Robertson)*

19: *Cockpit shot of a standard F-84E. Of note are the engine fire and overheat lamps below the light-coloured placard in the centre. If these lamps flicked on, the pilot would generally need to eject.*

during ejection — if the seat fired, that is. Bob Page from the 31st FEW recalls that:

"..at the time, many pilots didn't trust the F-84 ejection seat system. One of them successfully exited after engine failure by freeing seat belt and shoulder harness, releasing the canopy, rolling inverted, trimming nose down and effectively being thrown from the cockpit. Unfortunately another guy tried the same stunt while towing a target. He forgot to jettison the target first and stalled out".

From a maintenance standpoint, the view was no better, as 123rd FBW and 513th FBS Crew Chief Paul Fry explains:

"My memory of the F-84E is that it had at least two weaknesses; the wings developed stress cracks at the leading edge wing root. We stop-drilled cracks in the skin and most planes were limited to five or six Gs. The other major problem was engine failures — catastrophic failures when the compressor blades 'let go' and penetrated the main fuel tank behind the cockpit. Our squadron, the 513th, lost two or three planes in the air, probably related to engine failure".

The Thunderjet would have proved woefully inadequate as a bomber escort, had it come face to face with Soviet MiG-15s. Indeed, during the Korean War, the straight-wing F-84s employed in the fighter-bomber role often encountered this superior aircraft, and usually to the detriment of the Thunderjet. But by this time, the F-84's true vocation — in the 'air-to-mud' role — had been recognised, and at this the Thunderjet excelled.

All Wing aircraft on deployment departed for the UK on 26 December 1950, on a mission that was code-named Fox Able 10. This Air Echelon was commanded by Col. Cy Wilson, who accompanied the support air-craft. Wilson and his staff positioned themselves at each stop along the route, and via communications links with SAC, launch decisions were made; the ul-timate decision rested with Col. Wilson. The tactical aircraft (F-84s) were led by the 307th's Capt. Albert S. Pouliot, whose brief was to escort any aircraft that encountered problems to a diversionary airfield and then to bring up the rear of the flight. Each F-84 and T-33 crew member had to wear an anti-exposure ('poopy') suit, a life preserver vest, parachute and C-1 emergency sustenance vest. Additionally, each air-craft was to carry a one-man life raft and an individual emergency radio. F-84s were equipped with two 230-gallon wingtip fuel tanks, while T-33s carried two 165-gallon tip tanks. The aircraft departed in flights of generally four or more aircraft, with the lead flight being assigned the call sign 'Fox Able Zebra', succes-sive flights taking call-signs in reverse alphabetical order ('Fox Able Yoke', etc). Individual aircraft used the flight call sign, plus a number relating to their position in the flight. The only exception was that the leader of 'Zebra' flight used the radio call 'Fox Able Leader'.

In order to ascertain actual weather conditions along the route, a Military Air Transport Service (MATS) B-29 preceded the main formation, whilst a reserve B-29 was on standby at Goose Bay. In addi-tion to this, Search and Rescue aircraft were stationed at Goose Bay, Bluie West One and Keflavik in case of emer-gency. Backing up this massive operation were two North Atlantic Ocean Station ships positioned such that one was between Goose Bay and Bluie West One, whilst the other was between Bluie West One and Keflavik. These ships were code-named 'Duck Butts'.

A core of 66 maintenance personnel and equip-ment to support the Air Echelon departed on 26 December 1950, aboard the seven MATS C-54 trans-ports. These aircraft followed the same route as the Air Echelon, and were timed to give support to the tactical aircraft en route. The only problem encoun-tered during Fox Able 10 was when T-33 49-921 was unable to depart Goose Bay due to an engine fault. Two engine mechanics from Turner AFB were dis-patched to change the engine. A replacement aircraft (49-945) was later grounded at Bluie West 1, and was dismantled and returned to Warner Robins Air Mate-rial Area for repair during June 1951. The majority of the 31st FEW aircraft arrived at Manston on 4 Janu-ary 1951, nine days after leaving Turner AFB.

Cargo for the detachment was transported on commercial flights commencing 12 December, when seven aircraft left Turner AFB for Manston. However, during December, SAC rescinded the right to trans-

port household goods to personnel on indefinite TDY, and this applied to 31st FEW. Luckily, only four shipments of personal items remained to be trans-ported at this time, but it was not until 16 February 1951 that a telex from HQ 2nd AF allowed the trans-port of these shipments — at government expense. The task of moving Wing personnel to Manston proved more straightforward, and was commenced on 14 December. One of the first maintenance per-sonnel to arrive at Manston was Gene Armstrong, then a Sergeant engine mechanic with 31st Mainte-nance Squadron. He takes up the story:

"Around mid-December 1950, while attending a factory course on the J35 at Allison Division, Gen-eral Motors in Indianapolis, Indiana, I, along with three others from the 31st, was recalled to Turner AFB for deployment to Manston. The movement was carried out primarily with wet-leased (Douglas) DC-7Bs from Delta Airlines, Boeing Stratocruisers from Pan Am and Lockheed Constellations from TWA, and took place during Christmas week 1950. My group flew from Turner on December 24 to Westover AFB, Massachusetts, where we stayed overnight. We de-parted Westover for England in the late afternoon of Christmas Day, stopping in St. Johns, Newfound-land for refuelling. When we arrived over Manston, the presence of fog forced our flight to divert to Heathrow, where we waited for conditions at Manston to improve, [before] finally making the short flight to that station".

On arrival at Manston, the component based in England was designated as Detachment 1 of 31st FEW. The Detachment would come under the control of RAF Fighter Command only when participating in exercises, or when training in connection with the air defence of the United Kingdom.

As the Wing settled into its new home, it was re-alised that facilities were — at best — basic. There was little hangar space and no proper fighter disper-sals to speak of. Aircraft were often parked on bare earth or PSP (pierced steel planking) due to a lack of parking space. During February 1951, however, the British and American governments settled on a Spe-cial Construction Programme agreement, which would lead to the building and upgrading of 26 air bases in the UK for both strategic and tactical air op-erations. As a result, the British government agreed to provide $63 million worth of assistance, with any expenses above that amount being picked up by the US government. Although Manston would have to wait 18 months for any firm results of the agreement to materialise, at least there was now light at the end of the tunnel.

To carry out aircraft maintenance at Manston, Detachment 1, 31st Maintenance Squadron came into being on 31 December 1950. The Squadron came under the command of Detachment 1, HQ 31st Main-tenance and Supply Group until 1 February 1951, when Wing Materiel took control. The 31st Maintenance Squadron detachment undertook all day-to-day servicing of the F-84s, T-33s and C-47s, while the 4217th Organizational Maintenance Squadron (OMS), attached to the 31st FEW since August 1951, was detailed to carry out Intermediate, Major and Special Inspections of Wing aircraft. Maj. Lester W. Robinson was assigned the duties of 4217th OMS Commanding Officer.

On 14 January 1951, four North American RB-45C Tornado four-jet reconnaissance bombers arrived at Manston. These aircraft took part in photo-mapping sorties over the Continent, and were detached from the 323rd Strategic Reconnaissance Squadron at Barksdale AFB in Louisiana. They were supported by three KB-29P tankers, and the detachment remained until 23 February. Four days after the departure of these exotic visitors, one of the few Lockheed T-33 trainers assigned to the 31st Wing crashed at Ash, south-west of Manston. The pilot on this occasion was 'Hank' Meierdierck:

"I had a tip tank that wouldn't feed, so I flew local-low level to burn out fuel. Then the main tank was feeding the engine, and some fuel from the full tip. As the main tank got low, I dropped the tips, the engine quit and I made a smooth landing in a nearby oat field, very muddy. All was well till I came upon a small ditch and the nose gear collapsed - no other damage".

The first of many F-84 accidents to befall the Wing occurred on 24 January 1951. The 308th FES had been briefed to fly a camera gunnery mission at an altitude of 15,000 feet (4573m), and following a squadron take-off at 11.55 am, the formation broke into individual flights of three aircraft for their practice mission in separate designated areas. One such Flight, callsign 'Norman White', lost an aircraft almost immediately when one of its pilots declared a delayed take-off, due to a 'wet' start. The remaining two F-84Es in the Flight continued the mission as briefed. In the number two position of the flight was Lieutenant Commander William D. Biggers, the Squadron Executive Officer, on secondment from the US Navy. The Flight arrived over its designated area in the region of Margate 15 minutes after take-off. Lt Comdr. Biggers, flying F-84E serial number 49-2105 then made camera passes on the lead aircraft, which were assessed as 'good'. On one steep pass, the no. 2 was unable to recover to level flight until 3,000 feet (914m) below the target aircraft, but other than that, the mission was going to plan. At 12.29 PM, 'Norman White 3', the delayed aircraft, called for a rendezvous, and joined the Flight over Manston six minutes later. No.3 immediately commenced his camera passes. Lt Comdr. Biggers then pulled into close formation with the Flight leader, and made his only radio call of the mission: to instruct one of the other 308th FES Flights to use its correct call-sign.

At 12.40 PM, Biggers' aircraft was seen to make a slow turn to the right, away from the lead aircraft. At about 17,000 feet (5182m), the aircraft commenced a slow turn to the left, and the leader of 'Hooter' Flight (another 308th gunnery formation) passed to the rear of the aircraft to make an identification, and dropped back to 500-600 feet (152-182m) astern. At that moment, Biggers' Thunderjet pulled up abruptly, and climbed about 1,000 feet (304m) and rolled into level flight. The aircraft then fell through a slow split-S and continued to fall into a vertical dive, pulling up momentarily 30-40° from vertical. The F-84 then made a fast half-roll and pulled through again, which continued several times until the aircraft began a slow roll until it hit the ground and exploded. The pilot made no attempt to eject, and was killed instantly. The Thunderjet came down in the garden of a house at 10 Nash Gardens in Margate, and the impact left a crater 20 feet (6m) long and 12 feet (3.7m) deep. USAF fire crews were called, and thankfully, no one else was injured. The cause of the accident was put down to contamination of the pilot's breathing oxygen supply, causing hypoxia, a common cause of many aircraft accidents at the time.

At this point, the Wing was still qualifying personnel, and pilots who had not yet converted onto the F-84 went through a 5-day Transition Ground School, which taught Cruise Control, Emergency Procedures and Standard Operating Procedures. This would be followed by an examination, which required a 100% pass mark. Finally, students would be taken out to an F-84 and given a 'hands on' Emergency Procedure check, before being blindfolded and asked to locate switches and instruments 'blind'. A novel idea tried out on 4 February was the use of four 31st FEW F-84s to search for three occupants of a rowing boat adrift off the coast of Thanet. No trace was found during the search, but the hapless individuals later turned up alive and well.

On 10 March 1951, Col. Snavely returned to Turner AFB to take up command of the newly designated 31st FEW (rear). With a rear echelon operating at Turner AFB, the process of transferring from Manston once the period of TDY had ended would be made considerably easier. On 19 March, an award recommendation for Air Medal was made for Capt. William R. Peters of 307th FES. Capt. Peters had been able to locate an RAF Avro Anson aircraft, whose pilot had become lost and low on fuel. Despite a high speed differential, Capt. Peters managed to guide the Anson to a safe landing at Manston. A Wing inspection by the new Commanding Officer, Col. E.H. 'Dingy' Dunham was carried out on 24 March, and was followed by an impressive flypast of 48 F-84Es drawn from the three squadrons of the 31st.

During the month, ten F-84 pilots from the 31st were detached to the Korean Theatre, where the F-84E-equipped 27th FEW had been operating for four months. Assigned to Far East Air Forces (FEAF), these personnel were not replaced until 19 May 51, and their temporary loss led to a marked degradation in

22: RB-45C 48-019 was detached to Manston along with six others from January to May 1951. (Paul Cooper)

23: USAF crews inspect the damage left by Cdr William Biggers' Thunderjet in Nash Lane, Margate 24 January 1951. Biggers was killed in the crash and his aircraft, 49-2105 was completely destroyed. Fortunately no-one on the ground was injured. (John T Williams)

24: *A pair of 307th FES 'A' Flight Thunderjets taxi along the north side of Manston's massive runway on one of their first missions from the base. Just visible on the fuselage side is the 31st FEW shield, which comprised a wyvern design set against a blue and yellow background. (Hank Crescibene)*

25 Above: *On 13 March 1951, 2/Lt Hank Crescibene crash-landed near Aachen after an engine failure. He escaped unharmed and after repair in Germany his Thunderjet also returned to service at Manston. Note that the aircraft is devoid of unit markings and minus tip tanks; the latter had been jettisoned just prior to landing. (Hank Crescibene)*

26: *Damage to Hank Crescibene's Thunderjet 49-2379 was light; this view shows the tail section, which was ripped off in the crash landing. (Hank Crescibene)*

operational effectiveness. Nonetheless, 1,119 sorties were flown in Thunderjets during the month, which broke down into 2,204 flying hours, of which 224 hours were in bad weather, and 167 were at night. Escort missions were flown with the B-29s and B-50Ds of 509th Bomb Wing (BW), which was detached to the UK from February to May 1951. Its aircraft were based at Lakenheath, Mildenhall and Wyton, and to simulate 'hostile' aircraft during these escort missions, the RAF provided Meteor and Vampire jets that attacked the formations, trying to lure the Thunderjets away from the bombers. These exercises were deemed to be of great use to both sides, giving the RAF a chance to practice its Tupolev Tu-4 interception technique.

Ground Controlled Interceptions (GCI) by 31st FEW aircraft were flown in conjunction with the RAF radar bases at Neatishead, Norfolk (callsign: 'Dunlop') and Trimley Heath, Suffolk ('Hand-Bill'). In addition, low-level fighter sweeps were flown against the bomber bases in East Anglia, notably Sculthorpe, Mildenhall, Lakenheath, Bassingbourn and Wyton, to test their defences. Dive bombing, skip bombing and air-to-ground gunnery was carried out at the Leysdown and Dengie Flats ranges. The Wing also successfully performed a four-ship landing, entirely under Ground Controlled Approach (GCA) direction, and this was incorporated as Standard Operating Procedure. At this time, a rigorous ground training syllabus was also being beaten out, and aircrew who had completed the F-84 Transition Course received training on Flying Safety, Emergency Procedures, Standardisation, R/T Procedures, Aircraft Recognition, Combat Intelligence, Navigation, Security, Armament, Gunnery Technique and Escape and Evasion.

Throughout March 1951, there were only two aircraft accidents involving 31st FEW aircraft. The first occurred on 13 March, when F-84E 49-2379, piloted by 2nd Lt. Henry 'Hank' A. Crescibene of the 307th FES, crash-landed after an engine failure. Hank takes up the story:

"The 307th Squadron was on a cross-country flight from Manston to, I believe, Fürstenfeldbruck, Germany and return to Manston at flight altitude of 40,000 feet [12,195m], led by Col. William Dunham. Somewhere on the return leg the engine failed and it was decided that I would try to make Liege, Belgium. I immediately jettisoned my tip tanks to possibly give me more gliding distance. At this point, we were flying above a solid overcast; I broke into the clear at 20,000 feet [6097m]. Major Al Pouliot was the flight commander, and I was White 3. He escorted me all the way to my belly landing, which ended approximately 50 miles [81km] short of Liege and near Aachen, in a farmer's field. I came in very nose high and the tail hit the ground first, separating the tail cone. Major Pouliot made a low pass to assure my well being as I got out of the aircraft, then continued to Manston. The aircraft was trucked to a depot in Germany for repair and eventually flew again".

'379 was initially sent to 35th Air Depot Wing for salvage, but was considered repairable (probably due to the shortage of F-84E airframes), returning to the resident 123rd Fighter Bomber Wing at Manston on 2 March 1952. 2nd Lt. Crescibene later flew F-86 Sabres with the 335th Fighter Interceptor Squadron (FIS) in Korea, and shot down two MiG 15s during his tour.

The other accident during March 1951 came whilst the 309th's 2nd Lt. Herman H. Babb was conducting an escort sortie. The canopy of Babb's Thunderjet became detached and flew off, striking the tail. The impact of the canopy on the tail assembly caused considerable damage to the control surfaces of the aircraft (thought to have been 49-2063), but Babb managed to coax her back to a safe landing at Manston.

Aircraft maintenance carried out by the Aero Repair Section during March saw 40 aircraft processed, items changed including aileron boost and trim tab motors and engines. At this time, there was only a rudimentary taxiway between the 31st Maintenance Squadron hangar on the eastern side of the base and the 4217th OMS hangar, situated on the western taxiway (the area used by Station Workshops and the Air Experience Flight until the early 1990s). The towing of aircraft between these two areas was proving difficult due also to the narrowness of this taxi strip, and in many cases, aircraft ran off the tarmac and became bogged down in the mud of a typical English winter. To remedy the problem, in late March, the strip was widened with the addition of PSP metal plating, and the problem was partially solved. Hangar space at Manston, however, was still lacking, and the 31st Maint. Sqn. Aero Repair could only work on three aircraft under cover at one time. Therefore, most work on the Wing's F-84s was accomplished outside, where it always seemed to be raining, and the PSP did not stop the area becoming muddy.

The General Radar Section ran two courses during March; Course A was for airmen with no experience of the F-84E's AN/APG-30 radar system, and consisted of three week's training on basic electricity, electronics and basic radar. The third week was spent with AN/APG-30 familiarisation. Course B was for experienced personnel, and consisted of two week's training on the A-1CM gunsight, and a two-week review of the AN-APG/30. A fifth week consolidated all the previous items. The pilots of the 31st FEW also received a two hour course on the A-1CM and AN/APG-30, instructors for all these courses were Mr. R. Quance and Mr. Ed Donigan of Sperry Gyroscope Corporation, Mr. Ed Carson of the Philco Corporation, and Mr. Joe Rubel of General Electric.

The Gunnery Systems Section, undermanned as seemed to be the case everywhere at Manston, supported the Wing Gunnery Program, which was striving to qualify all pilots. During March 1951, 27,577

27: *A group of 307th FES pilots prepare for a mass sortie in front of the squadron operations hut. L-R: 1/Lt Virgal Sansing, Capt Louis Vogt, Capt Robert Keen, Maj Elmer DaRosa, 1/Lt William Peters, Maj John C Fabringer. 2/Lt 'Buck' Green is in background at right. Both DaRosa and Fabringer would command 307th FES. ('Mac' McMurray)*

28: *31st FEW pilots wait their flight briefing; many would go on to serve in Korea. Front centre is Capt Edward Dame of 309th FES and seated just below the wall plaque at left is 2/Lt Louis C Setter. Setter later became a U-2 spyplane pilot. Standing at extreme right is Capt Albert S Pouliot of 307th FES. Pouliot had been the lead pilot for the wing's deployment to England. (Hank Crescibene)*

29: *Fully kitted-up for action, these are the men of 'C' Flight, 307th FES. L-R: 2/Lt Charles W Joseph, 2/Lt William 'Mac' McMurray, unk, Capt John 'Hank' Meierdierck. Capt Meierdierck was flight commander. ('Mac' McMurray)*

rounds were fired, and individual scores were kept by means of painting the ammunition a different colour for each pilot. When the target was recovered after a mission, the different coloured bullet holes would enable accurate scoring. Unbelievably, for a while, it was a shortage of bullet tipping paint that threatened to curtail the Wing Gunnery Program.

At the end of March 1951, there were 697 USAF personnel on TDY at Manston. On 28th of the month, the three squadrons took off from Manston in three formations of sixteen F-84s for an aerial review of the base, led by Col. Dunham. The aircraft formation flew over in 'reverse order', with the 309th FES leading. For the month of April, 1,326 sorties were flown, which amassed 2384:55 hours of flying time. Escort missions were again carried out with the bombers of the 509th BW, and a radar calibration mission was accomplished to test Sandwich Control (callsign: 'Onion'), which was due to come into service. The Wing Gunnery Program had started to yield results at this point, with a Wing average of 12%. This was for all missions, and could be considered fairly good for the conditions prevailing. There was a lack of a firing-in butt at Manston, so bore sighting the six .50-calibre machine guns fitted to each aircraft was difficult at best, and testing was carried out during the actual gunnery mission.

The only accident for the month occurred on April 17, when a 309th FES F-84, with 2nd Lt. Roland X. Solis at the controls, collided on the ground with another F-84, piloted by 2nd Lt. Albert B. Smiley. There were no injuries to either pilot, and both aircraft were repaired at Manston. The lesser-damaged aircraft required aileron and wing tip fuel tank re-placement, whilst 2nd Lt. Solis's aircraft needed a new wing leading edge.

At 1400 hours on 11 April, two F-84Es, 49-2061 and 2042 were delivered to 4217th OMS to have 6th Major Inspections. A 6th Major was an in-depth maintenance operation, and these were the first to be attempted at Manston. With hard work and perseverance, the Squadron managed to have '2061 ready for flight test at midday on 14 April, whilst the second aircraft was finished at 1000 hours on 16th. Average man-hours for each was 255. This was considered to be something of a record, and is indicative of the high level of combat readiness and proficiency, which the Wing had achieved in only a short space of time.

Early Cold War Developments

By mid-1951, the deployed USAF F-84Es at Manston were being included under the ultimate control of the RAF's Fighter Command in a war deployment role. Further permanent USAF assignments to the UK were mooted, and a number of airfields were designated for development in this role. In a letter to the Secretary of State for Defence dated 16 May 1951, HQ Fighter Command, under AOC-in-C Air Marshal Sir Basil Embry, detailed the USAF's fighter deployment to the UK in wartime thus:

Airfields for development-1st Priority

Manston	1 Group of escort fighters
Bentwaters	1 Squadron of defence fighters
Shepherds Grove	1 Squadron of defence fighters
Wethersfield	1 Squadron of defence fighters

30 Below: *Aircraft 49-2349 was the mount of detachment commander Col Eugene H Snavely in early 1951. Red, yellow and blue squadron colours are repeated on fuselage, nose and tip tanks. (via Bruce Robertson)*

Airfields for development-2nd Priority

Carnaby	1 Group of escort fighters
Woodbridge	1 Group of escort fighters
Dunsfold	1 Squadron of defence fighters
Lasham	1 Squadron of defence fighters
Beaulieu	1 Squadron of defence fighters

Airfields for development-3rd Priority

East Kirkby	Group HQ and 1 Squadron of escort fighters
Spilsby	2 Squadrons of escort fighters
Wigsley	Group HQ and 1 Squadron of escort fighters
Sturgate	2 Squadrons of escort fighters

Airfields for development-4th Priority

Blyton	1 Squadron of defence fighters
Sandtoft	1 Squadron of defence fighters
Holm-on-Spalding Moor	1 Squadron of defence fighters
Charter Hall	1 Squadron of defence fighters
East Fortune	1 Squadron of defence fighters
Winfield	1 Squadron of defence fighters

Such ambitious plans would no doubt have been extremely costly to implement, as many of these airfields had little support structure to speak of. Nonetheless, most were officially designated as reserve USAF bases, even though they saw little use. It is interesting to note that all the 1st Priority airfields became operational USAF bases, with further airfields at Woodbridge, East Kirkby, Spilsby and Sturgate also becoming home to operational USAF units at a later date.

The new Commanding Officer of Detachment 1, 31st FEW, Col. David C. Schilling, arrived at Manston on 28 May 1951, and took over from Col. Dunham on 1 June, the latter returning to command the Air National Guard's 146th Fighter Bomber Wing at Moody AFB in Georgia. Col. Schilling was a well-known figure within the USAF, and had made a name for himself during WW II as a fighter ace. As a member of the 56th Fighter Group's notorious 'Zemke's Wolfpack', (named after Col. 'Hub' Zemke, commander of the outfit) Schilling had scored 23 kills, and later went on to command the 56th FG when Zemke was shot down and taken prisoner. By a twist of fate, Zemke became Commanding Officer of 31st FEW in 1955, long after the unit had returned to the US from Manston, and by which time Schilling had moved on to higher things. Some time after the 31st FEW returned to the USA, Schilling was assigned to a staff post back in England, and returned to Europe for the third time. Sadly, on 16 August 1956, he was killed while driving his Allard sports car on the twisty road between Lakenheath and Mildenhall.

May 1951 was a busy month for flying, with 2,233 hours flown on 1,472 sorties. Aerial gunnery was carried out, and again escort missions were flown, this time with the B-50Ds of the 2nd Bomb Wing, which had recently replaced the 509th on TDY. Low-level sorties were carried out against the 2nd BW bases in East Anglia, and aerial targets were towed for the RAF three days every week. The low-level missions were taken very seriously, and seen as a realistic training environment. By April 1951, the Soviet Union was believed to have 500 Tu-4s in its arsenal, plus an unknown number of the much-vaunted MiG-15 fighter. At a Chiefs of Staff Air Defence Committee meeting in London on 20 April, the Vice-Chief of Air Staff, Air Chief Marshal Sir Ralph Cochrane had stated, *"We assume that the Soviets will not, during the period of (to) 1957, have produced atomic bombs capable of being carried in smaller aircraft than the Tu-4"*. This small consolation was tempered by the prediction at the same meeting that MiG-15 fighters could be within escort range of the UK within 1 month of a start of hostilities. Ominously, the Korean War would show that the straight-wing F-84 was no match for the swept-wing Russian fighter.

On 19 May, another aerial review was carried out, again with three formations of 16 aircraft. During a normal 6 day working week, each squadron would fly at least once a day, while additionally, night flying would be carried out on a Monday and Wednesday, with Wednesday afternoon usually set aside for Ground School. On three Saturdays per month, Wing battle formation training was carried out, which culminated in a formation fly-by. In addition, one fly-by was performed during May at the American Cemetery near Cambridge.

The Wing Gunnery Plan was continued through May, with the 309th FES completing its training on the 21st, being replaced by the 308th, which had a 12.9% average at the end of the month. By this time four hundred gunnery sorties had been logged. The 307th FES, the last of the three squadrons to do so, took over and completed its gunnery training during June. However, by far the biggest commitment for the 31st during May was on Exercise *Ombrelle*, which was designed to simulate an invasion of West Germany from the East. The exercise would commence on 23 May and continue for three days, with 7th Air Division providing 'enemy' bombing missions. The 31st FEW was tasked to provide one squadron per mission to act as bomber escort for the 2nd BW's B-50s, commanded by Brigadier General Frederick E. Glantzberg. The defending forces consisted of Dutch-based Vampires and Meteors from the RAF, plus Dutch and Danish Air Force Meteors, stationed at Gilze Rijen in Holland. In addition, Belgian Air Force Meteors, Spitfires and Mosquitos, and three squadrons of mainland-Europe based USAF F-84s would join the fray. To distinguish 'enemy' aircraft, the F-84s from the 31st FEW that were involved in the exercise had broad black bands painted on the wings and rear fuselage. Gun camera film was used to ascertain the effectiveness of attacks throughout the entire scenario. F-84s from Manston flew five missions, with one squadron of aircraft assigned to each as follows:

Raid A-1, 23 May.

F-84s rendezvoused with bombers at 0900 GMT over Hanover, West Germany. The fighters escorted the B-50s to Rotterdam and Charleroi, then returned to base. The bombers then proceeded on to Nuremburg, Amiens, Ulm, Troyes and Paris before turning home.

Raid A-3, 23 May.

F-84s rendezvoused with bombers at 0920 GMT over Heligoland and escorted the bombers to Cuxhaven and Gilze Rijen before turning for base. B-50s carried on to Nuremburg, Luxeil, Chievres, Hanover and The Hague before returning.

Raid A-5, 24 May.

F-84s rendezvoused with bombers over Heligoland at 1800 GMT and escorted the bombers to Oldenburg, Rotterdam and Paderborn, then turned home. The B-50s then proceeded to Wurzburg and Cap Gris Nez, before returning to base.

Raid A-6, 25 May.

F-84s rendezvoused over Hanover at 1205 GMT, then escorted the bombers toward Metz, before breaking off. The bombers then flew on to Metz, Brussels, Worms, Stuttgart, Metz (again), Luxeil and Paris before flying back to UK.

Raid A-8 25 May.

F-84s rendezvoused over Hanover at 1225 GMT, escorted the bombers towards Brussels and returned. The B-50s continued to Brussels, Worms, Stuttgart, Luxeil, Paris, Brussels, Dortmund, and Rotterdam.

For the purposes of the exercise, fighter escorts from the 31st FEW were assigned the radio call sign 'Little Photo'. The exercise was a great success, and was carried out without mishap.

There were few incidents of note during May, but at the end of the month, 2nd Lt. D. Fellows of the 309th FES had to put down on the disused airfield at Snetterton in Norfolk, after an engine failure. On the next day, Lt. R. D. Robertson, also from the 309th, made another unscheduled landing at a disused airfield, due to low fuel. This time the landing site was Woodbridge in Suffolk, which in just over a year would reopen to the sound of F-84s operated by one of Manston's previous USAF squadrons, the 79th FBS.

For the maintenance personnel, May was a busy month. A telex message (TWX - Teletypewriter Exchange, often called a 'twix') from 7th AD grounded all F-84Es, pending inspection of elevator push-pull rod assemblies. 240 assemblies were removed and sent to Erding AB in West Germany for crack testing,

and of these, fourteen were found to be defective. The serviceable items were, however, returned quickly and the aircraft were soon back in service. Aero Repair received thirty six aircraft, eleven of which were for modification to the wing fuel filler bowl. Technical Order 01-65BJC-36 detailed the fitting of a pipe to the refuelling point, which was designed to drain away rain water, and prevent its ingress into the aircraft fuel tanks when the fuel filler cap was removed. One of the Wing's T-33 trainers, serial No. 49-945, which was grounded at Bluie West One on the initial deployment to Manston during the previous January (!), was finally dismantled and returned to Turner AFB on 14 June.

June 1951 was remembered for the visit of Lt. Gen. Curtis LeMay, Commanding General of Strategic Air Command, who was accompanied by Major General John P. McConnell, Commanding General of 7th Air Division. A new Wing formation of 48 aircraft in two waves was flown for the benefit of the VIPs. Lt. Gen. LeMay's visit was preceded on 4 June by a 7th AD inspection which expressed the performance of 31st FEW as "...very satisfactory". The flying commitment for June remained similar to that of previous months. Captains Pouliot and Peters were rotated back to the United States, and immediately began training on the F-84G at Eglin AFB in Florida, as it was planned that the 31st would re-equip with the newer model upon return from TDY at Manston. In order to practise as many mission profiles as possible, all pilots of 31st FEW were given a Jet Assisted Take Off (JATO) familiarisation flight during the month. JATO (or more accurately — RATO — Rocket Assisted Take Off) enables a heavily laden aircraft to shorten its take-off run, and on the F-84 this was achieved by fixing four expendable rocket bottles to the rear fuselage. When ignited, each bottle gave an extra 1,000-lb (444kg) thrust at takeoff, nearly doubling the power available. On completion of the take-off demonstration, the JATO bottles were dropped in the English Channel. Though subsequent Thunderjet units at Manston did not carry out the JATO experiment, the 92nd Fighter Bomber Squadron, which arrived at Manston in April 1955, would routinely carry out JATO take-offs with their heavy F-84Fs, and they would likewise drop expended bottles in the sea.

To celebrate the 1951 Festival of Britain, four F-84Es from the 31st Fighter Escort Wing flew a display at Rearsby Aerodrome near Leicester on Saturday 2 June. The formation was led by now Major Louis R. Vogt of 307th FES. Practise alerts were carried out in June to test the Base Evacuation Plan, whereby pilots and ground crews were called to their dispersals and the aircraft taxied to takeoff position, before recall. On 24 June, a simulated attack was flown by eleven of the Wing's aircraft against airfields in East Anglia. The purpose of this mission was to test the effectiveness of GCI sites in detecting low-flying in-

31: *49-2372 was being piloted by 2/Lt William B Johnson of 309th FES at the time of this accident in June 1951; he forgot to lower his undercarriage, but damage was minimised by the drop tanks, which took most of the weight of the aircraft. (M Gen C.G. Cleveland via Dave Menard)*

32 Below: *49-2349 is parked to the side of the Western Taxiway, this view is looking towards the control tower (not visible). As with all aircraft belonging to 31st FEW, they were parked on PSP matting laid directly on the bare earth. (via B. Robertson)*

33: *Parlous state of the aircraft during their stay at Manston is illustrated by these two F-84Es. They had been cannibalised for spare parts and were still present in 31st FEW colours on Manston's eastern side during 1952, long after the wing had departed. Aircraft at front appears to be 49-2075, which was returned to service and flew with 513th FBS. (Ernest Panizzoli)*

truders, with the secondary benefit of providing anti-aircraft gunners at these bases some practice of their drills. At 1257 PM, the eleven F-84s, led by Lt. Col. John C. Fahringer of the 307th FES took off from Manston in two flights of four, and one flight of three. One of these aircraft was an airborne spare, in case one of the flight members had to abort. The flight formed up over the base, and set course for their turning point just off the Suffolk coast at Lowestoft. The turning point was made at 1.22pm, and the aircraft then set course for the Initial Point (IP) at Norwich. Landfall was made at 1.30pm, one mile north of Great Yarmouth. Two minutes after crossing the Norfolk coast, three RAF Meteors were sighted at nine o'clock high, but they did not attack. Over Norwich, the flight divided into elements of two aircraft each, which went on to attack their respective targets of Sculthorpe, Marham, Wyton, Lakenheath and Mildenhall, while the spare aircraft remained available in the vicinity of Norwich. The flight up to this point had proceeded at 300-500 feet. The first element received clearance from Sculthorpe and proceeded with their attacks until 1.55 PM. At that time, two Meteors were sighted, but they declined to engage. The second element proceeded to Marham, and came straight in on their first pass. After several more passes had been made, two Meteors were sighted and engaged, the element subsequently claiming two Meteors 'destroyed'. Shortly before breaking off for the IP, another two Meteors attacked and stayed in trail. The third element to Lakenheath sighted a military encampment prior to reaching their target, and made several passes before going on to Lakenheath. When the element broke off after attacking this airfield, two Meteors attacked and were engaged. En route to base, the element was again engaged by Meteors, but could only take evasive action as the Thunderjets were by now low on fuel. The Wyton element could not locate the airfield, and were

jumped by two more Meteors. The F-84 pilots on this mission admitted that, had it all been 'for real', they would have been destroyed. The element that struck Mildenhall made several passes, and observed no other aircraft.

Meanwhile, the airborne spare had spotted ten Meteors taking off from Horsham St. Faith and wasted no time in engaging them. The pilot claimed two Meteors destroyed, before being shot down himself. All hypothetically, of course. The whole flight then reformed on the return leg at 2.00 PM. Total flying time for all aircraft on the mission was 16 hours and 55 minutes.

The day after this attack was flown, four F-84Es were tasked with a mission to intercept ships of the Royal Navy which were sailing in the Channel north of Cherbourg. The object of this exercise was two-fold. Firstly, it would give practise to the Wing pilots of navigating at low level over water, and secondly, it would give the defence units aboard the ships a chance to be put through their paces.

At 1.00pm on 25th, the four Thunderjets roared away from Manston en route to Cherbourg at 2,000-2,500 feet (610-762m) altitude. When the aircraft arrived over Cherbourg, the flight descended to 500 feet (152m), and set a course of 308° to intercept with the ships at 50° 27" North, 1° 10" West. The ships were soon sighted ahead, and a shallow turn of 5° to the left was made to line up the flight on two heavy cruisers, which were the largest ships in the group. Actual contact was made 44 minutes after the flight had departed Manston. The first pass was made in line abreast, with one pair of aircraft targeting each cruiser. The individual elements then separated and attacked the cruisers and their destroyer escorts for approximately 5 minutes. The flight was then reformed into trail for the final passes. The force was assessed as comprising 2 heavy cruisers, 6 destroyers, 2 corvettes and 3 transports. No other aircraft were encountered during the attack, and at 2.08pm,

34: This view inside the 31st FEW engine shop illustrates the spartan conditions at the base during the early days. J35 engines can be seen in their transport stands at left, while combustion section flame tubes await installation at right. The engine shop stood on the eastern side of the airfield on the site of the present-day passenger terminal building. (Gene Armstrong)

the engagement was broken off. The flight then gathered into a close formation, performed one more pass, and set course back to Manston. Flying at 15,000 feet (4573m), the aircraft were intercepted by a lone RAF Meteor near Brighton, but the flight could not engage due to their low fuel state. Total time for the mission was 2 hours and 10 minutes per aircraft.

There were three notable accidents in June. The first occurred on the 21st, as 2nd Lt. Kenneth A. Hardigan of the 307th FES was taxiing at the start of an escort mission. As Hardigan moved into the take-off position, his aircraft, 49-2079, struck the right wing-tip fuel tank of Capt. Robert J. Keen's Thunderjet, 49-2090. The impact was slight, but was enough to puncture the tank, which exploded and caught fire. Both aircraft were engulfed in flames, but Capt. Keen managed to taxi his aircraft clear, and jettisoned his tanks. Fire trucks were soon on the scene, but the fire had largely extinguished itself by this time. However, a small conflagration under Hardigan's aircraft was put out. Luckily, both pilots had closed their canopies, and there were no injuries. Hardigan reported that his right brake had seized prior to the impact, but subsequent inspection could find no cause for this. It was ascertained that '079 could not be repaired at Manston as a result of the fire damage, and the aircraft was written off.

On 26 June, Lt. Peter Van Brussel of the 308th FES (callsign 'Culprit 60'), flying F-84E 49-2055, was towing a target through light overcast at 5,000 ft (1520m) when he heard a thud, followed by an explosion in his engine. He quickly made a 180° turn and dropped his target. On breaking through the overcast, Van Brussel spotted a suitable landing area, and put his aircraft down in a field of barley 5 miles north-east of Dover. The aircraft was brought in wheels-up, and the resultant damage was extensive. The Dover Fire Brigade soon arrived on the scene, and extinguished a small fire that had broken out beneath the wrecked machine. Van Brussel was unhurt and was later commended for the way he had handled the situation. It was estimated that '055 would take 3500 man-hours to repair, and as a result the aircraft was written off three days later. It would seem that the no. 2 engine bearing problem had struck again.

The final accident in June was a result of pilot error. 2nd Lt. William B. Johnson of the 309th FES brought F-84E 49-2372 in to land at Manston without lowering its undercarriage. Luckily, pylon tanks were fitted beneath the wings, and the aircraft screeched safely to a halt on the southwest side of the runway. Damage was restricted to the nose gear strut, dive brake and lower forward fuselage. The aircraft was repaired and flying within 48 hours.

Aircraft of the 31st Fighter Escort Wing deployed to Norway on an operation codenamed *Goodwill* on 5 July. The exercise was designed to test the 31st's ability to deploy over large distances. In preparation for this movement, Royal Norwegian Air Force personnel arrived at Manston to offer advice, while survey flights were made over the planned route. An advance echelon, led by Wing Communications Officer Capt. Frank F. Long and Wing Intelligence Officer Capt. Brainard L. Gally, departed Manston on 4 July 1950, and divided their efforts between Sola Air Base near Stavanger, and Gardermoen Air Base near Oslo, where staff of Headquarters, 31st FEW were positioned. These personnel set up administration, maintenance and liaison activities for the Operation. Norwegian communications personnel were utilised in setting up a radio net, which then relayed information, such as weather conditions, to Manston. The initial plan was for flights of 27 F-84s to depart Manston on the mornings of 5, 7 and 9 July, and fly to Sola. After refuelling, the fighters would then rendezvous with a USAF bomber formation and escort it to Heligoland. In order to co-ordinate the rendezvous, Lt. Col. Fahringer, C.O. of the 307th FES, was to be detached to the 2nd Bomb Wing at Mildenhall and would ride in the lead B-50D bomber during the mission. After breaking off over Heligoland, the fighters would then proceed to Gardermoen AB, stop overnight, and return to Manston. In practice, however, the deployment did not go as planned.

The first mission was briefed 1 hour prior to departure for Norway. The items covered in the brief ranged from the geography of the country to information concerning the customs, badges of rank and structure of the Royal Norwegian Air Force. Led by Col. Schilling, the first mission departed Manston at 7 o'clock in the morning on 5 July. The pilot of 49-2071 had to abort his take-off when the foot of his exposure suit became wedged under his F-84's rudder pedal. With a minimum of delay, the aircraft later took off successfully and rejoined the formation en route. However, the twenty-four aircraft plus three spares were soon depleted when after only forty miles, 49-2053 had to turn back after an overheat warning light came on in the cockpit. Excessive vibration in stick and rudder was also noticed, and the aircraft returned to Manston on reduced power. Subsequent investigation revealed a cracked engine exhaust tail pipe. 200 miles (322km) out of Manston, the pilot of 49-2023 noticed that fuel was not feeding from his right-hand tip tank. After heading home, both tip tanks were jettisoned over the Leysdown Ranges, and the aircraft returned to Manston, where it was discovered that the tip tank fuel supply solenoid was stuck closed. The remainder of the flight continued to Sola with no further problems, and the remaining twenty five F-84s touched down at 0840 hours GMT. The aircraft were then refuelled and twenty-four F-84s took off at midday GMT to escort the bomber formation. 49-2065 returned to Sola soon after takeoff as a result of another tip tank feed problem. 49-2064 also returned because of a rough engine, and was escorted back by 49-2084. With the flight now down to 21 aircraft they continued to the rendezvous point, and contact with the B-50 bombers was made with no further drama. The fighters assumed their escort positions, and two of the F-84s made simulated gunnery passes on the bombers. All aircraft of the fighter formation broke off 20 miles north of Heligoland, and set course for Gardermoen. Within minutes, two Royal Danish Air Force Meteors attacked the flight, but their performance was not considered aggressive, and they soon broke off. The flight landed at Gardermoen at 1405 hours GMT and remained overnight. The return leg to Manston departed at 1.00 PM the next day in squadron formations, due to poor weather.

The second mission to Norway was delayed by bad weather for three days, and as notice of the Wing's return to the US had then been received, Operation *Goodwill* was called off, and the unit prepared for movement. All remaining personnel returned from *Goodwill* on 11 July. During the entire operation, the positive attitude of the Norwegians was praised, and the mission was achieved with some success. It was considered, however, that Gardermoen was not suitable for F-84s carrying pylon tanks, as their take-off run compared to the runway length was marginal. It was anticipated that a forthcoming runway extension to 8500 feet (2591m) would alleviate this. The only other problem encountered was that, in order to move equipment and personnel, three Fairchild C-82 Packet cargo planes had been requested, but only two provided. This caused a decrease in the efficiency of the move.

July brought good news for the personnel of the 31st Fighter Escort Wing. On the 7th of the month, the unit received advance notification of its return to the USA, with termination of the TDY expected after the 15th. However, July started as a busy month, when 435 sorties were flown, for a total of 856 hours. 2.25-inch rocket adapters were obtained on 1 July, and a programme of rocketry qualification commenced. This was only partially completed, but a mission to Keevil Airfield in Wiltshire demonstrated their effectiveness.

After verbal orders from 7th AD had been received, four F-84Es were loaded with four, 2.25-inch rockets and six hundred rounds of .50-calibre tracer ammunition each. Led by Lt. Col. Ray M. Hilliard, the flight departed Manston at 3.15pm on 10 July. The formation arrived overhead Keevil 45 minutes later, and began orbiting. At 4.07 PM, they were vectored onto the range, four miles south of the airfield on Salisbury Plain. The targets for the first two passes were tanks, and each aircraft fired two rockets on each pass. The remaining four passes consisted of strafing attacks, with the first two firing on aircraft and the final passes made on a truck convoy. The demonstration was completed and the flight made a final pass at 50 feet and 590 knots. The aircraft then proceeded to RAF Boscombe Down, where they landed at half-past four. The Thunderjets were refuelled, and ground control radio crystals removed. The flight departed for Manston 30 minutes later, and was back home by 5.30 PM. Eight hours total were logged for the mission, which went entirely to plan, leaving several tons of scrap iron strewn across the Wiltshire countryside.

Many maintenance personnel were utilised during the early part of the month on Operation Goodwill. The spares required for the mission were transported on C-82s, and all were deemed adequate, with the exception of engines. Two were changed at Gardermoen AB due to roughness, and this required their airlift from Manston. Prior to return of the Wing to the United States, it was necessary to put all aircraft through corrosion treatment; all of the 31st FEW's F-84E aircraft would be taken over by the incoming 12th FEW. A mass-production process was initiated, and all aircraft were washed, treated and repainted with little problem. This helped their transfer to the 12th proceed relatively smoothly.

Once the notification of a move to the US was received, the Mobility Plan was put into motion. All units were ordered to pack equipment for transport, and this was placed in Hangar 4 (on the 'Loop' dispersal). Movement of personnel was achieved by utilising return flights of the aircraft used in the 12th FEW's deployment to UK. The mission to return the 31st FEW to Turner AFB was named 'Fox Able 11', even though their aircraft would remain in the UK. Personnel began to depart Manston on 18 July 1951, though other cargo flights began leaving on 13 July, and all bar six had done so by 28 July. In all, 726 personnel and 185,000 lbs (82,295kg) of cargo were shipped to Turner on these flights. The route followed by MATS aircraft was the reverse of the Fox Able 10 route. Civil passenger and cargo aircraft were also used, and they returned via Shannon, Ireland (if required) — Keflavik — Gander, Newfoundland — Idlewild Airport, New York, and on to Turner AFB. The first transport aircraft to return was greeted over Macon, Georgia on 19 July by a flight of 2 F-84Es from the 31st FEW (rear), and four F-47D Thunderbolts of the 108th Fighter Bomber Wing, Air National Guard, which had been based at Turner AFB since March 1951. Col. Thayer S. Olds, Commanding Officer of the 40th Air Division, greeted the returning personnel, including Col. Schilling. The last flight to return to Turner did so on 2 August, when an aircraft which had been grounded in the Azores for an engine change, touched down. During the operation, forty-eight C-54, nine C-97, one B-17 and three B-29 arrivals were logged at Manston, including the arrival flights of 12th FEW.

Back at Manston, six personnel of Detachment 1 Headquarters and Headquarters Squadron, 31st FEW remained to make administration changes, and to close down the detachment. At midnight on 6 August 1951, Detachment 1 of the 31st Fighter Escort Wing was officially inactivated, the base and all F-84Es were turned over to the 12th FEW.

Commanding Officers - Manston Era

Detachment 1, 31st FEW
Col. Eugene H. Snavely: Start of TDY to March 1951
Col. Earl H. Dunham: March to 1 June 1951
Col. David C. Schilling: 1 June 1951 to end of TDY

307th FES
Maj. Elmer G. DaRosa: Start of TDY to 1 March 1951
Lt. Col. John C. Fahringer: 1 March 1951 to end of TDY

308th FES
Lt. Col. Ray M. Hilliard: Full period of TDY (promoted to Lt. Col. 20 February 1951)

309th FES
Maj. William R. Young: Start of TDY to April 1951
Maj. Don V. Booty: April 1951 to end of TDY

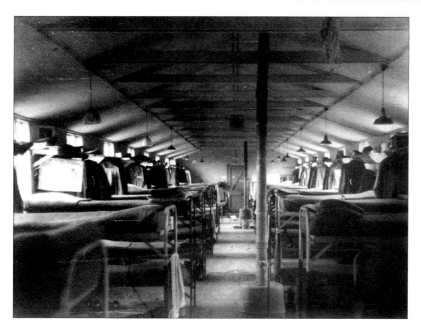

35: This is the inside of a typical wooden barrack hut at Manston during 1951. Ever-present pot-bellied stoves are placed along the centre of the room. Incredibly, some of these huts were still in use for transit accommodation into the 1980s. (Al Farnes)

36: These Maycrete buildings housed the Post Office (centre) and the 3917th Air Base Group headquarters (to the left). At far left is one of the main barrack blocks to the rear of the Officers Club. (Al Farnes)

THE 12TH FIGHTER ESCORT WING
Flight frustrated

In early July 1951, the 12th Fighter Escort Wing, based at Bergstrom AFB in Texas, was alerted of a move to Manston, as the next rotational unit to deploy to the Kent base. The 12th FEW had been reactivated on 1 November 1950 at Turner AFB in Georgia, where the 31st FEW had been stationed prior to its move to Manston. Concurrently, the 4219th Organizational Maintenance Squadron was designated, to be "..*organized at the minimum strength to perform squadron administration*". The 4219th OMS was assigned to the 12th Maintenance and Support Group of 12th FEW. The entire Wing was assigned to Strategic Air Command's 2nd Air Force, and was initially commanded by Capt. James M. Ross. Colonel Cy Wilson took over on 12 November, upon posting in from the Thunderjet-equipped 27th FEW in Texas. The fighter squadrons came under 12th Fighter Escort Group control; the Group was commanded by Col. Charles E. Gayle from 20 November. Another Thunderjet veteran, Gayle was transferred in from the 31st FEW.

The Wing was to be equipped with the F-84E Thunderjet, though during the period the unit was at Turner AFB, no aircraft were actually possessed by 12th FEW. On 25 November the Wing was instructed of a move to Bergstrom AFB.

Soon after arrival in Texas, the three fighter squadrons of 12th FEW — the 559th, 560th and 561st FES's — began to receive their first F-84Es. Immediately there began a period of intense activity to bring the Wing up to combat status. Among the missions carried out was that of gunnery training at Matagorda, an island off the Texas coast between Galveston and Corpus Christi. In addition, half a dozen Turkish Air Force officers were trained to fly the F-84 in preparation for their acquisition by that nation. Numerous bomber escort missions were also flown. On Monday 9 July 1951, the Wing personnel were informed of their move to Manston, UK.

The 12th FEW was to deploy to Manston without its aircraft, and would take over the F-84Es left by the outgoing 31st FEW. Prior to the move therefore, the 12th FEW had to transfer the majority of its aircraft to Alameda Naval Air Station in California, from where they would be shipped to Japan for use in the Korean conflict. At 1400 hours on 3 July 1951, the Wing received orders to ferry 40 F-84s to California, with all aircraft to be in place by the morning of the next day. This would prove a gargantuan task, and involved maintenance personnel working through the night to ready aircraft for departure. Test flights were flown until way after midnight. The pilots for the first section to leave were briefed at 1600 hours by Col. Wilson, and took off from Bergstrom four hours later. Subsequent flights left throughout the night and the early part of 4 July, and incredibly all aircraft were in place by midday on 4 July, less than 24 hours after the Wing had been given the initial order to move. The pilots spent the rest of Independence Day travelling back to Texas on transport aircraft.

Further problems awaited the Wing though. When the Operations Order for the move to Manston (code-named Fox Able 12) was finally received, it only allowed for 214,650 lbs (95,484kg) of cargo, plus 1,212 personnel to be moved. This strict allowance resulted in much head scratching, and although the target weight was finally reached, it was at the expense of much essential equipment. It was not until the Wing arrived at Manston that it was fully realised how little equipment was already in position, and how much vital equipment had been left back home.

Even so, this situation could have been considerably worse, had it not been for an ingenious idea that overcame many of the cargo problems. Before 12th FEW left for Manston, it was realised that certain items of essential equipment simply could not accompany the Wing on its deployment, and a hasty call to the 31st FEW at Manston arranged for a clever swap. In return for the 31st leaving a certain amount of equipment in the UK, 12th FEW would ferry a like amount of its equipment to Turner AFB, where the 31st would set up operations on its return from Manston. This proved to be a successful arrangement, being advantageous for both sides, but represented just about the only bright spot in this otherwise forgettable saga.

The Advance Party departed for Manston on 10 and 11 July, and was in place by the 13th. These personnel helped to set up the base for the main body of personnel, which started to leave Texas on 16 July. The majority of flights proceeded to Manston with the minimum of delay, but one MATS C-97 with 70 personnel on board lost an engine two hours out of Bergstrom, and had to divert to Andrews AFB in Maryland. The aircraft was delayed there for 26 hours awaiting spare parts. Two other C-97 flights encountered bad storms which gave their passengers a rough ride, while another aircraft flew four hours in the US with only three engines, and also made the crossing from the Azores to Manston in a similar fashion. Incredibly, all 738 officers and airmen of the Wing arrived safely, plus 419 personnel of the Air Base Group. By 21 July, the majority of men and machinery had arrived at Manston, though the cargo that had been shipped exceeded the Operations Order weight by over 30,000 lbs. (13,345kg). The last flight of the deployment left Bergstrom AFB on 27 July.

The Wing received 70 F-84Es from the 31st FEW on 21 July 1951, and these aircraft were found to be mainly of the E-1 and E-15 variants, which were considerably older than the aircraft that the 12th FEW had left in the USA. However, it could be argued that the newer aircraft were destined for combat, and as such, needed to be in tip-top condition. This, of course, was no consolation to the new residents at Manston, and although all F-84s were in commission upon receipt from the 31st, within a week many were grounded due to lack of essential spare parts. This situation would severely affect the flying that could be accomplished in July and had a knock-on effect during subsequent months.

At Manston, the 12th Fighter Escort Wing located its various squadrons in the same way as the outgoing 31st FEW, with the Engine Shop and Aero Repair taking over the facilities on the eastern side of the airfield and Periodic Maintenance taking over Hangar 3 on the western taxiway. The flying squadrons were located thus: the 559th on the western taxiway, the 561st on the eastern taxiway and the 560th FES on the 'Loop' dispersal. Parking areas were still mainly composed of PSP laid directly onto the bare earth. Unlike the 31st FEW, the 12th's aircraft carried fairly mundane colour schemes; the nose was painted with a scalloped band around the intake, the entirety of the tip-tanks also being painted. Both areas were in the colour of the relevant squadron: red for the 559th FES, yellow for the 560th FES, and blue for the 561st FES.

Operations began on 23 July when Cy Wilson took 18 aircraft on an orientation flight in the local area. This type of flying was performed on the next two days, and by the 26 July, when missions were flown over the USAF bases in East Anglia, the Wing was already getting the feel of operations in Europe. By the end of July, the 12th possessed 47 combat-ready pilots from a total of 109, and had taken over all F-84s. The maintenance problems during the early part of the deployment affected the amount of flying which was possible, and only 1,199 flying hours were logged in July, this total included the large amount of missions flown in the USA prior to departure.

August proved to be a better month for flying, and 2,339 hours went down into the logbooks. A lack of T-33 trainers, however, coupled with the grounding of many F-84s conspired to prevent any instrument training being carried out. When the Instrument Training Program was instigated during September, the problem had to be brought to the attention of 7th AD. Again, no solution was immediately found, and although 3917th ABG possessed an ageing AN-D-18 Link Trainer (a very primitive basic flight simulator), no permanent building had been found for it, and it was not erected for some time. The Link Trainer was eventually housed in a building on the technical site, near to where the RAF Officers Mess now stands. This item of equipment was, however, considered too old to be of any value to the combat pilots of the 12th FEW.

During August 1951, the 12th FEW participated in an exercise to test the defences of Norway. The Wing deployed to Sola AB, near Stavanger, and it appears that the whole mission was run in a similar fashion to Operation *Goodwill* carried out by 31st FEW during early July 1951. During the flight outbound to Norway, Capt. Bryce Long had to eject after his Thunderjet's engine died. He parachuted safely down through an overcast into Denmark. According to Bob Page, Long "..*had a date with a farmer's daughter before being picked up*"! Once at Sola, the 12th FEW flew 208 sorties for 433 flying hours on the whole exercise. The base at Gardermoen was not used this time due to its short runway.

Maj. Gen. John P. McConnell, Commanding General of 7th AD, paid his first visit to the Wing at

Manston on 10 August, arriving from RAF Northolt. Many more USAF 'top brass' would visit Manston during the early years of its USAF occupation, and Maj Gen McConnell visited again on 30th. On 14 August, two F-84s left Manston to take part in a sea search 75 miles south west of Calais, along with an SA-16 amphibian from the 9th Air Rescue Squadron Detachment at Manston. The information received for the search was very vague, and nothing was seen by any of the aircraft.

There were many other incidents to keep Manston's emergency services (still RAF-manned) on their toes. On 16 August, an F-84 flamed-out at 28,000 feet (8,536m) and was quickly turned towards Manston. Luckily the pilot managed to relight the engine, but not before the aircraft had lost 8,000 feet (2,439m) in altitude. Manston was also used as an emergency diversion airfield by other aircraft in distress. On 28 August, an RB-45C Tornado of the 91st Strategic Reconnaissance Wing (SRW) diverted into the base, only to be caught out by a cross-wind on landing, which resulted in two burst mainwheel tyres. The 91st SRW was by this time operating from Sculthorpe, having briefly stayed at Manston earlier in the year. One of Manston's T-33 trainers was also damaged in August due to faulty brakes, but the pilot escaped unharmed, and damage to the aircraft was minimal.

September turned out to be another lean month for flying. A 3-man maintenance team from 7th Air Division arrived on 3 September to inspect high-time aircraft with a view to scheduling them through the 59th Air Depot at Burtonwood for repair, as required. As a result, 44 F-84s were grounded on 22 September for Depot Inspection Reports (DIR), which incidentally also affected the aircraft detached to Libya, as detailed below. The further restrictions imposed by the 7th AD grounding of aircraft exacerbated the poor availability of F-84s, and only 1,321 flying hours were accrued during the month.

Simulated fighter escort missions were commenced in order to acquaint crews with the type of bombing mission flown in Europe. On 11 September, sorties were flown in support of the B-29s from the 22nd Bomb Wing, which had replaced 2nd BW B-50s at the bases of Mildenhall, Sculthorpe, Wyton and Lakenheath in East Anglia. A secondary benefit of this practice was that crews would be engaged in simulated combat, and could try out their long-range navigation and rendezvous skills. From the meeting point at Rouvray in France, the bomber/fighter formation travelled 925 miles up to Great Yarmouth, while being attacked from all sides by Vampire and Meteor jets of the Royal Air Force. In order to provide optimum efficiency, the escort mission was split into 11 separate sections, and in all, 69 sorties were flown for a total of 132 hours.

The task of providing escort practice continued, along with a few 'operational' tasks, including those for the RB-45C weather reconnaissance flights of the 91st SRW. The fighters generally commenced their escort missions in West Germany at Mannheim, breaking off at Basel on the border with Switzerland. Initially, three sorties were scheduled for the week of 16 - 22 September, but only two were actually completed after the 19 September mission was scrubbed.

The first of the Wing's gunnery practice camps to Wheelus AB in Libya was commenced on 19th September when the 561st FES deployed 23 F-84s along with support personnel, aboard C-47 and C-82 Packet cargo aircraft. Five days after flying out to Libya, ten of the Thunderjets had to return to Manston for urgent inspections brought about by the receipt of a 7th AD telex (Telephone Wireless Exchange, or TWX). As a result, aircraft with more than 500 flying hours were grounded temporarily, and this generally equated to the F-84E-1 variant, which would be brought up to 'late model' standard at Burtonwood. Despite the loss of these aircraft, the squadron at Wheelus managed to qualify 15 of its pilots in gunnery by the end of the month, and 374 gunnery sorties were flown in 342½ hours. By the end of its detachment, the 561st FES would have 23 qualified pilots.

Two aircraft accidents were reported during the month. On 10 September, whilst taking off from Neubiberg Air Base in West Germany on a return flight to Manston, one of the Wing's F-84s (thought to be 49-2368) experienced an engine failure. The aircraft was successfully crash-landed, and received major damage to its right wing. The pilot was unhurt. Ominously, the accident was put down to turbine failure, which was yet another engine-attributable cause to add to a growing list. Sadly, the J35 engine would prove to be the culprit in many other accidents during the reign of the Thunderjet at Manston, and it was only 6 days prior to the Neubiberg crash that another Wing F-84, callsign 'Turnkey Red 1' had suffered an engine fire. On this occasion the pilot was more fortunate, and after cutting his engine was able to relight at a lower altitude and return safely to Manston. Confidence in the J35 was not high, and the Manston F-84s were grounded during the last two weeks in September as a result of engine supply and failure problems.

The Wing's first fatal accident occurred on 13 September. As callsign 'Eggstar Red Tow', George D. Lee had been tasked with towing an aerial target for a gunnery mission, and reported an engine flame-out. He then gave the distress signal and stated that he was going to bail out, which it seems he achieved. An accompanying pilot saw his aircraft, 49-2088 roll onto its back at 4,500 feet (1,371m) and crash into the sea at a 45-degree angle. No cause for this accident was ever determined, as the aircraft had crashed into deep water off North Foreland. Number 2 engine bearing failure was suspected, but although it was planned to raise the aircraft from the seabed to investigate the cause, the USAF was advised that this would be a dangerous procedure due to the hazardous currents in the area. The aircraft and the body of its pilot were never recovered.

Maintenance operations were stepped up during September 1951, and a trickle of spare parts began to arrive to alleviate the Aircraft Out of Comission for Parts (AOCP) situation. On 9 September, 15 new J35A-17A engines arrived at Liverpool Docks, and were received at Manston two days later. The later modification J35A-17B engines were not scheduled to begin arriving until October, and as a result, 7th AD signalled SAC Headquarters for another fifteen J35A-17As before the receipt of the later engine variant. The delay in the arrival of the -17B was a direct result of the lack of modification kits, which would alter the F-84s airframe to accept the later engine type. Although Republic were producing these kits at a rate of six a day, only 17 had been completed and shipped by 3 September, though all remaining kits were promised by 1 October. Another engine modification that commenced during the month was the removal of intake screens from all engines. These screens were coarse, retractable filters, fitted on the forward face of the engine, and were designed to prevent the ingress into the engine of damaging foreign matter. In practice, as the ends of these screens were unsupported, pieces began to break off and were sucked into the engine, where they caused precisely the sort of damage they were installed to prevent! In addition, in certain weather conditions, ice forming on these screens could starve the engine of air and cause a flameout. Again, the removal of these screens was delayed by the lack of the special kit needed to complete the task. This equipment had been ordered on 13 August, but supplies were still short. One of the new engines supplied during the month was, thankfully, found to have the screen modification already embodied.

In addition to the modification tasking, the engine rejection rate during this period often exceeded supply capacity. The engine shop was also limited in the amount of work that could be carried out on the J35 before the engine would need to be sent away. In an attempt to increase the depth of work which could be done, and to prevent so many rejected engines going through the lengthy off-base reconditioning process, a request was sent to Air Material Command to enquire if it would be possible to carry out compressor casing top-half lifts. When approved, this procedure enabled maintenance personnel, under the guidance of the Allison Technical Representative, to blend out minor damage to the compressor blades due to foreign object ingestion.

On 22 September, a training programme for all maintenance personnel was put into effect. At this time, there was a fair spread of experience and ability on the maintenance side, and this training was designed to bring all ground crews up to the same standard, by providing background knowledge of the aircraft and its systems. To ensure standardisation of training, a request for a visit by a Mobile Training Unit (MTU) was submitted, whose pupils would also include the squadron pilots. Sadly, the MTU did not arrive at Manston until some time after 12th FEW had vacated the airfield. In the meantime, Base personnel would carry out training.

By the end of the month, there were eight F-84s still AOCP, mainly for engines, attitude gyros and fuel flow indicators, and along with these aircraft, examples of SA-16 (9th ARS), C-47 and C-82 (also 9th ARS) were in need of spare parts. By late September, up to three F-84E-1s at a time were being processed through 59th Air Depot Wing at Burtonwood for completion of DIR-originated maintenance, which involved wing pylon and oxygen system modifications.

At this point, it is worthwhile mentioning the maintenance organization that supported 12th FEW at Manston. In most flying squadrons, it is the aircraft maintenance activity that takes up more personnel than any other section, and the set-up at Manston was no different, there being 3 main maintenance squadrons, the first of which was the 12th Maintenance Squadron. This unit provided the field maintenance and engine build-up of all Wing and transient aircraft — that is, all non-scheduled maintenance and servicing, such as refuelling, after-flight servicing, and rectification of unserviceabilities. During September of 1951, six officers and 139 airmen were assigned, many working a 6 or 7-day week. In addition to the above tasking, 12th Maint. Sqn. personnel trained Royal Norwegian Air Force (RNoAF) officers and airmen on servicing aspects of the F-84. The RNoAF would later receive the F-84G Thunderjet.

The Engine Shop came under the wing of the 12th Maint. Sqn, and thanks to the ingenuity of the 560th FES's Lt. Robert Jacobsen, the engine testing facilities were greatly upgraded during September. Jacobsen was the maintenance officer in charge of the engine build-up section and devised a way of testing the J35 engine while still installed in its transportation stand. This meant that the engine did not have to be transferred to a test stand for running, and then removed again afterwards. Time spent in engine testing was reduced by up to 50% as a result. During an engine run, the transportation stand was secured to the ground by steel cables and a buried hook. This system worked so well that in later years it was modified for use with the F-86F Sabre's J47 engine. Although this system was subsequently tested with the F-86D's afterburning J47 engine, the model's extra thrust proved too much for the rig to safely accommodate. Robert Jacobsen recalls the problems with the J35:

"I recall performing frequent inspections on the F-84E engines. We found most of the engines had damage in the burner area. The [combustion section] interliners often had many cracks or small

pieces of the interliners missing - maybe 2 to 4 square inches of them missing. So my men replaced numerous interliners and when rebuilt we had to run-up each engine on the test stand. Many of the F-84E engines failed in flight so many of our pilots used the ejection seat. The main fault was the no. 2 bearing that failed. It was the thrust bearing and when it failed the stator and rotating blades of the compressor tried to occupy the same space, so the engine stopped abruptly. One of the engines failed close to Manston allowing the pilot to make a dead-stick landing on the runway. It was difficult to remove the engine from the airframe, as the engine had grown so large when the compressor exploded. Everyone was concerned about the health of the number 2 bearing".

The Engine Shop occupied a small building situated to the rear of what is now the main terminal for the Kent International Airport. Engine running and testing was accomplished in a purpose-built test cell, which was located mid-way between the Engine Shop and the main runway.

Typical of the maintenance activity carried out by 12th Maint. Sqn. during September 1951 was the replacement of all cockpit canopy bubbles. This task had previously been carried out by 31st FEW on these same aircraft, but it appears that the canopies were still giving much trouble. The braced canopy fitted to the F-84G was therefore rushed into the supply system and retrofitted to all early-model Thunderjets still in service. It was later discovered that nine of the new bubbles were unserviceable on removal from the pressure test stand, and in concert with the Republic Technical Representative, Mr. Seims, the defective canopies were returned to the manufacturer for further tests. Replacement of the remaining cano

pies was fairly straightforward, as the 12th FEW maintenance personnel had replaced the same item on the F-84s that they had left back in the States!

The second rectification unit based at Manston, the 4219th Armament and Electronics Maintenance Squadron, replaced the 31st FEW's 4217th A&EMS, and supported those aspects that its title implies. For example, on 13 September, a team of 1 officer and 19 airmen in the Armament Section were detached to Wheelus AB to support the gunnery mission. Including the firing in Libya, Manston-based F-84s consumed 19,875 rounds of ammunition during the month. Two Norwegian airmen commenced a six-week armament training course in September, and armament personnel of 4219th A&EMS provided instruction. The Communications Section of the squadron trained 3 other RNoAF personnel. The final section in 4219th A&EMS was the Electronics Shop, and during the month many of its personnel were also deployed to Wheelus to provide A-1CM gunsight radar maintenance.

The final maintenance outfit at Manston was the 4219th Organisational Maintenance Squadron, which was tasked with the scheduled maintenance of all aircraft. Like the 4219th A&EMS, the OMS took over from the 4217th when the 31st FEW departed. Maintenance generally included such items as engine changes due to time expiry, lubrication, and replacement of lifed items (components on the aircraft which require replacement after a certain amount of flying or operating hours have been accrued — generally equating to control system components and such like). During September 4219th OMS carried out 4 Intermediate Servicings and 9 Major Servicings, but the lack of available spares meant that 15 other aircraft had to be returned to the squadrons with main

38: Pictured during 1951, the old RAF Station Headquarters building housed a steadily decreasing number of RAF administrative personnel. Long-since demolished, it was situated across the road from the present-day Spitfire and Hurricane Memorial Building. (Al Farnes)

tenance incomplete.

On 8 October, the 560th FES replaced the 561st at Wheelus. In order to ease the load on the combat pilots and to save time, the 561st's aircraft remained at Wheelus for the incoming squadron, and would be handed over to the final squadron to undertake gunnery training when they rotated. Crews were rotated to and from Wheelus in the Wing's C-47 transports. 560th completed their gunnery qualification during the latter half of October, and in doing so amassed 284 flying hours, 311 sorties and qualified 17 pilots. The 559th FES replaced the 560th on 23 October for the final round of gunnery qualification, and by the end of the month had flown 145 gunnery sorties and qualified three combat pilots.

Back at Manston, two Practice Combat Alerts were called, which involved pilots and ground crews deploying their aircraft as quickly as possible. These practices were designed to show that all in-commission aircraft could be airborne after the alert had been given, day or night within a set time. Forty hours of Ground Training was commenced for the Thunderjet pilots, designed to keep these personnel abreast of current developments, including lessons being learned in Korea. These ground schools were very helpful in retaining the currency of Wing pilots, because the spares problem had been getting steadily worse, and only the very basics of proficiency flying could be carried out. Engines again proved to be the critical item, and during October, the AOCP rate rose to 35%. Other items in short supply were F-84 tyres, and a TWX to 59th Air Depot at Burtonwood revealed that stocks there had been exhausted, with resupply overdue from the US. Thus, the majority of flying was done at Wheelus, as a result of the urgency of completing gunnery qualification. However, even at Wheelus the lack of certain items began to be felt, not least of which was the difficulty in obtaining material for making towed targets. As a stop-gap, a TWX was sent out from Manston to the 560th FES, detailing the fitment of a secondary cable to the tow cable, which hopefully would lessen the likelihood of the target being shot off and lost before scores could be assessed, which would also preclude its further use. Numerous requests were made for the supply of the Aero 25 target, which was easier to score. The previously used A-6B target was also proving difficult to supply, and as a final solution fifty A-60B polythene targets were flown out from Bergstrom AFB in Texas. In use, these targets proved to be more durable than the A-6B.

From 29 September, Exercise *Pinnacle* was initiated, finishing on 7 October, and was followed immediately by Exercise *Cirrus*. *Pinnacle* was designed to practice defence of the United Kingdom from mass raids by day and night. There were six phases to the exercise, involving the afternoons of 29 September, 30 September and 3 October, and the full days of 6 and 7 October. One night-time phase was planned

for the night of 2/3 October, but bad weather meant that it was re-scheduled for 9th/10th of the month. These exercises involved 12th FEW F-84s on escort missions across the UK and Europe. Exercise briefings were given throughout by the 12th FEW Detachment Commander. On 7 October, B-29s from the 22nd Bomb Wing accompanied by escorting 12th FEW Thunderjets flew a practice mission against Glasgow, arriving overhead at 20,000 feet (6,097m). This was typical of the missions flown, but the final raid of Exercise *Pinnacle* saw F-84s escorting a sole B-45 bomber from France on a mission to Birmingham. The latter aircraft was assigned to the 91st Strategic Reconnaissance Wing at Lakenheath, and made its 'attack' at 35,000 feet (10,670m).

Despite the relatively low hours being flown, and largely as a result of the degradation in aircraft condition, there were numerous accidents during October 1951. On the 6 October, a pilot was returning to Wheelus from a tow target mission, with damage to his aircraft. The pilot stated that his F-84 would not trim properly, and that he would make a straight-in approach. As the pilot approached the base, difficulty was experienced in getting the flaps down. With so much going on in the cockpit, the pilot did not realise until too late that his undercarriage was not lowered, and though he tried to pull up, the aircraft settled onto the runway on its belly. Damage was restricted to the air brake door, bulkheads and components. The pilot was unhurt.

On 13 October, the flight leader of a gunnery mission at Wheelus suffered an engine failure approximately 3 minutes after take-off. The pilot made an emergency landing on a runway that was incomplete and in the process of being laid. As a result of the extremely rough terrain, the landing gear collapsed and the aircraft was destroyed, while the pilot walked away unhurt, cursing his luck. Again, this failure was the result of the number 2 engine bearing breaking up. On the 19th of the month, a 560th FES F-84, serial number 49-2034, hit the ground while flying low over 22nd Bomb Wing's base at Mildenhall and crashed near the village police station. The aircraft was a total write off; the pilot was fatally injured. Fortunately, there were no casualties on the ground.

One bizarre accident occurred on the night of 30 October, and was definitely not the result of mechanical failure. At approximately 5.10 PM, the pilot of an F-84 was making a landing approach to Manston, and immediately prior to landing, saw a dark object loom in front of him. Despite the immediate application of full power, the pilot was unable to avoid the object, which turned out to be the RAF Blind Approach Beacon System (BABS) vehicle. As 15,000 lbs of Thunderjet slammed into the van, the nose gear of the F-84 was nearly ripped off, and further damage was sustained by the underside of the aircraft. Somehow, the pilot managed to pull his mount staggering into the air and completed a circuit before executing a crash-landing with the main undercarriage down and the nosewheel in the 'up' position. The aircraft then sustained further damage to the forward fuselage, before bringing its hapless pilot safely to a halt. The BABS vehicle was a complete write-off, though it was unoccupied at the time.

The maintenance and supply aspects proved to be no less fraught during the month. At 0600 on 24 October, the Base Flight building was burned out by a fire started by an exploding oil stove. Forty dinghies borrowed from the 2nd BW at Mildenhall, along with much personal equipment and tools were destroyed. The 12th Maintenance Squadron also discovered the reason for the failure of so many canopy bubbles on the test stand — too much pressure was being applied. As a result, the pressure applied to the canopies was reduced from 12 to 5 psi and no further problems were encountered.

In early November, the return to Bergstrom AFB was announced, and the 559th FES on gunnery training at Wheelus curtailed its activities and returned home to Manston on 6 November. During the first week in the month, the 559th had qualified two more pilots and flown 34 sorties for a total of 70 hours. The Wing in total flew only 695 hours during November, in the main as a result of the serious lack of spares for the F-84. As an example, there were no J35 engines available anywhere in the UK, and the AOCP rate rose to 49.5%. A positive side to the low consumption of flying hours was that there were no accidents during 12th FEW's last month in the UK.

Maintenance activity centred mainly on getting the aircraft up to a condition where they could be handed over to the incoming unit, 123rd Fighter Bomber Wing. However, such was the state of the aircraft that it was not possible to get all of them serviceable, and three AOCP F-84s were handed over by the 12th Maintenance Squadron alone. The advance party from 123rd FBW arrived in mid-November, and immediately set about receiving aircraft, training on the F-84 (having been flying the F-51 Mustang previously), and getting the base sorted out for the arrival of the main party. On 15 November, 4219th OMS received 13 maintenance personnel from 123rd FBW for this purpose. In addition, two days later, 24 personnel from 59th Air Depot Wing at Burtonwood arrived to carry out DIRs and corrosion inspections on all F-84s. November was a busy month for the groundcrews, and to put a final spanner in the works, 42nd Air Division allotted five airmen for the 35-day Aircraft Jet Engine Mechanics Specialized Course (J35) at Chanute AFB, Illinois, which began on 8 November.

The 4219th A&EMS also received airmen from the 123rd, this time six underwent indoctrination, while four personnel from the 4219th stayed behind to hand over equipment. The Communications Section really had its work cut out during the handover phase, as it had just commenced the removal of all ARC-3

and ARN-6 radios from the Thunderjets for routing to Burtonwood for anti-fungus treatment. These items were serviced on a rotational basis, with 20 radio sets being worked on at Burtonwood at any one time.

Once the 12th FEW Movement Order was received, things progressed swiftly, and an Advance Echelon of Wing personnel left Manston by air on 24 November. This advance group consisted of 297 men, who were loaded onto nine MATS aircraft, which then routed from Manston to either Iceland or the Azores on their way west. Strong head winds were experienced on both routes, which resulted in some personnel and baggage being offloaded to ensure that the aircraft would reach the US safely.

The main body of the 12th FEW was ordered — at 72 hours notice — to proceed to Southampton Docks on the south coast, and departed by sea on the USNS *General W. G. Haan* at 3 o'clock in the morning of 30 November. Five hundred and forty seven personnel were accommodated on a troop ship capable of carrying 3,200 troops, and conditions were generally very comfortable. The voyage lasted eight days, and on 8 December, the *Haan* docked at New York. Personnel were then airlifted from Newark Airport in New Jersey to Bergstrom AFB on thirteen MATS-controlled civil flights. Baggage was generally transported by truck.

By the end of November, 261 personnel had returned to the US or were en-route by air, 547 were in transit on the USNS *Haan*, 31 were awaiting immediate airlift, and 271 Rear Echelon personnel remained at Manston. These personnel would return to Bergstrom once 123rd FBW had accepted all aircraft, and concluded its F-84 indoctrination. During December, 12th FEW personnel carried out the transition training of 17 123rd FBW pilots, which included ten hours of F-84 flying time each. This training was completed on 10 December.

The final large movement from Manston transported 243 of the Rear Echelon personnel aboard five MATS aircraft during 21 December 1951. Like the earlier 12th FEW flights, these aircraft encountered strong headwinds, and 6,700 lbs (2980kg) of cargo had to be offloaded in the Azores as a result. This cargo was not received at Bergstrom until early January 1952. The final 37 airmen and one officer of the 12th FEW Rear Echelon completed the hand-over of Manston to the 123rd early in 1952 and returned to Bergstrom AFB on 18 January.

It is fair to say that the 12th FEW had little chance to prove itself whilst at Manston. The shortage of spares, allied to the already poor state of the aircraft in general, conspired to make its TDY a frustrating experience. However, despite only staying at the base for something less than five months, many Wing personnel would cite their brief spell at Manston as the best TDY of their career.

Commanding Officers — Manston TDY

12th FEW
Col. Cy Wilson

560th FES
Maj. McCreery

559th FES
Lt. Col. Joe McKeon

561st FES
Lt. Col. Virgil 'Mike' Meroney

39: A group of 561st FES pilots confer prior to a mission. This view is unusual as the aircraft are parked along the edge of the main runway. Typical restrained 12th FEW markings can be seen on these machines. (Elliot Bouck)

40: Manston's control tower has changed little since the 1950s; the building also housed the base weather office. Air traffic control at Manston was RAF-manned until 1954. (Ernest Panizzoli)

41: Prior to departing for England, 123rd FBW trained its Thunderjet pilots using borrowed F-84s at Godman Field, Kentucky. Note raccoon-tail flying helmet in foreground, a 167th FBS trademark. (via Jack H Smith)

42 Above: F-84E of the Skyblazers aerobatic team; John O'Brien's aircraft was 'FS-237'. (George Pennick via Pete Hutting)

THE 123RD FIGHTER BOMBER WING
'Fortune assists the brave'

The outbreak of the Korean War on 25 June 1950 proved to have far-reaching consequences, and soon affected events on the other side of the globe. In the United States, 66 Air National Guard (ANG) squadrons were called to active duty, commencing in October 1950. The ANG is a combat-ready force, which backs up active units upon mobilisation, as in the case of the Korean War, and either supplements USAF units, or frees them for overseas deployment. ANG squadrons are generally manned by 'part-time' personnel, and are attached to the State in which they originate.

On 10 October 1950, the 123rd Fighter Bomber Wing was created to consolidate three ANG squadrons and was called to active duty at Godman AFB, Kentucky. To control the three combat squadrons, the 123rd Fighter Bomber Group was organized on the same day, subordinate to the Wing. Assigned to Tactical Air Command of USAF, the 123rd FBW and its three squadrons, the 156th FBS North Carolina ANG, 165th FBS Kentucky ANG and 167th FBS West Virginia ANG were flying the F-51D Mustang. The new commander of the Group became Lt. Col. William Payne. On 26 October the Wing was officially activated, with Col. Philip P. Ardery as Commanding Officer. Ardery had seen combat during WWII with 389th Group in the Middle East, and then with 2nd Combat Bomb Wing in the North African and Europ-

ean Theatres. He was subsequently awarded the Silver Star, the Distinguished Flying Cross with 2 Oak Leaf clusters, the Air Medal with 3 Oak Leaf clusters, the Croix de Guerre with Palm and the European Theatre of Operations Ribbon with 5 Stars.

At the time of Ardery's assignment, the nucleus of the 123rd's airmen had been drawn from the three states of its attached squadrons, and called to active duty for 21 month's service. The initial strength of each squadron was 30 officers and 122 airmen, but from November 1950, 46 personnel from the Georgia ANG were added to the strength of the 123rd FBW. Soon after moving to Godman AFB, the Wing's personnel were further augmented by those from Reserve and Regular US Air Force units.

There then began several months of intense training in order to come to operational readiness, although the Wing would retain its ageing F-51s for the time being. It is worthwhile to note that many of the Wing's pilots and maintenance personnel were new to the F-51, having previously been assigned to F-47 Thunderbolts or bomber types. On 24 June 1951, three pilots from the 123rd FBW were sent to Alexandria AFB in Louisiana, for training with 137th FBW on the F-84 Thunderjet. These were the first personnel from the Wing to undergo jet conversion. Subsequently most of the 123rd pilots received up to ten hours of F-84 time at either Alexandria or Shaw AFB in South Carolina.

During its build-up, the Wing started a series of gunnery camps at Eglin AFB, Florida, which not only qualified the Wing pilots, but also gave personnel from the 123rd experience of deploying from their home base. It was during one such detachment that Maj. Woodrow W. Sutherland of the 167th FBS was killed. His F-51D collided with another aircraft while taxiing at Eglin. On 8 April, three days after this accident, a C-47 bearing the Honour Guard for the Major's funeral crashed on approach to Charleston Airport in West Virginia. Nine officers and twelve airmen from 167th FBS were killed. As a result of this loss, many personnel were hurriedly posted in to the 123rd FBW who had little fighter aircraft experience. This was at a time when many of the experienced Wing personnel were being 'lost' to Far East Air Forces (FEAF) for service in Korea. The newly arrived replacement pilots were quickly put through an F-51 checkout, and after a month or so of intensive flying were integrated into the 123rd, and went through the F-84 qualification programme. Many of the 'real' fighter jockeys recall that, although the majority of these newly-qualified personnel had only flown transport aircraft prior to April 1951, they went on to become first-class fighter pilots.

On 19 September 1951, the arrival of a message from USAF Headquarters confirmed rumours which had been circulating for some time: that the Wing would deploy overseas — less aircraft — and would inherit aircraft already in position. The message alerted the Wing for: *"Foreign service and permanent change of station [with a] tentative readiness date of 1 December,...to a mild temperate zone"*. The only clues given were that an advance echelon of flight and maintenance personnel was authorised to proceed to the new duty location in order to train on the F-84E. This would prove to be the new equipment for 123rd FBW, and training would be given by 12th FEW personnel, which the message failed to mention, was based at Manston, UK...

It was not until the following month, however, that the Wing was 'officially' notified of a move to Manston. Despite the impending move and conversion onto the Thunderjet, at the end of September, only 21 pilots were jet qualified, and to speed up the process the remaining crews were sent to other F-84 units to train. In the period 3 - 25 October, 47 of the Wing's combat pilots were passed out in the Thunderjet by 20th FBW at Shaw AFB. Using F-84Bs and Cs borrowed from 137th FBW at Alexandria AFB, 123rd FBW pilots completed 199 flights and 223 hours between them for the 3-week period. Milt Markowitz, who was assigned to the 167th FBS explains:

"Shortly before transfer to England, all [nonqualified] unit pilots were sent to Shaw AFB, South Carolina for initial qualification in the F-84. It turned out to be a very basic checkout. A couple of hours of ground school and four local flights in the

F-84B with a chase pilot riding 'herd' on the student. I got a total of about 4¹/₂ hours on this checkout. Within three months, we were at Manston flying training sorties with a goal toward attaining combat readiness".

According to 20th FBW records, the ground school consisted of four classes of approximately 18 pilots, instruction taking one week per class. The target of 10 hours flying time per student was not achieved due to adverse weather. A further 17 of the 123rd's pilots were returned to the Wing without completing the full course, for a variety of reasons such as previous jet experience, being required to attend other education and being grounded after physical examination. Staff at the 20th FBW made their dissatisfaction with the training known, but by the time anything could be done, the 123rd was on its way to England. The relative inexperience of the Wing's pilots was, however, of minor importance compared to the problems which surfaced relating to eligibility for overseas service, the basic requirement being for personnel to have 9 months active service left. However, as the Wing would have been on active duty for 14 months (out of a total of 21) at the time of departure for UK, most personnel were not officially eligible for posting to Manston. In addition, many of the personnel who were new to the Wing had recently returned from the Korean Theatre, and did not fulfil the requirement of 12 months service in the US prior to another overseas move. Thus, at the end of September 1951, of 1,309 Wing personnel, only 551 were eligible for movement to Manston.

Two methods were used to resolve this problem. Initially, an influx of some 900 USAF and USAF Reserve airmen and 22 officers relieved the difficulty to some extent. Alas, the majority of these personnel were not experienced on the F-84, and in conjunction with manufacturer's courses such as the Allison J35 (F-84) engine course at Indianapolis, many of the maintenance personnel were rushed through intensive on-the-job training sessions. Some experienced F-84 pilots were also posted in from other units, notably from 111th FBS Texas ANG. On the maintenance side, Paul Fry was one of those who were hurriedly posted into the Wing:

"At least four of us [later to serve] in the 406th Group were among the first class of jet mechanics to be trained at Amarillo AFB in Texas. We were then assigned to Godman Field in Kentucky, where the Kentucky Air National Guard (we learned) had been activated for overseas duty. Obviously, the Guard personnel were very familiar with P-51 Mustangs [but] knew very little about jet engines. They probably weren't too happy at that point. At Amarillo, our training was on both F-80s and F-84s, so we studied both axial and radial flow [centrifugal] jet engines. It was about a six-week course".

The second method to overcome the manpower

problem was that regulations were revoked, and many personnel who had not originally been eligible to do so, accompanied the Wing to Manston. Additionally, many officers signed Indefinite Career Reserve agreements, which would retain them on active duty until May 1953.

In order to determine the adequacy of RAF Manston for the operating purposes of the 123rd FBW, on 16 October 1951 two liaison officers left Godman AFB for Manston on ten days temporary duty (TDY), for the purpose of co-ordinating the overseas movement. In addition, on 8 November, three officers and two airmen were detached to the New York Port of Embarkation to liase with Troop Movement and Initial Equipment Division at Brooklyn Army Base, so that the sea-borne movement of personnel to the UK could be accomplished smoothly.

The details of the movement of the 123rd FBW from Godman AFB to Manston were incorporated in a comprehensive movement order. The first personnel to move were the Advance Detachment of 13 officers and 96 airmen, who on 6 November departed Godman AFB, bound for Standiford Field in Kentucky, and on to Westover AFB, Massachusetts. Colonel Ardery departed Godman AFB ten days later by air for Manston. The Advance Detachment departed Westover AFB in two C-124 Globemaster aircraft on 9 and 11 November, and arrived 19 hours later at Manston. Upon arrival, this group of officers and airmen immediately started their F-84E indoctrination course under direction of 12th Fighter Escort Wing personnel.

The first, and perhaps the major project for this group was of checking out — under the supervision of 12th FEW personnel — seven 123rd FBW pilots in the F-84, who would then assume the role of instructors when the main body of the wing arrived. Unlike previous Wings that had flown the F-84 at Manston, the 123rd had not been flying the F-84 operationally prior to arrival, and the help of 12th FEW personnel during the training process was essential. The administrative personnel of the 123rd FBW detachment were immediately put to work cleaning and straightening up quarters and offices in preparation for the arrival of the remaining Wing personnel.

Don Sidak, another pilot with the 167th FBS, arrived at Manston as part of the Advance Detachment, and was assigned the task of checking out further Wing aircrew in the Thunderjet:

"I was on the advance party arriving about a month before the main party. We flew over in the C-124 and I might add that very few of the pilots had any jet time before arriving. The Guard pilots like myself had been flying P-51s, and before coming over, a few went to Shaw AFB and had two rides in the F-84. We had no 'dual' rides before checking out in the F-84 and our ground school was a briefing by an instructor pilot at Shaw, the day before we crawled in, and with the help of an experienced pi-

lot, got the jet started...an hour later, we were checked out in jets. Those that didn't get a check ride in the States went through about the same checkout procedure at Manston".

To expect such inexperienced (on the F-84) personnel to carry out the duties of check pilot so soon after their own conversion seems ludicrous. Fortunately, the standard of pilot on both sides allowed the process to follow through fairly uneventfully.

On 17 and 18 November, the main body of the Wing was transported by 514th Troop Carrier Wing Curtiss C-46 transports of the Air Force Reserve to Newark Airport in New Jersey. From Newark, the Wing was loaded onto buses and taken to Camp Kilmer, New Jersey, prior to embarkation. The 123rd FBW was split into two echelons before leaving Godman AFB, and the first arrived at Camp Kilmer on 17 November, the second on 19 November. Confusion reigned when two days later nearly 200 airmen, newly assigned to the Wing, arrived unannounced at Godman AFB for immediate shipment to Camp Kilmer. As with the earlier deployment of the 31st FEW, some juggling of personnel and equipment was made, and the rest of the operation ran relatively smoothly. On 19 November, the Air Echelon, composed of seven officers and five airmen, began the long ferry flight of the Wing's two C-47 aircraft. They departed for Westover AFB, enroute to Manston, under the command of Capt. Calvin Sefton and arrived in the UK a week later.

On 23 November, the first echelon left Camp Kilmer by train for New York City and embarked aboard the USNS *General Maurice Rose*, which docked at Southampton on 1st December 51. From Southampton these personnel were transported by bus to Manston. The second echelon left New York on 29th November aboard the USNS *General Hersey*, also bound for Southampton. Staff Sergeant Gregory Kirkwood was one of this second echelon, and takes up the story of the far-from-uneventful voyage:

"The Hersey *already had 2,000 troops on board and we made it 3,500 total. The ship was way overloaded by the figure of 1,000-plus men. Of note on the previous in-bound [voyage] from Bremerhaven, in early November, the* Hersey *had collided with an Argentinian freighter, sunk the freighter and seriously damaged the bow of the* Hersey. *A general-purpose temporary bow was fixed to the ship and we departed on November 29, 1951 for Southampton. The weather was blowing a full nor-easterner and conditions were very bad. The temporary bow was taking water and the Captain hove-to. During the first 24 hours at sea, we covered 27 miles! As nature has no pity on the wicked, when we entered the English Channel, a full gale was blowing. The ship started to take water and list to the starboard side. All 3,500 of we passengers were required to come up on to the deck and stand on the port side to keep the ship on a relatively even keel. Then, to top things*

off, a major fuel line [running] *across the bridge area broke a coupling and sprayed oil all over the bridge 'greenhouse'. The Captain had to lean out of the bridge and shout instructions to the helmsman!"*

The *Hersey* finally docked at Southampton on 9 December 1951, and the personnel of the second echelon were taken to Manston by bus. Finally, the rear echelon departed Godman AFB for Camp Kilmer via Newark Airport on 21 November. The Wing was officially in place at Manston on 9 December 1951.

When the Advance Detachment of four officers and 50 maintenance personnel arrived at Manston on 10 and 12 November 1951, they found that, because of the non-availability of parts and the presence of serious corrosion, a large number of F-84s were out of commission upon receipt from the 12th Fighter Escort Wing. By 19 December 1951, a total of 62 aircraft had been accepted by the 123rd, of which 30 were in commission, 7 were AOCP (aircraft out of commission for parts) and 34 were AOCM (aircraft out of commission for maintenance). The discrepancy in these figures is due to the fact that one aircraft could be AOCM and AOCP at the same time!

PFC Richard T. Grace from Cincinnati, Ohio, was just one of over 1,300 airmen now finding their feet at Manston. Following his Aircraft & Engine Mechanics Course at Sheppard AFB in Texas, Dick Grace had been assigned in October 1951 to the newly activated 156th FBS at Godman AFB. He arrived in England aboard the USNS *Rose* with the first echelon.

"After being assigned barracks, issued tools, etc., I was told I would be an Assistant Crew Chief, and work with S/Sgt Milton Harrington, Crew Chief on 49-2391. Capt. David Martin, 'B' Flight leader, was assigned as pilot of this aircraft".

"The first few weeks were spent going over all the planes doing inspections to verify their airworthiness. As it turned out, only about half were, in our opinion, ready to fly. The others had various problems ranging from inoperable radios and cut tyres to fuel leaks. Most of these aircraft were repaired and put back into service in 4 to 6 weeks; but some, because of a shortage of parts, would become 'hangar queens' and remain out of service for several months. Milt Harrington and I were lucky, maybe because we were both Irish [but more likely because it was a Flight leader's aircraft — 'Rank hath its privileges'], *because '391 was one of the better maintained aircraft and saw a lot of flying time".*

"During the early months of 1952, most of the mechanics on base were given some additional technical training known as 'The F-84E Mechanics Familiarization Course'. Shortly after completing this school I was promoted to A/2C. Milt Harrington was moved to another job and I was made Crew Chief of '391".

The squadrons, as with earlier detachments, took over the corresponding facilities vacated by the outgoing unit. The 156th FBS, commanded by Captain John Rose, took over the dispersal on the 'loop' at the north-western end of the runway. The other two squadrons were based on the other side of the airfield, the 165th — with Major Alma Flake as CO — on the western taxiway. Flake had previously flown combat missions in Korea with the 67th FBS, flying F-51Ds, and was one of only a few Mustang pilots to get a 'kill' in that conflict. The final F-84 squadron at Manston, the 167th FBS, was deployed on the eastern side of the airfield where the civilian air terminal stands today. Leading the 167th was Major James Covington. Each squadron was assigned a colour: 156th yellow, 165th red and 167th blue, and these colours were taken over from the aircraft handed over by the 12th FEW. There is, however, one interesting point to note here; in the past, the lowest-numbered squadron had been assigned red as its colour. Due to the fact that the 156th FBS had taken over aircraft and facilities at the 'loop' dispersal which had previously been assigned to the 12th FEW's 560th FES, the 156th FBS took over yellow-coloured aircraft. To save time, these colours were retained; indeed, the colour schemes worn by 123rd FBW Thunderjets were the same as had been applied to them by the 12th FEW. Each squadron of the 123rd was further broken down into flights, which were assigned the colours yellow, red, white, blue and green. A squadron would have four flights, and each flight would be assigned a colour. These flight colours were painted in a broad band around the tail cone, and on the vertical fin tip. An average flight would be assigned six pilots, generally led by a Captain.

The facilities available at Manston in the early months of 1952 were primitive to say the least, and it was not until August 1952 that the Y-shaped fighter-type dispersals were laid down. The aircraft taken over by the 123rd were generally badly corroded due to the deposits of salt and dirt that had accumulated over an extended period of time. Manston lies within sight of the sea, and a corrosive atmosphere is always present. It appeared that little, if anything had been done to rectify this condition by the 12th FEW, though in their defence, the 12th FEW maintenance personnel had hardly been idle during their brief stay at Manston. To remedy the corrosion problem, aircraft were scheduled through Burtonwood for treatment, with the first two F-84s taking more than a month to rectify. A programme of corrosion prevention training was started, and by the beginning of 1952, many of these major problems had been alleviated; though the condition of the aircraft, and the lack of spare parts would continue to hound the 123rd throughout its short time at the Kent airfield.

To carry out flying tasks not assigned to the fighter bomber squadrons, the 123rd Air Base Group Flight was formed under the leadership of Lt. Col. John R. Bennett. Initially, three C-47 transports were allocated to the Flight, and these were utilised for both cargo and personnel transportation. Three T-6

43: *Ray Simone (left) and Dick Grace, maintenance personnel with 156th FBS, pose with an air compressor on the 'loop' dispersal. Note 'rustic' wooden boarding ladder. Aircraft in background is 49-2057, which was written off on landing at Manston on 12 March 1952. (Richard T Grace)*

44: *These 167th FBS Thunderjets are parked on Manston's eastern side, close to the present-day civil terminal. Aircraft second from left is 49-2363, which was badly damaged during an engine run-up on 23 May 1952 and subsequently scrapped. (Dick Forsgren)*

45: *Typical overcast weather is apparent in this winter 1951/52 shot along Manston's 'main drag'. The station's 'Astra' cinema can be seen at the far end. (Al Farnes)*

46: *123rd FBW gained three T-6F trainers by just signing them out under Col Ceuleers' name. These noisy aircraft became known as 'Ceuleers' Air Force' and remained at Manston for some time. (Donelson)*

47: *The 'Skyblazers' aerobatic team pass towards the 167th FBS dispersal, 23 May 1952. Less than 30 seconds later Capt John O'Brien's aircraft crashed, killing the pilot. (Ernest Panizzoli)*

48: *Capt O'Brien's funeral service was held in the station's Astra cinema. USAF police personnel stood guard at the doorway. (Ernest Panizzoli)*

trainers were also acquired for the Flight, by a somewhat devious route. Gregory Kirkwood recalls these noisy aircraft:

"The Vice Wing Commander, Col. George Ceuleers found out that he could check out airplanes from the depot at Erding AB, Germany just on his signature. He had a Wing C-47 fly him and a couple of buddies to Erding (near Munich) and he signed a 'hand receipt' for three T-6s. He and his friends then flew them back to Manston. It was his own private air force. He had them painted bright yellow with red, blue and green fan-type tail decoration. In those days, the runway was 750 feet wide, (and) he and his friends would take off in formation using the runway width to take off".

It appears that this rather irregular use of these aircraft was overlooked until, in May/June 1952, a Third AF team of inspectors, who were present at Manston for accident investigation (of which more later), discovered the presence of the T-6s, and, to put it lightly, took a dim view. In the event, through what must have been some deft manoeuvring, the aircraft remained on 'indefinite loan' at Manston.

The 123rd FBW spent a great deal of time during December 1951 and the early months of 1952 in training ground crews and transitioning its pilots onto the F-84E, and as early as the first week of December 1951, the Wing had flown F-84 missions. One of the first was programmed for Tuesday 4 December 1951, and proved to be a somewhat problem-filled exercise. Three aircraft took off at approximately 10.40am for a long-range cross-country flight to Brussels, Frankfurt, Munich, Strasbourg, Lyon, Le Bourget, Coxyde and then back to Manston — a total of around 1,400 air miles (2,258km). Shortly after takeoff, one pilot returned to base because of a problem with his aircraft, leaving the remaining two F-84s to proceed with the mission. The flight was uneventful until the Munich-Strasbourg leg, when Capt. Ken Hoylman of the 167th FBS, flying F-84E 49-2053 reported that his tip tanks had emptied of fuel. An accompanying pilot gave Hoylman's aircraft a look over, and confirmed that fuel was siphoning from the tank vent. This was later pinned down to a faulty buckeye valve in the main tank, which had pumped nearly all of the fuel from the Thunderjet. The Flight Leader tried to get a steer from the Paris VHF Direction Finder, but other traffic prevented this, and although Frankfurt DF was contacted, they were unable to help.

Finally, the Flight Leader managed to get a fix, but unfortunately as a result of its proximity on the VHF band, Luxembourg radio beacon was received rather than Paris Le Bourget. The flight then commenced a letdown. Soon it was noticed that the ceiling and visibility were so bad that it became impossible to stay in visual contact with each other, so a climb was initiated to clear the cloud. However, in short time, Hoylman noticed that his fuel quantity was reading only 200 to 300 lbs (88-133 kg) and he realised

that there was nothing left for him to do to save the aircraft. He then decided to eject, but his canopy would not jettison and the seat failed to fire. Thinking quickly, Hoylman inverted his aircraft, dropped out and parachuted to earth safely. The Flight Leader climbed to 28,000 feet (8,536 m), radioed Manston Tower and returned to base.

The problems did not stop there, however, and Hoylman's short drop earthwards was brought to an abrupt end by a tree, where he remained for nearly three hours until freed by a farmer. It was only then that Ken Hoylman realised that he had crashed in Luxembourg, near the town of Vianden. The unfortunate F-84 had crashed in a fish hatchery, destroying property estimated at $3,000. 49-2053 was completely destroyed.

Minor accidents also occurred at this time. On 15 December 1951, an F-84E was taxiing behind a parking area when the nose undercarriage collapsed after hitting a concrete block. After breaking off the lower portion of the nose gear, the remaining section struck the far side of the block, then slid off and penetrated into the ground. The aircraft came to a rest with three inches (75 mm) of clearance between the ground and the nose gear fairing door, the pilot being uninjured. This was just one of many minor accidents of this sort to occur at Manston, and only serves to show the state of the airfield at this time. However, plans were in hand to drastically improve the aircraft handling areas, and later in the year, the modifications were started.

Charles 'Chuck' Crawford was Engineering Officer with 165th FBS during the stay at Manston. Chuck was well-qualified in this post, and had been working at North American Aviation on the F-86 Sabre irreversible tailplane control system prior to being called up:

"When we arrived at Manston, the CO made me Engineering Officer, as well as being one of the regular pilots in the squadron. It was my good luck that some very experienced jet mechanics had also been assigned to the unit and joined us at Manston. I had seven Master Sergeants [under my control] so I had top-notch guys to see that our maintenance crews did things quick, accurately and correct! I made three of them line chiefs of 6 or 7 airplanes each, two were my inspectors, one was my parts warehouse manager, and the last was [in control] over the other 6".

"Each of the squadrons had two T-33s and that's what we used to check out the other pilots in the F-84, after they finished their ground school. Then, later we used them for simulated night and weather flying with hoods, blinders, etc. We flew a lot of practice missions to bases in Germany, where ground troops were engaged in maneuvers. Some days we were the 'good guys' and sometimes we were the 'bad guys'. We were a low-level ground support unit, so our runs were strafing and skip bombing very close

to the ground. For me, it was old times as that was the way I flew in WW II".

The first quarter of 1952 was a difficult time for the 123rd FBW. The change from propeller-driven aircraft to jets, the move to a foreign country and numerous supply and material problems combined to make life difficult for the Wing personnel. In addition, a complete Ground and Transition Training Programme was instigated for pilots. The biggest problem for the Wing, other than the condition of the aircraft, was that of checking out the tactical pilots in the Thunderjet. The earlier efforts to have 12th FEW personnel check out 123rd aircrew soon paid dividends, and through a co-ordinated effort, the remaining Wing pilots were gradually processed through F-84 training. This program proved very successful, and the 156th FBS Transition Training was 94% complete at the end of March 1952, by which time 165th FBS had completed 85% of its transition and 167th had completed 80%. This Transition Training encompassed 20 hours of Ground School, covering all aspects of the aircraft and its operation.

The 12th FEW furnished most of the instructors for these classes. A total of 18 hours of tuition was followed by a written exam that required a 100% pass mark. There then followed the customary blindfold cockpit check, after which the transition pilot began the flight programme, which required the completion of 15 different training missions. These ranged in difficulty from Mission 1, which was accompanied by an instructor pilot, and practised stalls and landing patterns at 20,000 feet, to Mission 15, which was a long-range cross-country flight with three other aircraft and relied upon the student to plan the flight and prepare maps for the mission. The instructor pilots for these missions were required to have over 1,000 hours total flying time, with 100 hours in the F-84. Pilots who had been previously checked out in the F-84, and had over 25 hours of F-84 time were required to complete only 6 transition missions.

The 123rd's ground training commenced in a limited form on 2 January 1952. During the month, all units of the 123rd FBW began classes in Military Training, Physical Training, Information and Education, and 1 hour each in the following subjects: Atomic, Biological, Chemical, Character Guidance and Security. In order to further implement the training program on the F-84E aircraft, a Mobile Training Detachment arrived at Manston the first week in January. It was immediately set up and classes commenced on 7 January 1952, the last class completed training on 11 March 1952. Total attendance for all courses was 527, with 500 successful completions. During the months of February and March, the rate of ground training was stepped up, with 14 hours per man accomplished in February, and 16 hours per man in March.

The operational difficulties encountered in November and December were carried over into Janu-

ary 1952. The departure of the 12th FEW resulted in the loss of much aircraft test and support equipment that had been on loan to the 123rd FBW. This resulted in an inability to handle and operate the aircraft, and consequently all F-84s were grounded on 3 January 52. This seems an incredible situation for a front-line fighter bomber wing to be in, and to no great surprise, Third AF hastily made arrangements to borrow a minimum of essential equipment from the 81st FIW, flying F-86As at Bentwaters and the 86th FBW, which was operating the F-84E at Neubiberg, West Germany. The aircraft took to the skies once more on 13 January 1952, though a lack of equipment, allied to poor weather and a shortage of aircraft parts accounted for the low flying time and In-Commission rates for the month of January.

On Friday 4 January 1952, the 123rd FBW suffered its greatest loss during the period of tenure at Manston, raising the spectre of the crash at Charleston during the previous April. One of the 123rd Air Base Group's C-47 Dakotas had flown up to the Burtonwood Depot near Liverpool. These flights were routine and positioned aircrew for picking-up or dropping-off aircraft as well as serving as supply runs. Greg Kirkwood takes up the story:

"The aircraft had landed at Burtonwood and had completed its mission, the crew was to return to Manston with four passengers. They taxied to the active runway run-up area and completed their pre-flight duties. The weather was relatively bad with a 300-ft overcast, half-mile visibility and fog. They were told to hold their position for a landing by a US Navy P2V [Neptune]. The P2V landed approximately 900 feet short of the runway, veered to the right and struck our C-47 at the rear of the pilot's seat, the no.2 engine of the P2V broke loose and went through the crew compartment and down the length of the cargo/passenger compartment. The pilot, the radio operator, S/Sgt Robert Kidwell, who happened to be my roommate and four passengers were killed. Of the survivors, the co-pilot was badly burned and the flight mechanic was very severely burned".

The P2V had been returning to Burtonwood after aborting its run up to Keflavik in Iceland, the result of the bad weather. The accident came as a blow to the Wing's morale, but incredibly marked the last fatal aircraft crash at Burtonwood. Less than two years later, the crash of another Manston-based C-47 would have an even higher loss of life. It is a sobering thought that even in times of peace, men can still lose their lives in the defence of their country.

As with the previous rotational F-84 units at Manston, the commitment to simulate strafing attacks on airfields in East Anglia was initiated soon after commencing operational flying. This commitment involved simulating low-level attacks on three major airfields in East Anglia, three times weekly. At the time, the 93rd Bomb Wing's three squadrons of B-50D bombers were based at Lakenheath and Upper

Heyford, and in addition, on 27 January 1952, three giant Convair B-36 bombers from the 7th Bomb Wing at Carswell AFB, Texas arrived at RAF Sculthorpe for a brief period of TDY. In wartime, 123rd FBW would provide long-range fighter escort for these SAC bombers.

Accidents continued to punctuate life for the 123rd, and the March to May period brought an unprecedented number. On 12 March, shortly after four Thunderjets from the 156th FBS had departed Manston, number 4 aircraft of the formation (callsign 'Westwind Red 4') experienced a possible explosion in the cockpit and momentary vibration. The flight leader advised number 4 to abort and return to land immediately. Just after starting the gear down and at approximately 90 degrees on break for landing, a complete loss of power occurred. Due to the lower than normal traffic pattern being flown, the pilot was unable to reach the runway. He selected a small field and started the gear back up. Concurrently, the engine began to oscillate between negligible and 80-85% power, and the pilot then decided to continue his effort to reach the safety of Manston's runway. Due to his low altitude and airspeed, coupled with the momentary losses of power, he was able to make only a very shallow turn, which brought the aircraft onto the runway at approximately a 45-degree angle from the right or south side. This angle of approach would permit initial contact on the 900-ft (274m) wide runway, and with a right turn of approximately 10 degrees after landing, a run of grass of approximately 6,000ft (1,829m). Unfortunately, because of the lack of a taxi strip, it was necessary for other aircraft to use the north side of the runway for taxiing, and at the time of this accident, there were three F-84E aircraft taxiing in such a position that a turn to avoid them was necessary before contact with the ground. This turn resulted in the aircraft stalling and it dropped in on the right gear and wing tip. The impact bent the right main undercarriage leg at right angles at the top of the wheel, and when the left wheel slammed down, the left gear and nose gear were sheared from the aircraft which then skidded to a stop on the runway. Estimated damage to aircraft 49-2057 was $183,000. The cause was put down to water in the fuel system; the pilot received a strained back.

On 21 March, as two F-84s from the 156th FBS were carrying out a formation take-off to the east, the number 2 aircraft, piloted by Lt. Roy E. Jennings, Jr. experienced vibration and loss of power about 6,000 feet (1,829 m) into his takeoff run. The pilot immediately retarded the throttle and shot past the end of the runway still travelling at over 100 mph (161 km/h). Because of his high speed and the uncertain terrain in the overshoot area, Lt. Jennings attempted to raise his undercarriage. The nose and left main gears folded, and the aircraft came to a rest in a field of Brussels sprouts, in a nose-down attitude,

which caused the ingestion of a large amount of soil (and vegetables!) into the engine. Damage was estimated at $25,000, and the pilot was uninjured.

Less than an hour later, Lt. William F. Vogel from 'Red' Flight of the 156th FBS (callsign 'Westwind 25') left Manston on a routine mission. At about 6,000 feet (1,829 m), the fuel ice warning light came on. The pilot could not correct this indication, but as he had previously experienced trouble in checking out his aircraft's overheat warning system, and as no change in the condition of the aircraft was apparent, the flight was continued. On passing through 16,000 feet (4,878 m), however, an explosion occurred, again in the cockpit area, which was followed by severe vibration, and the engine overheat light came on. Lt. Vogel immediately throttled his engine back to idle, and checked for signs of fire. With no fire apparent, the aircraft was turned towards Manston for an emergency landing. Vogel tried to radio his situation to Manston tower, but no contact was made. Luckily, however, a flight leader in the vicinity picked up the broadcast, and suggested that Lt. Vogel contact Manston on the local frequency for a VHF/DF (directional) steer. Once DF contact had been made, steering instructions were passed to the stricken craft. On descending through 4,000 feet (1,219 m) the aircraft broke from overcast into clear air about three miles from Manston, and Lt. Vogel peeled off over the runway at 3,000 feet (914 m). As the pilot began to turn base leg onto runway 29 however, the aircraft began losing height rapidly. An attempt to apply more power produced no response from the engine, and the weight of the aircraft, along with the drag from the lowered undercarriage prevented the aircraft reaching the runway. On realising his predicament, Vogel wisely raised his undercarriage and landed the aircraft in the undershoot at approximately 60° to the runway heading. The canopy spontaneously jettisoned due to the impact and the left wing tip tank was wrenched off and caught fire. The aircraft slid for about 1,000 yards (914 m) and came to a stop behind a farmhouse, approximately 500 yards (457 m) from the runway threshold. Damage to the aircraft (49-2327) was estimated at $158,670.00, and although the Wing records stated that *"..the pilot escaped with slight facial injuries"*, William Vogel remembers it differently; *"I was injured when the canopy separated from the airplane, hit my helmet and tore my nose, which a wonderful doctor was able to stitch back to my face"*.

Six days later, on 27 March, the pilot of another Thunderjet was practising approaches to Manston. The first two approaches were made without incident but on the third approach the undercarriage warning light stayed on and the pilot could not get a 'down' indication for his nose gear. All attempts to get a nose gear green light were unsuccessful. After checking with the Runway Control Officer, who stated that the gear appeared down, a landing was made, guarding the hydraulic pressure with the hand pump. The landing roll was completed without incident, and the maintenance section was called to install the nose gear safety pin. The line chief installed the safety pin in the nose gear and cleared aircraft to taxi back to the parking area. But as the aircraft taxied on the rough pierced planking taxi strip the nose gear collapsed causing slight damage to the aircraft. The pilot was uninjured.

A more serious accident occurred on the 27th, when Capt. Charles E. Mack, the 167th FBS Maintenance Officer, took off on a transition flight with a chase pilot. Although it was Mack's second flight, it was in fact detailed as a 'third F-84 transition' mission. Presumably, as a result of Mack's previous experience (1,026 hours), he was permitted to skip one of the preliminary check flights. Captain Mack had only 4 hours and 20 minutes in the F-84E prior to this flight. The sortie was detailed as follows:

Supervised by instructor pilot in area, 150 gallons fuel in each tip tank.

(1) Climb to 10,000 feet (3,048m) at 98% RPM. Check time and fuel consumption.

(2) Cruise at 300 Kt. IAS at 10,000 feet; time fuel consumption for 6 minutes. Note airspeed, tailpipe temperature and fuel pressure.

(3) Cruise at 96% at 10,000 feet; time fuel counter for 6 minutes. Note airspeed, tailpipe temperature and fuel pressure.

(4) Practice dives and zooms.

(5) Practice stalls, chandelles and lazy eights.

(6) Practice ADF approach.

(7) Enter traffic pattern with minimum of 1,000 lbs (444 kg) fuel. Make a practice go-around (minimum altitude 200 feet/61 m). Observe tail pipe temperature and acceleration.

The climb out from Manston to 20,000 ft (6,096 m, rather than 10,000 feet/3,048 m) was normal and the mission was performed as briefed, ending with a series of aileron rolls, lazy eights and chandelles. However, approximately 30 minutes after takeoff, at approximately 11.05am local time, Capt. Mack's machine entered a slight diving left turn as if entering a lazy eight. The dive continued to steepen and at approximately 6,000 or 6,500 ft (1,829/1,891 m) the aircraft apparently went through a mild pitch-up and entered a dive leading to the left. Mack ejected somewhere between 6,000 (1,829 m) and 3,000 ft (914 m) but it seems that he was injured when he left the plane. He made no attempt to separate from his seat or open his parachute, and was killed. The aircraft, 49-2044, came out of cloud at 3,000 feet (914 m) with wings level in a thirty-degree dive. It then rolled to the right and struck the ground at a 65-70° angle. The crash occurred west of Canterbury, with wreckage spread over a large area.

One rather unusual chain of events came to light soon after Mack's crash. Just prior to the accident, 1st Lt. Don Sidak took '044 up for a spin, and what subsequently happened is particularly poignant:

"I had flown the airplane the day before, got airborne and something did not seem right, so I entered down wind and landed with a full fuel load. I never could determine what was wrong — maybe a gut feeling, but on the next flight, it crashed. He [Mack] was flying with my flight gear, as we were short on equipment. He had my parachute, flight jacket and possibly my helmet (the doctor originally filled out the death certificate in my name), and his crash was never really resolved as to what went wrong. He bailed out at low altitude with the aircraft in a steep spiral and the 'chute never opened and he landed in the seat, face down on the concrete in front of a pub".

The most likely cause would again seem to have been lack of, or contaminated, oxygen. At the briefed altitudes, oxygen would certainly have been required, but we will never know the full story. Don Sidak, however, had plenty of reason to thank his pilot's intuition.

From April 1952, the 123rd FBW began to fly an average of two missions per week in conjunction with the GCI sites, taking on the role of defending interceptors. Previously, all GCI missions carried out by the Wing had been purely 'enemy' in content. On 1 April, gunnery and bombing missions were commenced on the three ranges at Manhood, Dengie Flats and Leysdown. A lack of range facilities, however, meant that the use of these ranges was not possible on a regular basis. During the month, a Combat Operations Section was set up which was manned 24 hours a day by intelligence specialists and apprentice operations clerks. This section tracked the progress of all missions, and plotted their movement on a WW II-style master map, while direct telephone lines linked the section with all the individual squadrons as well as control tower, Neatishead and Trimley Heath GCI sites and the 9th Air Rescue Squadron. In addition, the Combat Operations Section controlled base defence, and instigated exercises during which certain base personnel would act as 'enemy' agents and try to infiltrate the base defences and 'destroy' key installations.

By the end of the month, the 156th FBS had flown 476 hours in Thunderjets, compared to 706 for the 165th FBS and 563 hours for the 167th. During April, the squadrons were assigned an average of 28 officers and 136 airmen, the combat Group possessing a further 11 officers and 24 airmen. The Group was at this time commanded by Lt. Col. Delynn Anderson, with Maj. William Preble as the Group's Operations Officer. From May 1952, Major Preble replaced Capt. John Rose as CO of the 156th FBS, Rose in turn taking up the position as the squadron's Operations Officer. Finally, Capt. C. Morris was assigned to Group as Operations Officer from 167th FBS. Many such reshuffles were necessary as key members of the Wing rotated back to the United States.

49 Above: *T-33A 49-1000 belonged to 165th FBS: it sported the squadron's red colour on its tip tanks. The aircraft was lost in a crash off Margate on 20 November 1952; both crew survived. (via Paul Cooper)*

50: *This 1997 view in St Peters, Broadstairs shows the exact place that Capt Clifford Fogarty's 165th FBS Thunderjet crashed. Fogarty's aircraft approached from the left and impacted where the car is seen in the centre; three civilians were killed on the ground, and ruined houses were never re-built. St Peters church can be seen in the background at right. (Author's collection)*

51: *On 25 May 1952, 1/Lt Joseph Glass's Thunderjet caught fire at the eastern end of Manston's runway. Glass, a pilot with the 167th FBS, was uninjured; his aircraft, 49-2363, had to be taken to Burtonwood for repair. Buildings in foreground are on the site of the present-day civil terminal buildings. (Dave Keep)*

A 'typical' week of flying in the spring of 1952 would see the 156th FBS performing night training missions on four days, with air-to-ground gunnery taking place at the Dengie Flats range. Meanwhile, the 165th would fly gunnery sorties at Manhood range, near RAF Tangmere, in addition to night flying duties. The 167th FBS could then carry out its gunnery training at Leysdown, as well as night practice. All of this depended on the availability of the ranges of course, along with the supply of bullet marking paint, which was again in short supply. In parallel with the F-84 flying, the Wing's T-33 trainers were utilised to the fullest extent in order to maintain jet proficiency.

Sadly, the task of performing these training missions continued to take its toll. On Sunday 27 April 1952, along with three other pilots from the 165th FBS, Capt. Clifford Fogarty had been detailed for two Sunday Standby Transition Training flights. The first mission took off at 9.15 am, and went without a hitch. On return to Manston two hours later, Capt. Fogarty commented *"I have got the best plane and the best crew chief in the outfit"*. The second mission of the day was to be a flight of four aircraft led by Major Alma R. Flake, commanding officer of 165th FBS. The finger four formation roared off Manston's runway at 12.15 pm, and almost immediately Capt. Fogarty was in trouble. Only 45 seconds after lifting off, No.3 in the formation radioed that Fogarty's plane, 49-2111, was on fire in its left wing. Major Flake took control of the situation and called Fogarty: *"Cap, you are on fire, put it down in the first flat space you see"*.

Things soon got very serious, and Fogarty turned inland over Ramsgate, trying to find a clear field. Over Dumpton, only a mile or two further, there was a muffled explosion, and as the aircraft passed over Broadstairs, a larger explosion occurred. Almost immediately, the aircraft went out of control, dived to the ground, and crashed on houses at St. Peters. Captain Fogarty had no chance to successfully eject and was killed instantly. His body was found 30 feet from the crash scene. It was generally thought that Fogarty was trying to steer his aircraft away from the built-up area when the explosion happened, after which the plane went out of control. One of the other pilots in the flight backed this up: *"I was flying with him and we reached between 800 and 1,000 feet (243 and 304 m) when his plane caught fire. With our speed he could have used his ejector seat at that height, but I am convinced he stayed with the aircraft and tried to get it away from the built-up area. He was trying to get over St. Peters to open country"*.

As it hit the ground, Fogarty's aircraft had demolished a sub-branch of Lloyds Bank in the High Street and flattened a wall in Ranelagh Grove. Two civilians, Mr William Read (79) and Mrs Evelyn Read (55), were found dead at the scene. A further victim, Mrs Ellen Collier, died later of her injuries.

One positive point to note was that the congregation of St. Peters Church, merely 100 yards from the crash scene, had been detained an extra ten minutes by the sermon of their vicar, the Rev. L.C. Sargent. Had this not been the case, then at the time of the crash, the streets of St. Peters would have been filled with people returning home from church, and many more would have been killed. Following the accident, the body of Capt. Fogarty was flown to Burtonwood, and then on to Brooklyn, New York for burial. The only other aircraft incident during April involved another Thunderjet, which made an emergency landing at RAF Tangmere, though thankfully with no damage to either man or machine.

Just over two weeks after Fogarty's accident, on 14 May, Capt. C. Kenneth Walker, Jr. of the 156th FBS was flying his F-84 (49-2074) over the Thames Estuary, heading for Manston. As he was approaching Margate, Capt. Walker's aircraft caught fire and crashed into the sea 1 mile off Foreness Point. Luckily, Walker was able to eject, and after 23 minutes in the water was picked up by the Margate pilot boat and taken, uninjured, to the Manston Base Hospital. Walker described the incident:

"With two other pilots, I had been on a normal mission. We had been at altitude for a short time, and I was leading. As we came down, my wingman told me I was on fire. At the same time I felt a lot of vibration in the cockpit. We were between four and six miles out to sea, just northwest of Margate, flying at about 1,500 feet. I pulled my 'plane up a bit and then banked left to make sure the aircraft would avoid Margate and crash in the sea. I floated down by parachute and dropped into the water. When I hit the sea, I became entangled in my 'chute and had difficulty inflating the dinghy. My wingmen circled above me all the time to let the rescue boat know exactly where I was. That's all there was to it. But I sure want to thank the man in the rescue boat. He did a wonderful job. That water was very cold".

This accident led to the grounding of all F-84s by Third AF HQ on 15 May, pending further investigation. Despite thorough and painstaking analysis, no cause could be pinned down, and the F-84s were passed as fit to fly. Then, however, an oil strike in the USA affected the availability of jet fuel, and the aircraft were again prevented from taking to the air. As if that were not enough, when aircraft finally could be recovered to flying status, bad weather further curtailed airborne activity, and total flying for the three squadrons was down to 968 hours for the month.

Nonetheless, on Wednesday 21 May, another Thunderjet crashed at Manston, and the pilot was killed. Two days later, the 36th FBW Skyblazers F-84 aerobatic team from Fürstenfeldbruck AB in West Germany flew a display at Manston to restore faith in the aircraft among 123rd FBW personnel. Sadly, during one of the final manoeuvres of the display, the aircraft of Capt. John P. O'Brien, 49-2237, crashed and exploded. The pilot was killed outright. Captain O'Brien was a pilot with the 36th FBW's 22nd Fighter Bomber Squadron, and had been flying with The

Skyblazers since the team's first display in September 1948. Chuck Crawford was a witness to the sad events on that day:

"It was a lovely day and everybody who could get there was there. The four aircraft had pulled up into their vertical climb and had split into the four major compass points, looping over for low-level passes across the field, close to each other but in opposite directions. The number 5 man, who was in charge and watched from above, dove down to make his low-level pass. He was most of the way down the runway, about 25 to 30 feet above it and started to pull up into his vertical climb. As he got the nose up about 10 degrees, approximately half of his right wing came off. The airplane made a very quick roll and went in upside down, then bursting into flames. The pilot of course was killed. Luckily, there was no one in the area where he crashed and no one else was injured. This was very hard to take for some people — my son (not quite 3) was bothered by it for some time, as he knew I was flying the same kind of airplane".

This run of tragedies during May was brought to a close two days later. As the 167th FBS's 1st Lt. Joseph W. Glass checked the emergency fuel system of his F-84 near the threshold of Manston's runway 29, the aircraft exploded and caught fire. Luckily, the pilot was able to escape the aircraft without injury. Damage to aircraft 49-2363 consisted of a wrecked fuselage skin due to all the thrown engine compressor blades, and in addition the tail section suffered fire damage. The engine was completely destroyed. The damage to the aircraft was classed as 'substantial', requiring 4,000 man-hours to rectify at a cost of $35,000. As explosion followed by fire had been a common factor in many of these accidents, a thorough investigation was carried out. Rumours of sabotage were firmly denied, and experts from Third AF, 123rd FBW and Rolls-Royce tried to come up with a root cause. In the end, no common fault could be found, and a system of extensive and rigorous maintenance was put in motion to rectify any inherent problem. The cause of the explosion in Glass's aircraft was later put down to a faulty fuel control unit. Thankfully, there would be no other major accidents while the Wing was at Manston.

Personnel from the 123rd FBW Maintenance, Operations, Material and Medical sections departed for Rhein-Main AB in West Germany on 18 May for a 'paper war', entitled Exercise *Maytime*. This exercise was designed to acquaint personnel with the aspects of running an air-support operation. All aspects of this exercise were simulated, and as an example, the first 'mission' flown was a bombing sortie to Berne, Switzerland, during which 3 aircraft were 'lost'. Realism was the key to the successful completion of *Maytime*, and even C-47 cargo resupply flights were planned during the exercise. *Maytime* was concluded satisfactorily on 21 May.

During the week of 2 - 8 June, in conjunction with RAF Metropolitan Sector, the Wing flew missions directed by Sandwich GCI. During these missions, two F-84s played the attackers, while another pair of Thunderjets, under the GCI direction of Sandwich, acted as interceptors. On 13 June, the Wing was tasked with making dummy strafing attacks on the Royal Navy battleship HMS *Vanguard*, which was sailing in the North Sea. Eight F-84s from Manston performed two attacks, one at 1100 hours and one at 1500 hours. The aircraft approached *Vanguard* at between 1,500 and 3,000 feet (457 and 914m), dropping down to 200 feet (61m) for their final approach. The ship returned fire, using blank ammunition in her anti-aircraft guns.

The Wing's gunnery training moved to Wheelus AB in Libya on 14 June. Starting with 165th FBS, which left for Wheelus on 14th, each of the Wing's squadrons would spend 20 days overseas. Ground personnel were shipped to Wheelus on 60th Troop Carrier Wing aircraft from Rhein Main AB in West Germany, around 128 men with each squadron. In addition, the C-47s of the 123rd FBW were utilised to transport essential equipment to Libya. One of these aircraft had departed Manston earlier in the month with an advance party and equipment such as parachutes. This aircraft then positioned to Rome on 13 June with maintenance personnel, where, the following day, minor maintenance support was rendered to the 165th's Thunderjets, as they deployed out from Manston.

The first four Thunderjets had departed Manston at 0800 hours on the 14th and arrived at Fürstenfeldbruck AB, West Germany 1 hour and 45 minutes later; further flights of four aircraft departed Manston at 15-minute intervals. The first flight then departed Fürstenfeldbruck at 1045 GMT, bound for Rome, where they arrived just after midday. From Rome, the flight to Libya took about an hour and a half. During the first deployment, 391 gunnery sorties were flown, plus 86 camera sorties, for a total of 585 flying hours. The maintenance personnel worked wonders during this deployment, and the In Commission rate rose to an unprecedented 75.8%. The only incident of note occurred when an F-84 burst a tyre on landing at Wheelus and swerved off the runway, causing extensive damage to the nose leg. Chuck Crawford has numerous recollections of the 165th's gunnery camp:

"When it was time for aerial gunnery qualification, we went to Wheelus Air Base in Tripoli. I was recovering from a bad cold so I had to go down with the support equipment and personnel, in the transports - Manston to Marseilles to Tripoli. Shooting at the target sleeve down there let our spent ammo fall into the Mediterranean Sea. When our aircraft were in the air, we always had one of our pilots up in the tower with the controllers. We could not expect them to know the aircraft, its emergency systems etc, [so an experienced pilot was put there] just in case.

Since I had the cold still, I spent eight days in that tower. This situation was also routine at the tower back at Manston. Finally, I qualified at the aerial gunnery and flew one of the F-84s back to Manston when we were finished. On that trip we stopped overnight in Rome and then flew around Switzerland on the way back to Manston".

From 18 to 26 June, aircraft from the 156th and 167th FBS took part in Exercise *Castinets* (sic), which involved attacking a group of ships sailing in the North Sea and English Channel. Strafing and bombing took place at altitudes ranging from 200 to 10,000 feet (61 to 3,048 m). Four F-84s were provided for each of twelve missions detailed. One mission was cancelled when haze prevented the convoy being sighted whilst another was cancelled prior to leaving Manston. On two of the missions, aircraft from RAF Fighter Command participated as opposing forces. Attacks were flown in the final stage at altitudes as low as 200 feet (61 m), no problems were encountered on any of these missions. Maintenance problems stretched Wing capability, however, as the gunnery training at Manhood, Dengie Flats and Leysdown was continued through this period. One final accident in June involved a T-6 training aircraft, which struck a tar-burning truck on the runway. Damage was not too serious, but the right wing of the T-6 had to be replaced.

At the end of June, there were still 60 ANG officers assigned to the wing. Third AF ruled that the Indefinite Career Reserve statements, which these officers had signed in February 1951, were invalid, and alerted these personnel for return to the United States. Fifteen officers requested release from active duty. USAFE HQ reversed this ruling, however, and with their hopes dashed at the last hurdle, many would be retained on active duty for another year. During the first week of July 1952, the caretaker 3917th Air Base Group was awarded a 7th Air Division ground safety award for the months April/May/June. Maj. Gen. John P. McConnell presented the award to Maj. William H. Noel of the 3917th.

On 5 July, the 167th FBS began to replace the 165th at Wheelus, and began its gunnery training. By the time it came for the 156th to complete the programme, the Wing would no longer be in existence. On 10 July 1952, the 123rd FBW was returned to state control from active duty, and the squadron designations reverted to their respective states, 21 months to the day after activation. Certain key personnel, such as Lt. Col. Lee Merkel returned to the United States, and assisted in setting up their old ANG squadrons. Finally, in October 1952, Col. Ardery and the majority of the ANG personnel returned home. Philip Ardery took up command of the newly redesignated 123rd Fighter Interceptor Wing. The majority of Wing personnel, who were by this time active USAF, still remained at Manston and were ready to take over immediately as the newly-reactivated 406th Fighter Bomber Wing.

Commanding Officers - Manston Era

123rd FBW
Col. Philip P. Ardery:
26 October 1950 to 10 July 1952
(continued as CO of 406th FBW until October 1952)

156th FBS
Capt. (later Maj.) John M. Rose, Jr:
5 September 1951 to May 1952
Maj. William E. Preble:
May 1952 to 10 July 1952

165th FBS
Capt. Alma Ross Flake:
6 September 1951 to 10 July 1952 (?)

167th FBS
Maj. James C. Covington:
16 May 1951 to 10 July 1952 (?)

52: *Three blue fuselage bands denote that 51-639 is the aircraft of 167th FBS squadron commander Jim Covington. 123rd FBW Thunderjets wore the same scheme as taken over from 12th FEW. (Ken Hoylman via Smith and McLaren)*

THE 406TH FIGHTER BOMBER & FIGHTER INTERCEPTOR WING
'Rise and defend'

Mid-1952 heralded a new era at Manston; finally, an active USAF combat unit was assigned to the base. That unit, the 406th Fighter Bomber Wing, was assigned on 25 June 1952, and reactivated on 10 July, taking over all aircraft, personnel and assets from the 123rd FBW, whose squadron designations reverted (on paper) back to US State control. Previously, the 406th Fighter Group had operated P-47 Thunderbolts in Europe during World War II; the Group inactivated at Nordholz in Germany on 10 August 1946. The different sections within the reactivated 406th FBW were as follows:

HQ, 406th Fighter Bomber Group
512th Fighter Bomber Squadron with twenty-five F-84Es
513th Fighter Bomber Squadron with twenty-five F-84Es
514th Fighter Bomber Squadron with twenty-five F-84Es

HQ, 406th Maintenance and Supply Group
406th Maintenance Squadron
406th Supply Squadron
406th Motor Vehicle Squadron

HQ, 406th Air Base Group
406th Communications Squadron
406th Air Police Squadron
406th Food Service Squadron
406th Installations Squadron

The 3917th Air Base Group still carried out the duties of running the base. Pilots and aircraft were assigned to the three fighter bomber squadrons of the 406th FBW in such a way that those from the 156th FBS were generally transferred to the 512th FBS, those from the 165th went over to the 513th FBS, and 167th personnel and aircraft became 514th FBS assets. The aircraft colour schemes were similar, with the tip tanks and tail fin tip in the squadron colour and a flight-colour band around the tailpipe. Now, however, the nose scallop colour demarcation was extended rearwards below the fuselage on the lower portion. In addition, many aircraft received the squadron badge on the left side of the nose. These emblems, based on those of the WWII 406th Fighter Bomber Group consisted of a bulldog's head wearing a flying helmet superimposed over an F-84 silhouette and three bombs for the 512th, a stylised flea riding a flying bomb for the 513th, and a stylised bomb with legs and arms, dressed as a boxer for the 514th. Only the 512th badge differed greatly from its WWII version, replacing the P-47 silhouette with that of its younger brother, the F-84.

At the time of the 406th's activation, the 165th FBS was completing its gunnery training at Wheelus AB. When the squadron returned at the end of July — now re-named the 513th FBS — its place in Libya was scheduled to be taken by the 512th FBS, returning from its planned 20-day deployment on 15 August 1952. A Readiness Inspection Test, scheduled for August, meant istead that these plans were cancelled and aerial gunnery was completed during July on the Bradwell Bay (Dengie Flats) range northeast of Manston. Prior to this, all 512th aircraft were flown to Germany to have their guns boresighted. One aircraft returning from Germany experienced fuel trouble, the pilot quickly blew off the tip tanks, and made for an emergency landing at Brussels. Both main gear tyres were blown upon landing but the aircraft and pilot were otherwise undamaged. Sadly, a combination of causes meant that the 512th's gunnery back in the UK was largely a waste of effort. Firstly, a lack of airworthy aircraft made maximum utilisation impossible, and poor refuelling facilities at the time merely exacerbated the problem. And even when F-84s could get airborne, the targets (themselves towed by F-84s) were either lost on take-off, necessitating a return to land, or were lost on the way back to Manston, which wasted the whole mission. By the end of the month, there were no targets or tow cables available at Manston as a result. Finally, when missions did prove to be successful, the gun camera film expended on gunnery often proved useless for training purposes, due either to camera malfunctions, poor film or incorrect processing. To round off a thoroughly miserable period for the 512th FBS, on Tuesday 23 July, Capt. Harold Eyrich's Thunderjet ingested the tow target after he had shot it off the cable. Dick Grace, by this time an F-84E Crew Chief with the 512th, remembers the incident well:

"This accident occurred during aerial gunnery training near Manston. The pilot, while making a pass at the tow target hit the steel bar, which kept the target straight and stretched out behind the tow plane. The bar went into the air intake at the nose of the plane, penetrated the radar/radio compartment, came through the lower part of the cockpit, breaking the rudder pedal and exited out the side of the fuselage, taking with it part of the aileron boost system".

Some debris went into the engine, causing it to fail, breaking the rudder pedal, injuring the pilot's foot and left very little, if any, rudder control. Knocking out the aileron boost is like losing your power steering in a car, so this left him with manual control of the ailerons. I believe, but am not sure, there was limited, if any, use of the elevator".

"To say the least, the pilot had a problem. He

decided to bring the wounded bird home. So with no power, no radio, no hydraulic pressure and very little directional control he headed back to Manston. He did an emergency landing gear extension, found the runway, and proceeded to make a perfect dead stick landing and coasted the plane right up to the front doors of Hanger 4 [loop dispersal], where he parked it and climbed out, suffering only a bruised foot. The aircraft was used for parts and never flew again".

Another pilot on a gunnery mission experienced an engine flameout, but managed to re-start the engine and returned to Manston. The incident referred to by Dick Grace represented the last accident to befall the 512th at Manston.

After a brief lull during the summer of 1952, the F-84 safety record again took a dive. On 29 July, 1st Lt James E. Sims from the 513th FBS, flying 49-2342, (actually a 512th aircraft), took off on a gunnery mission to the Dengie Flats Range on the Essex coast. As the three-ship flight, with Sims as no.2 reached the range north west of Manston, the flight leader immediately commenced his camera passes. The initial pass was made from 7,000 feet (2,134m) at a 35° dive angle. The second pass was from 9-10,000 feet (2,743 to 3,048m) at a dive angle of 40-50°, pulling out at 5,000 feet (1,524m). The final pass was the same as the second pass. On completion of his passes, the flight leader heard his number two call that he was commencing his run. Lt. Sims' aircraft was seen in a 40° angle diving on the target at a normal speed for this manoeuvre. Sims' right wing was, however, seen to drop slightly as the dive continued, and though a decrease in dive angle was noticed, the aircraft failed to pull out, and the right wing struck the beach. The Thunderjet cartwheeled down the shoreline and exploded in a ball of flame. There were no indications of a problem prior to the impact, which snuffed out the life of the hapless pilot. A dismal day was rounded

54: *The 512th FBS 'bulldog' squadron badge adorned this board outside the operations hut on the 'loop' dispersal. F-84 plan view was later modified for an F-86 when the unit converted to the new type. (Richard T Grace)*

55: *August 1952 saw the commencement of major construction on the airfield; troops from the US Army's 817th Engineer Aviation Battalion immediately set to work on upgrading runways and taxiways. Here 817th EAB personnel are laying Y-shaped fighter hardstandings alongside the western taxiway on 10 August. (USAF)*

56: *Manston's aircraft often flew missions for the Air Ministry photographers, mainly so that photographic coverage of new types could be placed in 'Recognition Journal' magazine. Milt Markowitz from the 514th FBS flew as backseater for this T-33 mission on 5 August 1952. Note the lack of ejection seats on this early-model aircraft, 49-1006. (Milt Markowitz)*

57: *In November 1952 a number of 406th FBW pilots were tasked with ferrying F-84 Thunderjets to NATO nations. Milt Markowitz took this photo of Randy Steffens' aircraft on one of the trans-atlantic legs. 51-10755 would later serve with the Royal Danish Air Force. (Milt Markowitz)*

58 Above: *512th FBS Thunderjet 49-2054 parked on bare grass during the summer of 1952; concrete hardstands would come by the end of the year. Note how the painted nose differs from the 123rd FBW 'scallop'. (Merle Olmsted via Dave McLaren)*

59: *Among the improvements put into place during the early 1950s was this large concrete apron on the eastern side of the airfield. Aircraft in background are from 514th FBS while those at front are recently arrived with the Wing from 86th FBW at Neubiberg in West Germany. Runway 29 runs left to right on the horizon. (Dave Keep)*

60: *Busy scene inside Hangar 4, 'loop' dispersal. Among the 512th FBS Thunderjets can be seen a couple of 406th ABG C-47s and a 66th Air Rescue Sqn H-19 helicopter. (Richard T Grace)*

off when the SA-16 amphibian scrambled from Manston to assist in the recovery operation ran aground. In any case, there was little that the crew could do.

In May 1952, Third Air Force had contacted the Air Ministry to request that the USAF be given exclusive use of the Dengie Flats range. Up to this point, it had been jointly utilised by USAF and RAF aircraft. Initially, Fighter Command agreed to this, on the proviso that USAF personnel manned the range, and that the RAF could use it when required. In a letter to AOC-in-C Fighter Command, however, Wing Commander N.H. Fresson stated on 31 July 1952 that the RAF still had an urgent need for Dengie Flats, and would only go as far as conceding that USAF personnel could share aspects of range ground operations. This proved to be the case for its future use.

August 1952 saw numerous minor accidents among the 406th's aircraft, starting on the 5th, when F-84 callsign 'Entreat Red 2' undershot on landing and struck the approach lights at the end of the runway. The aircraft was damaged, but the pilot escaped injury. On 10 August, T-6F 44-81777, one of 'Ceuleers' Air Force', called an emergency over the sea, 15 miles east of the airfield. The aircraft was short on fuel, but managed to make the runway. On the 13th, F-84 callsign 'Thread Blue Leader' crashed on the south side of runway 29 on take-off, after the elevators jammed. Again, the pilot walked away. The next day, 406th FBW T-33 51-4474 declared an emergency in company with 49-1006, which was siphoning fuel. Both aircraft landed safely.

A more serious accident occurred on 20 August, when 'Thread Red 2', on a local night flying exercise, caught fire. The pilot ejected successfully from his burning machine, which crashed 1 mile (1.6km) west of Deal. The aircraft, 49-2349, was destroyed. This rather eventful month was brought to an end when F-84G 51-932 from the Woodbridge-based 79th FBS crash-landed on the 28th with a damaged undercarriage; there were no injuries to the pilot, Richard J. Fox. The 79th FBS was one of the three squadrons making up 20th FBW, which had only arrived back in the UK two months previously. The 20th had been the first F-84 unit based at Manston in July 1950.

Around this time, it was decided that F-84 bombing accuracy could be improved if a forward air controller was airborne in the vicinity of the target, to advise pilots of how they were scoring. Whether the Wing instigated this idea is not known, but as a result two little high-wing Stinson L-5 Sentinels were obtained. Lt. Milt Markowitz of the 514th FBS was involved with these spotter aircraft from day one:

"I happened to be the pilot who brought in our first L-5. They dropped me off at Burtonwood, where the US maintained a depot and the next day I got a rudimentary checkout in the aircraft in some 20 minutes and three quick landings. Due to inclement weather, I cooled my heels for four days before taking off with low ceilings. I put in at Bovingdon [after] about an hour and a half of harrowing, low altitude flying and waited two more days before being able to get back to Manston. I was then checked out as an Instructor Pilot and gave a few instructional rides before being rotated back to the US".

Assigned to the 406th Air Base Group, this L-5, plus another which was ferried in soon after, got little use and were returned to Burtonwood in early 1953, one in February, the last departing in April. On average, the spotters had flown less than four hours each per month and the trial was dropped. But the value of forward air control would be demonstrated in both the Korean and Vietnam conflicts.

August saw the commencement of major construction on the airfield. During the month, 130 troops and five officers from 'A' Company of the 817th Engineer Aviation Battalion, US Army, had arrived at Manston with their tractors, bulldozers and graders to start the building of taxi strips and hard standings. Work was to involve the installation of a large aircraft servicing platform (ASP) beside the control tower, a linking taxiway, and 72 Y-shaped concrete fighter-type hard-stands. By February 1953, the hardstandings were complete, and work started on those at the 'loop' dispersal, used by the 512th FBS, plus the construction of the ASP. The improvements at the 'loop' were finished the following month, and the ASP was ready for use in April 1953. With this work behind them, the US Army troops were replaced by those of 'A' Company, 803rd EAB, and numbers reduced to less than thirty. They began work on the resurfacing the centre of runway 29/11. This was expected to last for some months and until construction was complete, aircraft used the runway to either side of the renovation work, such was its width. The Runway was fully reopened on 8 August, and the only remaining work required was the repair of runway lighting, which was completed on 19 October 1953. Minor tarmacking of taxi tracks continued into December, but one year after the start of this major building work, the USAF finally had a fully equipped, operationally viable airfield at Manston. Through subsequent years, further buildings and facilities were added, and Manston was upgraded to meet the demands of an expanding Air Force.

Unfortunately, September of 1952 began with the 406th's second fatality. Captain Roscoe Nemer of the 513th FBS had only recently joined the squadron as Maintenance Officer. Though he had previously flown over 1,200 hours in such types as P-38 Lightnings, P-40 Warhawks and T-33s, much of his flight time was in non-fighter aircraft. Prior to this transition flight, Captain Nemer had only flown $7\frac{1}{2}$ hours in the F-84. Nemer, flying wing to an instructor pilot, departed Manston on the afternoon of Thursday 4 September to practice QGH (ground-controlled) letdowns. Initially all went to plan, but during one 195° turn at

11,000 feet (3,353m), the flight leader lost contact with Capt. Nemer's aircraft, and, after he failed to return to base, the emergency services were alerted. Following an extensive search by the Margate lifeboat, two SA-16 amphibians and the two newly-arrived H-19 helicopters from the 9th Air Rescue Squadron detachment at Manston, F-84 wreckage was found on Margate Sands, five miles off the Thanet coast. The aircraft, 49-2347, proved to be Nemer's aircraft; he had been killed. The wreckage was not recovered, but Capt. Nemer's body was returned to base by helicopter. This was the only major accident to happen during the month, and the entire Wing flew 1,196 hours for an accident rate of 48 per 100,000 flying hours.

September also marked the end of a busy time for the 406th Maintenance Squadron. A new version of the F-84 engine, the J35A-17B, had just been brought into service and all aircraft were retrofitted with it at the soonest opportunity. By the end of September, the last five aircraft had been thus modified. J35 engine life was not fantastic with the F-84; 80 to100 flying hours between installation and removal were the norm. At this time, the scarcity of spares was again being felt, with such items as radar set wave guides, wing access panels, fuel booster pumps and even fuselage aft sections topping the short supply list. And again, A6B tow targets were becoming difficult to obtain, with a resulting decrease in gunnery training activity. Throughout its time at Manston, the Thunderjet was plagued with such problems.

During the latter half of 1952, 406th FBW Thunderjets flew exercises for the first time. On 14 September, Wing personnel and aircraft travelled to Neubiberg AB in West Germany for the rather unimaginatively titled NATO exercise *Blue Alliance*. Ground crews travelled from Manston in the customary C-119s, and were away for ten days. The big annual UK air defence exercise, *Ardent*, followed in early October 1952. As with *Pinnacle* in 1951, Manston-based F-84s flew many missions as bomber escorts. The exercise was broken down into three phases:

Phase 1
0001 hrs, Saturday 4 October - 1700 hrs, Sunday 5 October

Phase 2
2200 hrs, Thursday 9 October - 0200 hrs, Friday 10 October

Phase 3
0900 hrs, Saturday 11 October - 2200 hrs, Sunday 12 October

Attacking forces comprised UK-based F-84s from Manston, escorting the 2nd Bomb Wing's three B-50D squadrons, which were on TDY at Upper Heyford. The UK-based bomber effort was backed up by the permanently stationed B-45As and RB-45Cs from the 47th Bomb Wing at Sculthorpe. The Royal Air Force supplied bombers in the shape of Lincolns, Washingtons (RAF B-29s) and Canberras. In addition, Twelfth AF in Europe supplied USAF B-26 bombers and F-84s. Finally, many NATO countries provided aircraft to attack the UK.

For the purposes of the exercise, Manston was declared as an emergency diversion airfield, and on 4 October, six Dutch Air Force F-84s involved in *Ardent* diverted into Manston, short on fuel. The Dutch were flying the later F-84G version of the Thunderjet by this time, and many 406th personnel must have wondered when their turn to re-equip would come.

One week later another pair of Dutch Thunderjets diverted under similar circumstances. Exercise *Ardent* confirmed that the Royal Air Force was in dire need of more modern fighters, such as the Swift, Hunter and Javelin. However, it was of more importance to the 406th FBW in that it demonstrated the inferiority of the F-84 as a fighter. RAF Meteor pilots from 41, 74 and 245 Squadrons all confirmed that the Thunderjets were even easier to attack than piston-engined aircraft such as Seafires, Sea Furies and Fireflies during the exercise.

The Wing flew 1,018 hours during October, much of it during the two weeks of *Ardent*, and thankfully there were no major aircraft accidents. There were, however numerous minor incidents to punctuate life. On the 6th, F-84E 49-2350 of the 512th had a canopy blow off in flight. The pilot made a safe, but windswept, landing. Ten days later, the pilot of another Thunderjet 'Thread White 2' called an emergency after experiencing incorrect functioning of his controls. This potentially hazardous situation was also brought to a close with a safe landing. Finally, on 18 October, unlucky 'Thread White 2' radioed that he had experienced engine vibration and a subsequent flameout. Through deft piloting, the aircraft was jostled to a 'dead stick' landing at Manston.

During November 1952, many of the pilots of 406th FBW became involved in the delivery of F-84s to NATO countries. Previously, many of these aircraft had been transported from the USA on aircraft carriers, but the corrosion incurred by the aircraft during the voyage often caused a great deal of maintenance work to rectify damage before the aircraft could be delivered. It was decided therefore to deliver subsequent batches of aircraft by air.

Lt. Milt Markowitz was one of these pilots, and ferried an F-84G to the Royal Danish Air Force.

"The ferry flight was quite an experience for us. For whatever technical reasons we had to originate the trip from Denmark. We were sent there commercially, then flew to New York on Pan Am. It was a Silver Anniversary flight for them in the Boeing Stratocruiser and those were the days when passengers were able to go into the cockpit, which we found very interesting. We flew into New York then down

61 Above: *49-2328 is a 512th FBS 'Black' Flight aircraft, denoted by the coloured band around the tail cone. This view shows the yellow nose band to good effect, bordered in a thin black line. (via Bruce Robertson)*

62: *Corrosion prevention was an important part of life in Manston's seaside atmosphere. Here, 512th FBS personnel clean F-84E 49-2391; note traces of 12th FEW/123rd FBW nose scallop. (Richard T Grace)*

63: *This F-84E is undergoing undercarriage functional checks following scheduled maintenance on Manston's east side. (Ernest Panizzoli)*

64: *A pair of 406th FBW Thunderjets undergoing maintenance attention on Manston's eastern ASP. The aircraft in the background is a 512th FBS aircraft while the machine at the front has its aft section and engine removed. (Ernest Panizzoli)*

65: *Thunderjets were returned to the United States via the Burtonwood depot in the north west of England; this view was taken there in 1954 of 49-2068, an ex-512th FBS aircraft, awaiting return. In the background at left can be seen the mortal remains of 49-2330, which burned out on the ground at Manston in early 1954.*

66: *Personnel of 513th FBS parade alongside the western taxiway, late 1952. Newly-laid Y shaped hardstandings allowed two aircraft to be parked on each dispersal. (Paul R Fry)*

to Warner-Robins AFB, Georgia, where we picked up the 'planes".

"We then flew them to Westover AFB, Massachusetts, where we were fitted for immersion suits, got emergency portable radios and other survival gear for overwater and cold climate emergency conditions. We also received an extensive overwater briefing covering emergencies and navigational problems to be encountered during this trip. The next leg was to Goose Bay, Labrador where we were met by members of the USAF fighter unit stationed there [59th FIS, flying F-94B Starfires] with a cold beer for each of us. It was very gracious of them, but cold beer in an open cockpit in Goose Bay in November is no great thrill".

"The next leg was our first real overwater leg of the trip. A couple of hours before we departed, a Grumman SA-16 Albatross took off before us and sent out a homing signal which made our navigation very simple. Another Albatross departed Narsarssuak (Bluie West 1) in southern Greenland and also sent out a homing signal for us to follow. We then homed in on a station at the tip of Greenland and flew up a fjord, turning left where the fjord split at the site of a crashed B-47 bomber, and to the airport at the end. It was a short runway for F-84s and slightly uphill, covered in ice and all in all a fairly hairy situation".

"We were restricted to clear weather, daylight flying only for this trip so we did spend a few days at each stop to assure that all conditions were met. We did not have a great time window in which to fly at these northern latitudes. At this time of the year we watched the sun come up at about ten in the morning and zip across the horizon setting at about 2 P.M. The next leg was to Keflavik, Iceland and we used the same navigation procedures. Somewhere on one of these legs, I took 16mm film of my lead, Lt. Randy Steffens. The next leg to was to Prestwick, Scotland without the use of the Albatrosses and thence via jet airways to Copenhagen. We were gone for about 28 days for this entire episode, and in those early days of jet flying, it was indeed an adventure".

The 406th Fighter Bomber Wing was shown the shape of things to come on 6 November when two Canadair Sabre Mk. 2s from No. 1 Wing of the Royal Canadian Air Force, based at North Luffenham landed with low fuel. The Canadair Sabre was a Canadian license-produced version of the famous North American F-86 Sabre, which was proving to be an effective MiG killer in Korea; the Mk. 2 was roughly equivalent to the American F-86E. These were the first Sabres to visit Manston, but by no means were they to be the last.

And still the losses mounted. At one minute to three o'clock on 20 November 1952, T-33 49-1000 took off from Manston on a familiarisation flight in VFR (visual flight rules) weather. Aboard was Capt. Charles B. Gresham of 513th FBS, and in the rear

seat was Capt. Herbert Kipp from the Air Base Group as instructor. A quarter of an hour after departure and by now over the sea, Capt. Gresham decided to return to base as the weather was deteriorating. On contacting Manston Tower, Gresham was informed that he was number two for GCA (Ground Controlled Approach), and told to wait on the GCA frequency. As Gresham turned towards Manston, and at 20° of left bank, the controls were neutralised to establish straight and level flight, but the aircraft failed to respond and continued banking, in a shallow climb. After about 270° of roll, the aircraft started buffeting (a sure sign of imminent stall), followed by a second undemanded roll to the left, which was much tighter, though now in a slight nose-down attitude with continuous buffeting. To make matters worse, the fire and low fuel level lights illuminated during the roll. The pilot then decided to abandon the aircraft and jettisoned the canopy, simultaneously informing Capt. Kipp to bail out, if he was in any doubt by this time. Gresham then decided to eject, but the first attempt to fire the seat was unsuccessful, and though the second try did the trick, Capt. Gresham sustained head injuries. Captain Kipp ejected slightly after the pilot, and both parachuted safely into the sea. 49-1000 crashed a short distance away, 11 miles NNW of Manston, 23 minutes after take-off.

After some time in the water, both airmen were picked up by the Margate pilot boat, with Capt. J.C. Strich of the ARS detachment aboard. After return to Margate jetty, the crew was returned to Manston by H-19 helicopter. The cause of the accident was undetermined.

November was rounded off with another crash, on the night of Sunday the 30th. Capt. Raymond. L. Denanny was an experienced F-84 pilot, with 261 Thunderjet hours, and was assigned to the 513th FBS. Capt. Denanny had spent the day at RAF Sculthorpe, home of the USAF's only Europe-based B-45 Wing. In mid-afternoon, Denanny's flight of Thunderjets began the return leg to Manston. After flying for about an hour, and with the winter sky darkening, the flight arrived over Thanet, where it was decided to practice a let-down and penetration through the overcast. As the fight approached Deal, and in a straight and level climb after the let-down, Capt. Denanny, (call-sign 'Air Force 103') flying 49-2071 experienced a violent explosion accompanied by the bright glare of overheat warning lights in his instrument panel. Denanny was informed by his wingman that '071 was on fire somewhere in the region of the under-fuselage dive brake. The pilot then realised that the situation was hopeless, and ejected above the overcast, watching his dying Thunderjet plummet, burning and shedding a wing, into the swirling cloud below. The aircraft had suffered a terminal compressor failure.

By a twist of fate, Lt. Forrest Smith, another Manston F-84 pilot, was enjoying a day off at his house on the cliffs near Deal, and saw the last moments of the accident and watched as Denanny's aircraft crashed into the sea off the Kent coast:

"On that day I was outside in the driveway working on the seat of my Consul sedan. Hearing a roaring sound, I looked up and saw an F-84 aircraft arcing across the sky at about 500 feet [153m] above the ground, one wing gone but a red tip tank plainly visible. It pitched over the edge of the cliff just a few hundred yards away and plunged into the sea. Tiny pieces of metal came down from the sky like falling leaves. I grabbed my camera and ran to the edge of the cliff and took a photograph of the burning spot in the sea and a few minutes later, took another of the area, but this time there was a tanker in the background".

"All the while, I looked for a parachute but saw none. The base of the overcast was around 1,000 feet [305m]. Due to the rising terrain south towards St. Margarets Bay, and the overcast, I could not see Denanny's parachute as he landed in the Channel. He got into his dinghy and was picked up by the tanker that had appeared in my second photograph! Soon, a helicopter bearing Capt. Strich, MD, flew over and picked up Capt. Denanny from the deck of the tanker".

Nearly 40 years on, Raymond Denanny and Forrest Smith were neighbours in the same Indiana town. Sadly, Forrest passed away at the start of 1996.

The Coronation Year, 1953, began quietly for the Wing. The decrease in flying had the effect of reducing the accident rate, but aircraft from other units had their own problems. On 26 January, a pair of Thunderjets, callsign 'Frontier Romeo' from the 20th FBW at Bentwaters called Manston tower, with only 10-15 minutes of fuel left. These aircraft were homed in to land safely. Four days later, one of the 406th's F-84s 'Thread 23' declared an in-flight emergency after experiencing engine vibration. Unable to maintain height, and flying in poor weather, the pilot landed safely back at Manston.

February proved no better for flight safety. On the 6th, two Thunderjets on a mission near Deal collided and crashed. The pilots, Capt. Phil Conserva (aircraft 49-2383) and Lt. Clyde Jones (49-2062) from the 514th were killed. Lt. Jones had been on a solo mission to complete his monthly 4-hour flying requirement. The weather was 10,000 feet (3,048m) overcast, with good visibility below the overcast. Capt. Conserva meanwhile was leading a four-ship flight up through the overcast to practice formation flying and approach patterns. As the flight entered the cloud, off airways and without radar contact, Lt. Jones' descending Thunderjet struck that of Capt. Conserva, a long-time 123rd FBW pilot, Air Force Cross holder and Korean War veteran. The three remaining aircraft returned to base, undamaged. As a result of this and the large number of other losses suffered by the Manston Thunderjets, numerous air-

craft began being drafted into the 406th from other USAF units. Among these were four F-84E-5s, which arrived during May of 1953 from the 86th FBW in Germany. Despite the arrival of these aircraft, however, by mid-1953 the squadrons were running at far below the optimum level for adequate combat readiness to be maintained.

In early 1953, there were roughly 140 officers and 1,330 airmen assigned to the Manston Wing. In addition, there were 28 officers and over 100 airmen assigned to the Air Rescue Squadron, plus numerous detached personnel, such as the Army battalion engaged on airfield work. Close on 800 personnel were living in tented accommodation, although efforts to house USAF personnel in the surrounding area was having an effect. The tents had been erected around the end of 1951, and numbered nearly 140 on the domestic site alone.

Diversions into Manston continued through this period. On 10 February, a B-29 bomber (44-87601) from the 301st Air Refuelling Squadron based at Brize Norton flew in after it had experienced engine trouble. The nose undercarriage was also indicating a malfunction. A safe landing was made on three engines. Fourteen days later 47-082, a B-45 from the 84th Bomb Squadron at Sculthorpe, made an emergency call with two engines out. After arriving overhead Manston, the crew decided that they could make their home base, and completed their mission without further mishap.

Across the world in Korea, fighting still continued, but by the start of 1953, the build-up of the FEAF's Fifth Air Force was beginning to have an effect on the Communist offensive. To satisfy the need for experienced fighter pilots, squadrons throughout the world supplied personnel on TDY as and when required. Two such pilots were 1st. Lts. Dale P. Connolly and Roy E. Jennings, Jr., both from the 512th FBS. Roy Jennings recalls these detachments:

"Dale and I were both pilots in the 512th squadron (and prior to that, the 156th) arriving in January 1952. Most of the pilots in the Wing arrived by ship from the US while I flew over in a C-47 via Greenland and Iceland. The C-47 was assigned to Base Flight Operations along with one T-33. In the winter of 1952-53, Dale Connolly and myself were sent on TDY assignment directly to Korea where we each flew 20 missions prior to returning back to Manston. Then we both returned to civilian life in the fall of 1953".

Jennings slightly undersells himself. Fighter-bomber missions in Korea were no joy ride, and on their return to Manston both pilots received the Air Medal from base commander Col. Conrad Herlick. During the ceremony, held on 27th March 1953, the local press was told how Jennings (29) and Connolly (27) were being decorated *"For meritorious achievement while participating in aerial flight as a pilot of an F-84 Thunderjet over Korea".* The Third AF

Band accompanied their award ceremony. By this time, three Thunderjet units were operating in the Korean Theatre: the 49th, 58th and 474th Fighter Bomber Wings, and many Manston personnel were deployed on these 60-day TDY stints, straight into combat. Sadly, Dale Connolly died of a heart attack in April 1993 while sailing his boat from Ramsgate to Flushing.

During May, the Wing commenced gunnery training, one squadron at a time at Wheelus Air Base in Libya for around 30 days TDY. 558 hours were flown at Wheelus during the month, and an additional 453 hours in June. The 513th FBS completed its gunnery training during September. Wing pilots ferrying a T-33 trainer from the Lockheed factory at Burbank, California for the 512th flew another 44 hours. Accident rates at this point were finally coming down; the sole aircraft damaged during this period was a T-6F, which received minor damage while being operated by a non-Wing pilot. The aircraft struck a runway tar burner while taxiing.

The summer of 1953 was largely uneventful for the 406th; there were no major accidents, and flying carried on as normal. On 23 July, Exercise *Coronet* started and lasted for 11 days. The 406th had deployed its Thunderjets to Wiesbaden, West Germany for the first part of the exercise, and many missions were flown as aggressors against NATO bases in Germany. In the course of *Coronet*, both airfields and ground forces were attacked. Dick Grace:

"About half of the 512th went to Wiesbaden to participate in Coronet. *Wiesbaden was Headquarters for USAFE and the people there greeted us upon arrival with a nice welcoming ceremony, parade (including floats) and a delicious banquet. We were supposed to be on manoeuvres, but were treated like visiting royalty. However, the party ended abruptly".*

"After several days, we were told our make-believe enemy was overtaking the base, and we hastily evacuated our aircraft, loaded our equipment into some C-119s that were brought in, climbed on board and departed — destination unknown. We ended up at a base that was just being completed, which was Sembach AB, near Kaiserslautern, Germany".

"We continued to operate out of Sembach until Coronet *was completed. As usual, at the end of these TDY trips we sent off our aircraft then loaded and boarded the C-119s for the flight back to Manston. As I recall, the weather wasn't the best and we waited around for quite a while before the decision was made to depart. Upon our return to Manston, as it turned out, the weather had gotten worse and blanket fog covered the base. All of the C-119s were placed in a holding pattern and were brought in, one at a time by the GCA people. Because of the number of 'planes, this took a long time".*

"When we finally landed, we noticed our F-84s parked randomly along both sides of the runway,

some of them had gone off into the grass. What had happened was that upon their (the F-84s) return to Manston, several hours before us, they also had to be brought in by GCA. But when they landed, the fog was right down on the ground, and visibility so poor and fuel supplies so low, that there was no alternative except to taxi over to the sides of the runway and park. All of our guardian angels were working overtime that day".

A new shape was seen in the skies over Thanet during the summer when the first Boeing B-47 Stratojet bombers began practising GCA approaches to Manston. Powered by six J47 engines, these aircraft came from the 306th Bomb Wing normally based at MacDill AFB, Florida, and stationed on 12 weeks TDY at Fairford, Glos. B-47s became a common sight transiting through Manston, but local protests led by the Member of Parliament, Mr. W.R. Rees-Davies brought about a reduction in their presence until in late November 1955 the USAF stated that B-47s would no longer be making approaches to the base. Then, as now, protecting the peace was a thankless task.

By mid-1953, 406th Wing possessed around 50 Thunderjets, six T-33s, three C-47s and three T-6s, the latter two types were operated by the Air Base Group, the Harvards of 'Ceuleers' Air Force' still getting a lot of use, and the C-47s flying throughout the UK on supply missions, as well as regular daily 'milk runs' to Frankfurt. On 19 August one of the ABG T-6s was diverted from local flying to investigate a large 'splash' in the sea off North Foreland, but nothing was found. Similarly on the last day of August one of the T-33s was diverted along with an SA-16 to search an area 10 miles south of Littlestone on the south Kent coast. Search details were sketchy and nothing was sighted, but such was the variety of life at Manston in those days.

On 9 October 1953, one of the last cross-country training flights by Thunderjets of the 406th was undertaken. Leaving for Rome, 12 F-84Es from the 512th FBS were accompanied by a C-47 and 14 ground personnel to render maintenance support. Upon leaving Rome on 11 October, the 512th pilots were given permission to bring their Thunderjets in over the centre of the city 'low and fast'. Pulling away from the Italian capital, the formation set course for the return trip to Manston. Even the hard-worked ground crews had managed to have an enjoyable weekend in the Eternal City, marking a high point in the life of the F-84s at Manston.

Changes were afoot, however. In late August and early September the first examples of a new aircraft type to equip 406th FBW had arrived: the famed F-86F Sabre. The F-86F would take the Wing into a new era — now the pilots of 406th Fighter Bomber Wing would be relieved of their 'air-to-mud' role, and would take on the mantle of pure fighter-interception. Although the 'Fighter Bomber Wing' tag would remain for some months, the Sabre had already made its name in Korea as a 'MiG-killer'. Local residents were informed of its heroic exploits, tempered by a warning of sonic booms, but the appearance of the F-86 still came as a surprise to many. Once more local feeling took a marked downturn, and once more, Mr. Rees-Davies was at the forefront of the complaints. But the Sabre just begged to be flown to the limit, and for a while at least, the feelings of a few less-than-happy citizens of Thanet had little effect. David B. Tharp was assigned to the 3917th ABG during January 1953, and remembers the arrival of the first Sabres, among other things:

"I arrived on a cold wintry night via an open six pack [truck] with about five other young men. We were put in tents with no heat, and given a pile of blankets to keep us warm. It was late at night, we were cold, hungry and dead beat. We awoke the next morning only to find it was a holiday and nothing was open. They could not find the OD [Officer of the Day] so could not get us any mess passes. We went to the little snack bar and spent the day there. Incidentally, this holiday was followed by a Saturday and Sunday, so it was three days before we were acknowledged by anyone at our new assignment".

"I was assigned to the 3917th Operations Squadron and worked at Base Operations as a dispatcher. After the initial shock, we came to love the assignment. Margate was one fantastic town for young airmen — the Long Bar, amusement park, and lots of restaurants and bars to bide our time. We had only one airplane, a C-47, and so my job was mostly spent passing away the duty hours. When I arrived the 406th had three squadrons of F-84s; I vividly remember the arrival of the F-86s and how they sent a test pilot out to give us all a show of the new bird. He took off, then half way down the runway he flipped over on his back and went out of sight. It was one heck of a show he put on".

The remaining Thunderjets were quietly ferried back to the United States, where they were generally allotted to the Training Wings at Laughlin AFB, Texas, Luke AFB, Arizona and Nellis AFB in Nevada. Eventually, these ex-Manston Thunderjets went on to numerous Air National Guard squadrons, which were in the process of re-equipping with the F-84E. With their poor safety record and unreliability, neither air nor ground crews of the 406th mourned their passing.

By early 1954, most of the Thunderjets had been dispatched to the United States, but not all. On 20 January, Lt. Begley from 513th FBS had just taxied to its take-off point. Paul Fry was the assistant Crew Chief on Begley's aircraft, and describes what happened next:

"The first plane I was assistant Crew Chief on blew up on the runway just before releasing brakes to take off. Amazingly, the pilot unbuckled and jumped before the 1,300 gallons of JP fuel engulfed the plane. Minutes before this occurred, we had checked the engine for vibrations at 100% throttle, in the revetment. I've thought about that many times — crouched under the plane, reaching through the dive brake to feel around the accessory drive case for vibrations".

Had the aircraft still been in its revetment, the results of the explosion could have been catastrophic. As it was, the pilot escaped without injury though the F-84, 49-2330, was written off. Sgt. Till was the Crew Chief on this aircraft.

Perhaps it should come as no surprise then that only one of the 'Manston' Thunderjets appears to have survived; 49-2348, which currently resides with the Ohio Air National Guard collection at Rickenbacker ANG Base, near Columbus. '348 was accepted by the USAF on 1 June 1950, and delivered straight to the 31st FEW at Turner AFB in Georgia during November 1950. Along with the rest of the 31st's F-84Es, '348 made the long flight across the Atlantic during early 1951 upon detachment to Manston. Successively transferred to the 12th FEW on 20 July 1951, the 123rd FBW on 29 November 1951, the aircraft ended up with the 406th FBW, to which it was transferred on 27 July 1952. At the time of the reactivation of the 406th, '348 was detached to Wheelus AB in Libya. Following the phase-out of the Thunderjet by the 406th, the aircraft then returned to the United States, and passed to the 3645th Flying Training Wing at Laughlin AFB in Texas, then on to the 3600th Wing at Luke AFB, California on 3 July 1954. Assigned to the 2256th Wing at Niagara Falls, NY in December 1956, the aircraft ended its USAF days at Norton AFB in California, where it was struck off for reclamation during May 1957. Unlike so many other Cold War warriors however, '348 did not go into the smelter at Davis Monthan, and was purchased by the San Jose Technical College in California. Here the aircraft was utilised by the Aviation Department, and was maintained at San Jose Airport. It was during the period at San Jose that the aircraft's tip tanks were lost. Finally, in the early 1990s, the aircraft was scooped up by the Ohio Air National Guard, and after a thorough restoration, it is now displayed in the unit's colours.

The first Sabres for the 406th FBW arrived during August of 1953, direct from the North American factory in Ohio. These aircraft arrived with red-painted tail and wing tips as an aid to spotting the aircraft in the event of a forced landing in the snowy wastes of the North. 1st Lt. Drury Callahan was assigned to the 514th FBS at this time, and ferried three F-86Fs over to Europe at the end of 1953. Later, when the F-86F began to be superseded in Europe by the F-86D, he ferried one more F-86F back to the USA. Drury recalls:

"These [missions] were called 'Operation High Flight'. Since this was before the days of air-to-air refuelling, they had to take the following route: Eastbound: Macon, Georgia (origination point) to

67: *These unmarked 406th FBW Thunderjets are lined up on the estern ASP at Manston; most had been assigned from USAFE squadrons in Germany during 1953. Checkered drop tank on 49-2214 is a remnant from 86th FBW ownership. (Ernest Panizzoli)*

68: *Canisters for the F-84E's nose-mounted .50-calibre machine guns can be seen in this photo; hinged door provided access for arming. Also visible is the 514th FBS 'boxing bomb' squadron badge. (Betty Wright)*

69 Below: *49-2348 is the only known survivor of Manston's Thunderjets. Seen here at San Jose airport in the 1970s, the aircraft has since been rescued and restored by the Ohio Air National Guard. (David Phipp)*

Dover AFB, Delaware to Bangor, Maine to Goose Bay AFB, Labrador to Bluie West 1, Greenland to Keflavik, Iceland to Prestwick, Scotland, to Manston (or to France or Germany).
Westbound: Burtonwood, England (origination point) to Prestwick to Keflavik to BW-1 to Presque Isle, Maine to Dover AFB to Macon".

"Specifics of my trips:
1. F-86F 51-13456. Departed Macon, Georgia 17 August 1953, arrived Manston 22 August 1953. Total flying time 11:40.
2. F-86F 52-5332. Departed Macon 30 October 1953, arrived Manston 10 November 1953. Total flying time 11:40.
3. F-86F 52-5386. Departed Macon 26 November 1953, arrived Chaumont AB, France (48th FBW) 16 December 1953. Total flying time 11:20.
4. F-86F 52-5300. Departed Burtonwood 29 November 1954, arrived Macon 12 December 1954. Total flying time 12:15".

Soon after the Sabre's arrival at Manston, North American Aviation pilot Bob Hoover arrived to give a demonstration of the aircraft's ability. Drury Callahan was closely involved in this chapter:

"The demonstration was on the morning of 30 September 1953. The F-86F that he used was 51-13505. The aircraft was configured with two 200 gallon drop tanks (which were empty) and carried only 1,800 lbs [800kg] of internal fuel and no ammunition or ballast. Had the aircraft been fully loaded, it could never have performed as it did. The cockpit was carefully vacuumed to get rid of any dirt which could fall into Hoover's eyes during the inverted and negative-G manoeuvres".

"After the demonstration at Manston, Hoover put on an identical show at Bentwaters on 1 October 1953 using the same aircraft, 51-13505. Because of Air Force regulations, Hoover could not fly the airplane cross-country to another base, so I was selected to fly it to Shepherds Grove and to Bentwaters. My job was to fly it to those bases, ensure it was configured to Hoover's requirements, wait while he put on his demonstration, have a stiff drink ready for him after he landed, and then fly it back to Manston on the afternoon of October 1. All went well with no incidents. One thing I noticed though, was that Hoover's hands shook so badly after each flight that he had to use both hands to hold the drink I provided him".

Forty-odd years later, the author spoke to Bob Hoover, who confirmed that the Sabre display consisted of a roll on take-off (a Hoover trade-mark), followed by 4, 8 and 16-point hesitation rolls, an inverted pass and a series of Cuban Eights with 3 rolls on the 'down' side. Next, Hoover would put the F-86 into a series of upward vertical rolls followed by a series of tail slides. Then a double Immelman with a five-turn spin off the top leading to a succession of round, square and eight-sided loops concluded the first part of the display with the Sabre being brought in for a landing. But this was no ordinary landing. Prior to his display, Hoover had the 406th's personnel place a marker 2,500 feet (762m) from the runway threshold, and now, Hoover landed his aircraft in that distance, turned around — out of the wind — and took off again in 2,500 feet. To bring the demonstration to a close, he then rolled the aircraft all the way round the traf-

71: *The first F-86Fs for 406th FBW were assigned in late August 1953; the six aircraft here still have their tail sections painted insignia red for the ferry flight to Manston. Nearest aircraft is 51-13508, which was assigned to 406th FBW on 30 August; it became a 514th FBS machine. (via Dave Keep)*

72: *Dick Bingaman poses in the cockpit of 2/Lt Herman E Griffin's F-86F, 52-5384. Aircraft was assigned to 512th FBS, and this view shows the 'new' squadron badge incorporating an F-86 silhouette. (Dick Bingaman)*

73: *Seven 513th FIS F-86Fs lined up at Nouasseur AB in late May 1954 – note the two 512th FIS examples at the rear. Aircraft at front, 52-5286, later served with the Peruvian Air Force. (Drury Callahan via Marty Isham)*

fic pattern, made a low-level roll straight into the landing run, and set the Sabre down onto the tarmac. But far from finishing the display, he then pulled the aircraft back into the air and performed one last low-level roll before completing his landing run.

The Sabres assigned to the 406th were all F-86F-25 variants, the F model being the most capable American fighter used in the Korean War. Though it would in effect become a fighter interceptor wing, the 406th for the time being retained its 'FBW' tag, and got on with the job of converting onto the Sabre and coming up to operational readiness. F-84E pilots generally converted straight over to the F-86F, after the minimum of ground school and a check flight or two. The maintenance personnel also went through familiarisation courses starting in November 1953, comprising of 82 hours of ground school. As an interesting footnote, on 26 February 1954, an 81st FIW F-86A (49-1074) was loaned to the 406th for one month, possibly for ground familiarization. As the 'A' and 'F' models differ considerably, however, such an operation would be of little benefit. Nothing further is known of the loan of this aircraft, which returned to the 81st FIW after use at Manston.

The F-86F Sabre

The F-86 Sabre was born of a WWII US Navy requirement for a jet-powered fighter. That design, the straight-wing XFJ-1 built by North American Aviation at Inglewood in California flew during September 1946, by which time the USAAF (soon to be USAF) had become interested in the aircraft. The Air Force version, which became known as the XP-86, was to be straight-winged, and the initial mock-up, approved on 20 June 1945, reflected this. It was soon realised by the Army Air Force and North American however, that performance of the XP-86 would be less than startling with its 3,800 lb thrust General Electric TG-180 engine. To remedy this problem, North American redesigned the XP-86 to include wings swept back at a 35° angle.

The first XP-86, powered by a TG-180 engine took to the air from Muroc, California on 1 October 1947, piloted by NAA test pilot George Welch. Production F-86A aircraft entered USAF service from February 1949, and were officially named 'Sabre' during the following month. The F-86A was powered by General Electric's J47 turbojet.

The F-86A was followed on the production lines by the F-86E, which introduced an 'all-flying tail', which enabled the Sabre to manoeuvre successfully at high Mach numbers. The E-model was followed by the F-86F, which was fitted with a 5,910-lb (26.29kN) thrust J47 GE-27 engine. The F-86F was produced in greater numbers than any other Sabre variant, being assembled at the NAA plants at Inglewood, California and Columbus, Ohio. In addi-

tion, further F-86Fs were built under license by Mitsubishi in Japan. Various sub-types of the F-86F were built, the F-86F-1 was the initial production version, followed by sixteen F-86F-5, thirty-four F-86F-10 and seven F-86F-15s. These early models differed little, with F-86F-20 denoting the first Columbus-built Sabres.

Built at North American's Columbus, Ohio, plant, the F-86F-25 differed from previous F-86Fs in that it had a 'dual store' wing, where provision was made to carry a 120 gallon drop tank or 1,000 lb (444 kg) bomb on the inner wing pylon, whilst a second, outboard pylon could accommodate a 200 gallon drop-tank. In this configuration, a ferry range of 1,600 miles (2,580km) was attained. In addition, from the 171st F-86F-25 off the production lines, the slatted wing of earlier Sabre variants was replaced with a 'hard-edge' unslatted wing of increased chord with a fixed wing fence at 70% span. This fence prevented airflow moving towards the wing tip, and the whole combination increased top speed at altitude and greatly improved the manoeuvring capacity of the Sabre, with only a slight, but significant, increase in stalling speed. Since the earliest F-86F-25 delivered to Manston was number 201 out of the factory, all the 406th's aircraft were thus modified.

The F-86F was well liked by its pilots, who revelled in the manoeuvrability and speed of their mount. For the maintenance crews, the Sabre also scored highly, according to the 513th FBS's Paul Fry:

"Somewhere in the late Summer or Fall of 1953, we received F-86[F]s. In February 1954, we were in Bitburg, Germany with them — probably for NATO exercises. The Sabre was a breeze to maintain and keep in-commission. Its low wing design made it easy refuelling and servicing otherwise. We took 16 aircraft to French Morocco [Nouasseur AB] in May '54 for gunnery practice near Casablanca. The 513th Squadron racked up over 1,000 hours flying time without even a flat tyre. It was a beautiful plane. I'm sure the pilots appreciated it too. We did lose one on take-off for a test flight, following Major Inspection. I believe it was a case of the aileron control jamming. The pilot was killed".

Squadron markings for the new aircraft consisted of a coloured band around the nose immediately aft of the intake ring, and the squadron colours were repeated on the wing tips and wing fence. On the tail, there were three diagonal stripes in the three squadron colours, which were bordered with a thin black line. Finally, the canopy rail was painted in the squadron colour and displayed its pilot's name in 4-inch high white lettering on the left side, with the crew chief's name on the right. In practice, however, the 'assigned' pilot rarely flew 'his' aircraft. Squadron badges remained unchanged except for the 512th FBS, which changed the F-84 silhouette in its emblem to reflect its new mount.

In the early afternoon of Wednesday 2 Decem-

74: *Dick Grace performs a pre-flight inspection on a 512th FBS Sabre 52-5274; note Grace's name on the canopy rail. Open side panel provided access for engine oil filler. (Richard T Grace)*

75: *Lt Joe 'JD' Smith (right) takes time out to pose with his crew chief and Sabre. JD's assigned aircraft was 51-13508, but he was flying 51-13490 when he was killed on 4 October 1954. (Dave Roberson)*

76: *50-hour engine inspection being carried out on a 512th Sabre at Nouasseur during the squadron's gunnery deployment of May/June 1954. KC-97 tanker aircraft are parked in the background. (Richard T Grace)*

77: *A quartet of 512th FIS Sabres await a gunnery sortie at Nouasseur. Nearest three aircraft lack the usual drop tanks as the 'clean' configuration posed less manoeuvering limitations for gunnery flying. (Richard T Grace)*

78: *Pilots gather round the gunnery 'flag' target to assess their gunnery skills. On any firing mission, each aircraft would carry differently coloured bullet tips and when the bullet passed through the target this colour would wipe off onto the flag. In this way, a number of aircraft could fly on the target during a single mission. (Richard T Grace)*

79: *512th FBS aircraft ranged on the 'loop' dispersal during the winter of 1953. Hangar 4 is at the centre of the photo. (Jay Blanco)*

ber 1953, Captain Lee F. Barrows of the 514th FBS, callsign 'Entreat Red 1' crashed off the Ramsgate end of runway 29. His aircraft, 51-13509, went out of control on landing and crashed 300 yards from the threshold of the runway. Captain Barrows, from St. Albans, West Virginia was killed instantly. Don Sidak, also from the 514th, remembers the accident:

"Captain Barrows crashed his F-86 [which] spun in on finals and [he] was killed. Capt. Barrows had some previous F-86 time, but it was in an earlier F-86 model that had leading-edge slats. Our F-86F models did not have the leading-edge slat on the wings and would stall without warning, and were more sensitive to stalling".

Three days later another F-86F, this time from the 513th FBS, callsign 'Thread Blue Leader', fell to earth near Ash, seven miles south-southwest of the airfield. The aircraft, 51-13484, was destroyed and the pilot, Lt. John A. Huerter was killed. An inauspicious start then to the operation of the Sabre at Manston. Compared to the recalcitrant Thunderjet, however, the F-86 was a real 'hot ship', and many accidents during the 'fifties were as much a result of over-exuberance as any design or maintenance condition.

The start of 1954 saw the three Sabre squadrons coming up to operational status at Manston. The new aircraft were integrated into the GCI network very quickly, as the Sabre had been a common sight in the skies over the UK since late 1951, when the Canadians began to deploy their aircraft to Europe. The F-86F proved to be a far more reliable aircraft than the preceding Thunderjet, and only niggling problems punctuated Sabre operations at Manston in the early part of the year. On 24 February 'Westwind 16' called an emergency with frozen controls, but the pilot managed to shake them loose and returned for a safe landing. On 29 March, two Sabres of 'Paris Red' flight returned to base on emergency, one with low fuel pressure, the other with a cracked canopy. Again there were no further difficulties. The 31st March saw three F-84Gs from the 20th FBW divert into Manston, one with tyre problems, another with a mis-feeding tip tank. It seemed that even though they had long departed the base, the old straight-wing F-84s just could not stay away.

Again the 512th was in the news when on 21 February, it logged the 577th accident-free day of flying. During this period, which included transition from the Thunderjet, the squadron had flown 5,828 hours equating to around $2\frac{1}{2}$ million miles (4.03 million km) of flight. Much praise went to Capt. Joe F. Marling, 512th's F-86F check pilot, who summed it up thus:

"A flying safety officer doesn't make flying safe. Much of our success is due to a healthy attitude, high morale, and proficiency of the ground crewmen — the men who put them on the line in tip-top shape in all kinds of weather".

Rare recognition indeed for the often unsung maintenance personnel. But the squadron's 82% in-commission rate for the Sabre spoke volumes for the effectiveness of these men. The 512th also made its prowess known in the field of air-to-air gunnery and devised the Mobile Aerial Gunnery Assessing Unit, which consisted of a 3 feet (0.91m) square opaque screen mounted on a 6 feet (1.8m) deep projector base, which enabled gun camera film to be viewed in daylight conditions when projected from the rear of the screen. This machine was fully portable and could be taken to gunnery camps where the effects of a pilot's shooting could be viewed with little delay. From a design by Major Thomas J. Cribbs, the Assessing Unit was built by squadron pilots 2nd Lts. Gordon H. Bruce, Murray P. Brush III, Joseph Nedel and James Toomey, under the supervision of Capt. Jack L. Butterfield.

It was not long before the 406th was up to combat status with its new mounts. And thus, participation in NATO exercises began during the early part of 1954. On 25 February, F-86Fs drawn from all three squadrons flew to Bitburg AB in West Germany to participate in *Magna Flux*, a one-week exercise. Ground crews again followed in C-119 transport aircraft. This was the first real test of the Sabres, and Dick Grace recalls that: *"The F-86s performed beautifully and were well received by pilots and mechanics alike"*. Many missions were flown with the Sabres acting as 'friendly' forces; those aircraft of the 'enemy' (among them Royal Canadian Air Force Sabres), were painted with black bands on nose and wings to denote their offensive nature.

On 5 March 1954, two RAF Meteor F. Mk. 8s from 245 squadron at RAF Horsham St. Faith were dogfighting with a Sabre over Deal. As they did so, the two RAF jets collided, causing serious damage to both. One aircraft, piloted by Squadron Leader Bowen, managed to divert to RAF Marham, where an emergency landing, minus flaps and air brakes was accomplished in relative ease. The second aircraft, with Flying Officer Humphreys at the controls, managed to home on to Manston's steering signals, and initiated diversion action, and shortly afterwards, F/O Humphreys radioed that he was bailing out. Neither Humphreys nor his aircraft was ever seen again. It is presumed that his aircraft plunged into the sea off the coast of Thanet, tantalisingly close to the safety of Manston's tarmac. There does not appear to be any mention of this incident in 406th FBW records, nor is there any recollection of it by the Manston pilots. It is quite conceivable that the Sabre pilot was completely unaware of the tragic outcome of his dogfight.

On 1 April, the 406th finally became a Fighter Interceptor Wing (FIW), to reflect the true nature of the Wing's mission. In turn, the squadrons became Fighter Interceptor Squadrons, though mission profiles and objectives remained the same. On 12 April, USAF took over operation of the Control Tower, leaving only a few RAF personnel at Manston, and in addition the 406th now ran the fire section. On the same day the 3917th Air Base Group, which had carried out the day-to-day running of the base since the arrival of the first USAF aircraft in July 1950, departed for East Kirkby. The 406th FIW now became responsible for all these duties. In addition to the USAF personnel at Manston, many local civilians were employed on the base, and by June 1954, 150 such employees were working, mainly on the domestic site, in what was being termed as 'The fourth phase of American expansion'. The effects of Third AF's 'Project Native Son', instigated during November 1953 had begun to bear fruit. 'Native Son' was designed to convert 5,000 US military jobs in the UK to civilian slots, and within 4 years, the number of locals working at Manston had increased threefold.

Obviously, throughout this period, personnel ranging from pilots to cooks were being posted in and out of the unit, now that it had gained 'permanent' status. A young 2nd Lieutenant posted in to fly for the 406th during the spring of 1954 was Dave Roberson:

"After finishing flying training in December 1953, I went through gunnery training at Del Rio. We flew T-33s, then on to Luke AFB for F-84s. We finished training in April 1954 and most all of the class was headed to Korea, but the war had ended so some of us were sent to England. I guess Korea was overloaded with pilots".

"I guess you could call us mavericks because by this time all the F-84[E]s had left the UK — of course, we didn't know that. In those days (the end of an era), everyone went to a processing center at Prestwick, Scotland, to get your end assignment. Of the group of four that I had travelled with, two of us, myself and Herschel Barnes were sent to Manston. The other two to Shepherds Grove. This was in May 1954".

"Herschel an I took the train to Margate and then caught a taxi to Manston. As we drove on base, we saw the F-86s all over the place. We queried the driver, and he advised us that was the aircraft they flew here. Wow! I had tried to get '86 school, but was sent to '84s. Anyway, we reported in a military manner to some Lieutenant in Group Headquarters, who said to come back tomorrow and he would give us our assignments. Appeared no one was expecting us. I went back the next day and was assigned to the 514th and Herschel was assigned to the 513th".

"The 514th of course was quite a distance away, and the Lieutenant had no suggestions on how to get there, so I walked. I finally found the shack the 514th ops was housed in and went in. No one was expecting me there either. Luckily, Joe Smith, who was a friend from my home area had arrived a few weeks before and took me in tow. The day I reported was the day that Harry Schurr (assistant ops officer) made Captain, so everyone headed to the bar quite early to start the celebration. As I recall, it was a Thursday. Everyone got smashed and had a great time. The following day, there was little or no flying, just nursing hangovers. Then, at quitting time, it was time to go to the club for Friday night beer call. The party went on into the wee hours and I ended up spending the night at St. Mildreds Hotel, which was where a great number of the pilots from all squadrons had apartments".

"The days that followed were great fun. Seems as though there was a party every night. I decided this fighter business was OK, but I wasn't getting to fly the '86. I had a couple of rides in the T-33, but no-one even mentioned the '86, and 2nd. Lts. don't make waves. I just drove the vehicle to take pilots to the aircraft, and did odd jobs around the squadron. I guess they didn't know what to do with me. But I was happy".

"Finally, on 23 May 1954, we were having another big party at St. Mildreds, and Major Grady Morris the Squadron ops officer (at about 1 am) asked me how I liked the F-86. I told him that I had never flown it (seems things weren't too well organized in those days). He said, 'By God you'll fly it tomorrow'. I then said I had better get off to bed if I was going to fly. He replied something to the effect of 'Fighter pilots don't sleep'. The following day, he followed up and had Lt. Mickleson help me fill out a questionnaire on the '86 and then proceeded to the aircraft. At this time I had never been in one, but he showed me how to start it, and away we went. I then had several rides over the next couple of weeks. The [hard edge] '86F had bad characteristics at low speed, and on 12 July 1954, the thing tried to snap roll turning final approach [in similar circumstances to Lee Barrows' fatal crash]. I managed to recover and got it on the ground barely under control. Scraped an aileron in the process. The flying safety officer came over and took a look and said that it didn't look too bad and we didn't need to bother with all that paperwork. As I said, things were sort of loose in those days".

"I had a grand total of 13 hours in the aircraft when we went into Operation Dividend [July 1954], but flew right in there with the big boys. Quite an experience as I look back".

On Wednesday 5 May a young Royal Cambodian Army Lieutenant took a flight in a 406th FIW T-33, becoming the first Cambodian to experience the thrill of jet flight. The Lieutenant was a member of a joint Cambodian/Lao/Vietnamese visit to the base. In the period from January to August 1954, over 1,200 people visited the base, which broke down into fourteen different nationalities, from all walks of life. But by far the biggest number of visitors were locals, both civilians and members of the part-time Territorial Army and Royal Observer Corps.

At the weekends, Manston's Sabres would often fly 'Rat-Terrier' missions for the Royal Observer

Corps. These were low-level high-speed missions that gave the ROC an opportunity to test their detection of low-flying intruders, which would otherwise be invisible to radar. The 406th pilots generally enjoyed the relaxed feel of these sorties. Another weekend pursuit was that of flying displays for the many countrywide airshows, which often entailed little more than a quick series of fly-bys to demonstrate the Sabre's speed before departing home. Such a display was flown for the 1954 Plymouth Air Display at Roborough aerodrome, when four Manston Sabres closed the day's flying.

The Manston Sabres began flying gunnery training missions during the spring of 1954, this time from Nouasseur Air Base in Morocco. Previously, the 123rd FBW had investigated using the other Moroccan base at Sidi Slimane for gunnery use, but at that time (early 1952), Sidi Slimane was insufficiently developed. By 1954, however, the base at Nouasseur near Casablanca was deemed suitable for the task, and during April 1954 the Manston squadrons deployed there, the 514th FIS being the first to arrive. On 23 April 1954, the squadron suffered a further loss. As Capt. Thomas J. Fox brought his F-86F (51-13465) in low over Nouasseur's runway to drop a towed target, his aircraft stalled and bellied onto the tarmac. Unable to jettison his external tanks, a fire soon ensued. However, although Fox managed to unbuckle himself and escape the inferno, he then had to run through the heavy, toxic smoke around the burning Sabre, and in doing so seriously damaged his lungs. Sadly, Capt. Fox died of pneumonia shortly after.

Around 24 April, the 513th FIS replaced the 514th at Nouasseur, its TDY overlapping that of the 514th, with the 512th flying out for a mere 17 days of gunnery training on 24 May. The reason for the 512th's curtailed training is not known — the other two squadrons served a full 30 days in Morocco. This would prove to be the 406th's only visit to Nouasseur — in future, all armament practice camps would again be flown out of Wheelus Air Base.

At Manston, exercises continued apace, and by now the skies over Britain and Europe were seemingly full of jet pilots trying to demonstrate their prowess. During Exercise *Dividend* the 406th FIW was tasked with defending the UK from attacking aircraft at high and very high levels, among them the Canadian Sabres from 3 Wing at Zweibrucken. The Canadians were equipped with their own license-built aircraft, similarly-configured to the USAF F-86F, even down to the broad-chord wing of the F-86F-25, but with one distinct advantage; they had the Orenda 10 powerplant. This Canadian-designed and built engine developed 6,355-lb (28.26kN) thrust (over 300 lbs (0.133kN) more than the F-25's engine at Military Power), and made the Canadians tough opponents. *Dividend* was designed to: *"..Exercise the air defences of the UK against possible types of attack by manned aircraft likely to be encountered in the first few days of war at the present time"*. The exercise was broken down into two phases:

Phase 1, running from 1900 hrs Zulu (GMT) 16 July to 1700Z 18 July.

Phase 2, running from 1400Z 22 July to 1700Z 25 July.

During Phase 1, the defences were severely stretched, with 1,784 attack sorties being flown against the UK. During the two-part scenario, cine cameras fitted in the intake lip of the Sabres were used for scoring purposes, with feet of film being expended in dog fights instead of rounds of .50-calibre. Among the aircraft that 'attacked' the UK were USAF KC-97s, B-47 Stratojets, F-80s, Canadian F-86s and the Thunderjets again from the 20th FBW. In addition, aircraft from the Fleet Air Arm and the French Air Force also took part. During Phase 2, when 3,942 raiding sorties were flown, B-45 Tornados joined the attacking force. The high-level B-47 attacks in particular proved almost impossible to intercept, and highlighted the superiority of this bomber, whose speed was a match for most fighters of the day. The UK air defence system fielded 877 fighters during the exercise, including 75 from the 406th at Manston, plus RAF Meteors, Vampires, Venoms and Sabres, as well as Canadian Sabres, which operated on both sides during the exercise. Around 30% of attacks were intercepted before they reached the coast of the UK.

The post-exercise scrutiny of *Dividend* highlighted the lack of 'Tu-4' (B-29/B-50) aircraft in the scenario, but more importantly conceded that the chances of intercepting the high-altitude (B-47) jet bomber raids was, at best, marginal. Clearly, Soviet bombers of this type could also have raided with impunity. Bad weather thwarted many missions during *Dividend*, and again, the need for all-weather fighters was evident. *Dividend* was the 406th's first NATO exercise with the F-86F, and served to qualify the Wing as combat ready following transition from the F-84E. It was also the first time that Manston-based USAF aircraft had defended the UK on an exercise. The Sabres acquitted themselves well, as demonstrated by their 244 individual high-altitude intercepts during Phase 2, compared to five for RAF Meteors in the same period.

The diversion of aircraft into Manston continued, and, strange for a military airfield operating some of the most advanced fighters in the world, commercial airliners arrived unannounced with annoying regularity. On 14 August a Trans-Canadian Airlines Lockheed Super Constellation flew in from a fog-bound Heathrow Airport, returning from the Empire Games in Canada. On board were British athletes, among them Jim Peters and Roger Bannister. The latter had famously broken the four-minute mile record barely three months earlier, and a cartoon in the base newspaper, *The Saber* [sic] showed a USAF reporter trying to interview the two runners as they jogged away from their aircraft.

Tragedy struck again on 23 August when another of the 406th's F-86Fs crashed. Major William 'Tex' Crawford, Operations Officer of the 513th FIS had just left Manston for a post-maintenance test flight when his Sabre (52-5420) exploded, showering wreckage over a large area near Littlebourne, to the east of Canterbury. The majority of the debris fell to earth near Sturry, the main portion carving a 70-yard furrow in the earth. The cause was put down to a disconnected fuel line, which sprayed kerosene into the engine area. The suddenness of the explosion gave Major Crawford no opportunity to eject, and sadly he was killed.

Of all the missions flown by the Manston Sabres, it was probably the cross-country flights which were the most popular; especially if a stop-over in one of the European cities was involved. One such flight carried out by the 514th during September 1954 saw four F-86Fs flying out to Rome. Jake Eicher led the flight, with Jay Blanco, Bob Gottfried and Dave Roberson as wingmen. Roberson takes up the story:

"We had a great stay in Rome, where we were shepherded around by a former American Mafia type, Ralph Ligorri, who was deported along with Lucky Luciano in the '40s. He was really interesting to listen to. Tried to get us to go to Naples and meet Lucky, but we declined".

"The return flight got pretty sticky. We filed to Chaumont, France and encountered some unexpected headwinds. (As later came out in the C-47 crash, the met. office in Rome left something to be desired). We arrived at Chaumont where they had 200 ft ceiling in rain and we were all at minimum fuel. I don't recall how much I got on the ground with, but Jay Blanco recalls he had 200 lbs, and I'm sure we were all pretty close to that. The rest of the trip was uneventful".

The 512th had at this time achieved a long run of accident-free flying, and in recognition of this the squadron commander, Lt. Col. Frank Haynie received a Third AF Citation for achieving the 10,000th safe flying hour in September. As a ground crew member, Dick Grace appreciates what a feat that was:

"The 512th only had one minor incident while flying F-86Fs. This occurred when a flight of planes that had been up on a routine night flying mission returned to Manston. One of the planes could not get a 'green' light on one of his landing gears while attempting to land, so the pilot went around and tried again. Each landing gear has a down-lock pin that moves out and locks the gear in place. Sort of like a door catch. When it moves fully into position, it engages a microswitch, which activates a green light on the control panel, thus letting the pilot know the gear is safe to land on. After several passes, the plane was about out of fuel, and still no 'green' light. The decision was made to land. By then, the crash crews were out and ready for the worst. However, they were not needed".

"The pilot did a magnificent job of keeping the weight of the plane off the faulty gear until his airspeed was very low, then that side of the plane dropped down. But since it was equipped with under wing auxiliary fuel tanks, which were now empty, the plane safely came to rest with part of its weight on the auxiliary fuel tank".

"The drop tank was replaced, the gear problem corrected and the plane was in the air again before noon the following day. This was not considered an accident because Air Force Regulations stated that any aircraft suffering damage that was back in service within 24 hours was considered only an incident".

The 512th had been redesignated on 8 August and became the 512th Fighter Day Squadron in preparation for a squadron move later in the year. The remaining two fighter interceptor squadrons kept their previous designations, and despite the apparent difference in job title, the three squadrons would remain assigned to 406th FIW for the foreseeable future.

One of the Wing's most popular members, 2nd Lt. Joe Daley 'JD' Smith was killed on Monday 4 October 1954. Smith was leading a mission over East Anglia at 35,000 feet (10,670m) when he spotted two RAF Meteor NF Mk 12s below. In those good old days any fighter pilot worth his salt would do anything to tangle with the 'enemy' to demonstrate his prowess and 'JD' Smith was no exception. Lt. Thomas Gordon, number two in the flight followed Smith in on his run:

"From my position, about 300 yards (274m) to the right, I saw him pull up behind a Meteor. He then started to pull away from it and in doing so, the wings of the Sabre and Meteor touched. A six-foot section sheared off the Sabre's wing and the aircraft began to spin to the left. I waited about 5 seconds to see if Lt. Smith called me. As he did not I radioed; 'You had better get out' ".

Sadly though Smith managed to eject, he did not separate from his seat, and was killed. The RAF Meteor, WS691 from No. 152 Squadron attempted an emergency landing at RAF Wattisham, but went out of control on approach and crashed 2½ miles west southwest of Needham Market, killing the crew of two. Smith's Sabre, 51-13490 came down near Valley Farm, on the Suffolk-Norfolk border, its canopy was later found near Bramfield, 14 miles north of Bentwaters. Dave Roberson knew Smith very well:

"I had known Joe and his wife since school days. In fact we got houses a few blocks apart in Broadstairs so we could bring our wives over. We had gone to work together that morning. I was scheduled for the Link trainer and he was on flying schedule. Shortly after I got back to the squadron we learned that he had crashed. After confirming he was dead, it fell on me to inform Mary Ann. I was accompanied by the Chaplain and Col. Hubler the

83 Opposite: *This aerial view of Manston shows the main runway with the western taxiway running into the distance at centre. Red-trimmed F-84Es of 559th FES can be seen parked beside the taxiway, as well as visiting C-119 transports. A solitary SA-16 of the air rescue service is also visible in the foreground. (Elliot Bouck)*

80: *Pictured at Turner AFB shortly before departure for the UK, F-84E 49-2097 was the Group Commander's aircraft, signified by red, yellow and blue bands around intake lip and fuselage. Coloured stripe to the rear of nose checks and tail fin tip were yellow. (B Butcher via Dave McLaren)*

81: *Slanted tail bands on this 514th FIS T-33 show that the photo dates from the 1955 period. Highly-polished finish is typical of the era. (Max Beasley)*

82 Far right: *Stalky nose undercarriage caused a number of problems at Manston. On a number of occasions the leg collapsed or snapped off completely. If the pilot was lucky it broke below the level of the gear doors, and damage was minimised. (Author's collection)*

84: *This view of the 561st FES operations hut shows the squadron emblem, a winged flying skeleton. Standing in front of the building is Col Cy Wilson, 12th FEW commanding officer. (Elliot Bouck)*

85 Below: *As the 12th FEW commander's aircraft, 51-645 carried these 'rainbow' markings to indicate the three squadrons under his command. Nose scallop is red, yellow and blue; repeated on the tip tanks, fuselage and tail fin. Aircraft in background are yellow-trimmed 560th FES machines. (Elliot Bouck)*

86: *Pilots from the 561st FES gather for a pre-flight cigarette during the summer of 1951; of note are the ever-present life jackets. At right is squadron commander Lt Col 'Mike' Meroney. This view was taken from the main airfield towards the 'loop' dispersal. The B2190 Minster to Manston road can be seen running left to right at rear. (Elliot Bouck)*

87: *These blue-trimmed Thunder-jets from the 167th FBS are parked on the airfield's eastern side, nowadays the location of the civil terminal buildings. Back in 1952, only pierced steel planking (PSP) kept the aircraft off the bare earth. (Ken Hoylman via Jack H Smith)*

88: *During Exercise* Coronet *in late July 1953, 406th FBW Thunderjets deployed to bases in Germany to act as 'enemy' forces. Here, 512th FBS aircraft are lined up at Sembach AB with 514th FBS machines further down. Black nose and wing bands were for exercise purposes. (Richard T Grace)*

89: *This F-84E's undercarriage is mid-way through the retraction process during functional checks outside Hangar 4. Three yellow fuselage bands denote 51-616 as the personal mount of 512th FBS commander Maj William Preble. (Richard T Grace)*

90 Above: *49-2330 was one of only a very few 513th FBS Thunderjets remaining at Manston when it caught fire on takeoff on 20 January 1954. Pilot Lt Begley escaped, but the aircraft was seriously damaged. (Forrest E Smith)*

91: *49-2102 was assigned to the 512th FBS, and like most of the squadron's aircraft, had a yellow-painted speed brake panel, as seen here. Aircraft is standing on one of the new Y-shaped fighter dispersals. (Richard T Grace)*

92: *F-86F 51-13477 was the personal mount of Capt H.D. Stallings; he was assigned to the 514th FIS. Note white disc on nose where the squadron's 'boxing bomb' badge will be painted. Photo was taken at Nouasseur AB in April 1954. (Glenn Stallings)*

93: *406th FIW personnel prepare to board an Air Base Wing C-47 for the deployment to Nouasseur in the spring of 1954. The wing had just changed from the fighter-bomber to fighter-interceptor tag at the beginning of April. (Richard T Grace)*

94: *A 512th FIS armourer loads .50-calibre ammunition prior to a gunnery mission from Nouasseur. Soot around the lower pair of guns shows that this aircraft has already fired on the flag. (Richard T Grace)*

95: *Though based in East Anglia, 512th FIS Sabres often visited Manston. This aircraft is 52-10035, later the subject of an Airfix plastic kit. The Mighty Mouse rocket tray is extended below the fuselage for maintenance. (Max Beasley)*

96 Above: *During 1957, USAFE F-86Ds began to be fitted with 'sugar scoop' cooling ducts on each fuselage side to aid heat dissipation in the tail section; they can be seen on this 512th FIS machine just aft of the fuselage band. 52-4185 was on display at Duxford for the station's 1957 Battle of Britain display. (via Jack Friell)*

97: *52-4063 carries the name of pilot 1/Lt G. Naber on its canopy rail; Naber was flying the aircraft at the time. Pilot's helmet was red with white lightning flashes. (Gerry Naber)*

98: *513th FIS aircraft wore this red and black 'sunburst' scheme once assigned to the 86th FIW. 52-4140 had flown with the 406th FIW from December 1954; it wound up with the Yugoslav Air Force in 1961. (via Jack Friell)*

99: *L-20A Beaver 52-6138 was the only one of its type to be flown from Manston. The aircraft is seen at Blackbushe airport on 10 September 1955, having taken squadron personnel to the Farnborough air show. (Bob Brinker)*

100 Below: *Jack Cotter prepares to board 52-6516 for a ferry flight to Lisbon in April 1956; the aircraft, an F-84F-35, was exchanged for a dash-45 model. This machine had been Bob Brinker's personal mount – his name appears on the canopy rail. (Bob Brinker)*

101: *Basic working conditions at Manston extended to the administrative side too – this is the 92nd FBS ops hut. In the background is Hangar 4 with F-84F drop tanks stacked alongside. (Bob Brinker)*

102: *Later-style 92nd FBS colours moved the squadron badge from the tail fin to the fuselage side. This 'hero' shot of Jack Austin also shows the thin black trim applied to the yellow areas on the squadron's F-84Fs. (Jack Adams)*

103 Far left: *A youthful Lt Bob Brinker poses beside the 92nd FBS buildings on the 'loop' dispersal, October 1955. Many of the buildings on the loop were still present into the 1980s. (Bob Brinker)*

104 Left: *A closeup of the vintage Rolls-Royce hearse used by the 92nd FBS as a crew bus shows off the unit badge.*

105: *Long after it had served at Manston, 51-0025 was still flying missions with the California Air National Guard. This is the aircraft that was beached at St Mildred's Bay on 17 August 1955 after hitting a submerged object. It is now preserved in the New England Air Museum at Bradley in Connecticut. (MAP)*

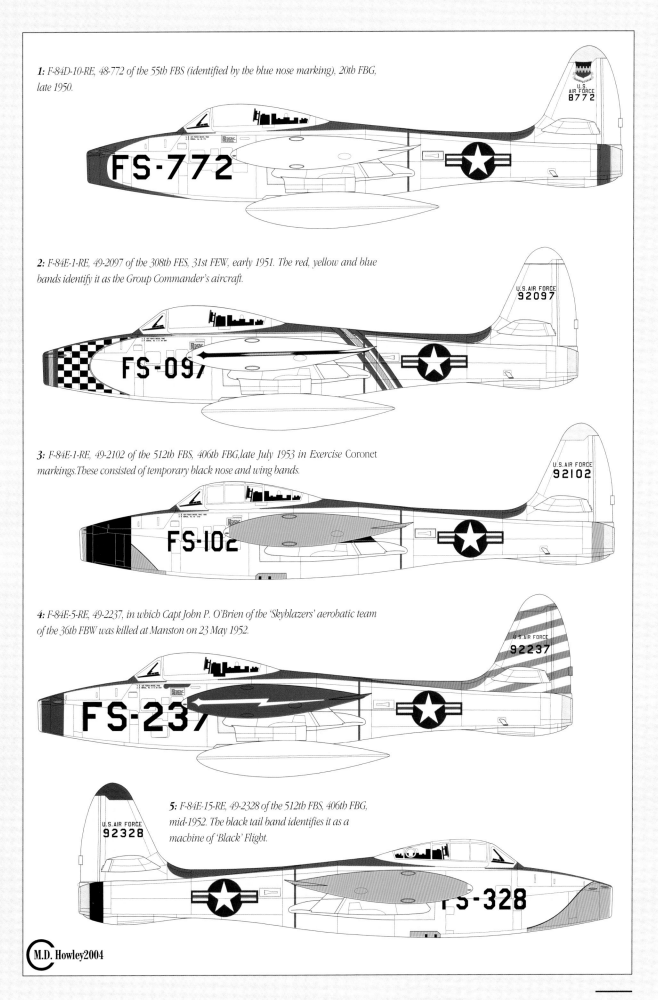

1: *F-84D-10-RE, 48-772 of the 55th FBS (identified by the blue nose marking), 20th FBG, late 1950.*

2: *F-84E-1-RE, 49-2097 of the 308th FES, 31st FEW, early 1951. The red, yellow and blue bands identify it as the Group Commander's aircraft.*

3: *F-84E-1-RE, 49-2102 of the 512th FBS, 406th FBG, late July 1953 in Exercise* Coronet *markings. These consisted of temporary black nose and wing bands.*

4: *F-84E-5-RE, 49-2237, in which Capt John P. O'Brien of the 'Skyblazers' aerobatic team of the 36th FBW was killed at Manston on 23 May 1952.*

5: *F-84E-15-RE, 49-2328 of the 512th FBS, 406th FBG, mid-1952. The black tail band identifies it as a machine of 'Black' Flight.*

M.D. Howley 2004

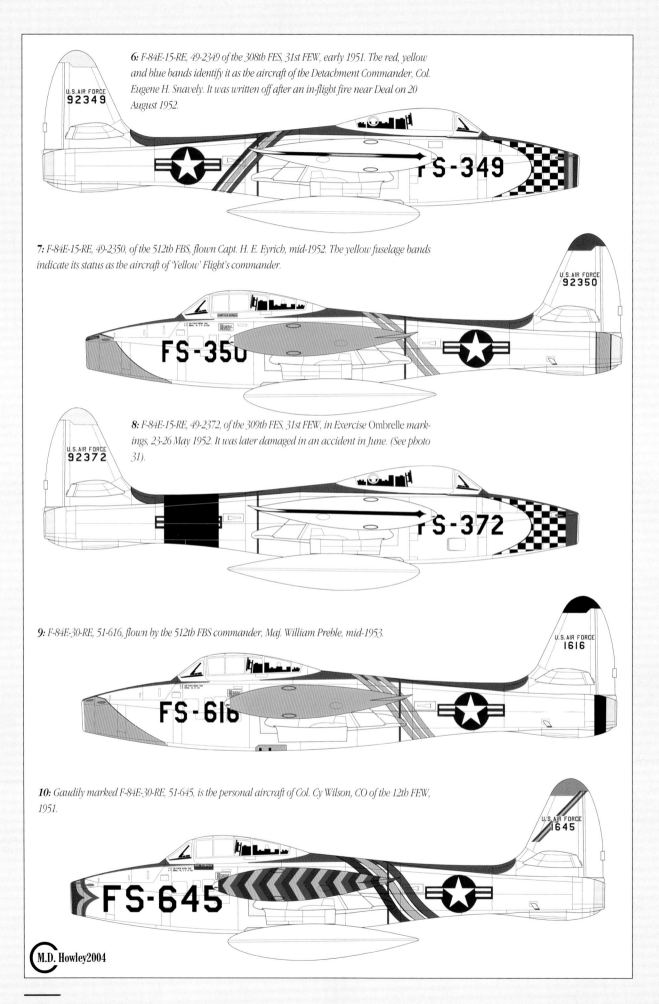

6: *F-84E-15-RE, 49-2349 of the 308th FES, 31st FEW, early 1951. The red, yellow and blue bands identify it as the aircraft of the Detachment Commander, Col. Eugene H. Snavely. It was written off after an in-flight fire near Deal on 20 August 1952.*

7: *F-84E-15-RE, 49-2350, of the 512th FBS, flown Capt. H. E. Eyrich, mid-1952. The yellow fuselage bands indicate its status as the aircraft of 'Yellow' Flight's commander.*

8: *F-84E-15-RE, 49-2372, of the 309th FES, 31st FEW, in Exercise Ombrelle markings, 23-26 May 1952. It was later damaged in an accident in June. (See photo 31).*

9: *F-84E-30-RE, 51-616, flown by the 512th FBS commander, Maj. William Preble, mid-1953.*

10: *Gaudily marked F-84E-30-RE, 51-645, is the personal aircraft of Col. Cy Wilson, CO of the 12th FEW, 1951.*

M.D. Howley 2004

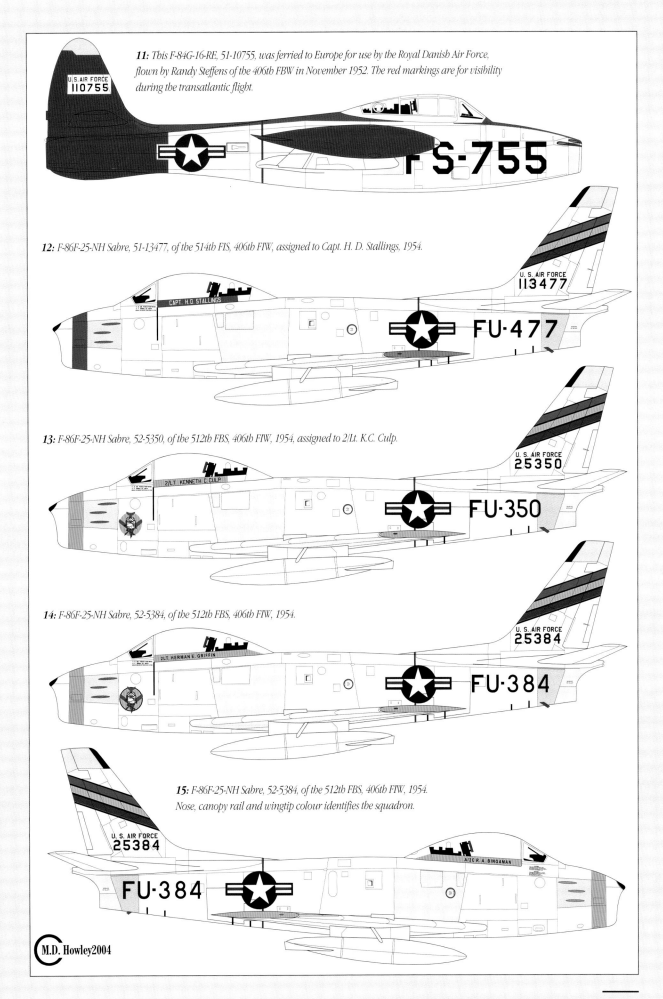

11: This F-84G-16-RE, 51-10755, was ferried to Europe for use by the Royal Danish Air Force, flown by Randy Steffens of the 406th FBW in November 1952. The red markings are for visibility during the transatlantic flight.

12: F-86F-25-NH Sabre, 51-13477, of the 514th FIS, 406th FIW, assigned to Capt. H. D. Stallings, 1954.

13: F-86F-25-NH Sabre, 52-5350, of the 512th FBS, 406th FIW, 1954, assigned to 2/Lt. K.C. Culp.

14: F-86F-25-NH Sabre, 52-5384, of the 512th FBS, 406th FIW, 1954.

15: F-86F-25-NH Sabre, 52-5384, of the 512th FBS, 406th FIW, 1954. Nose, canopy rail and wingtip colour identifies the squadron.

M.D. Howley 2004

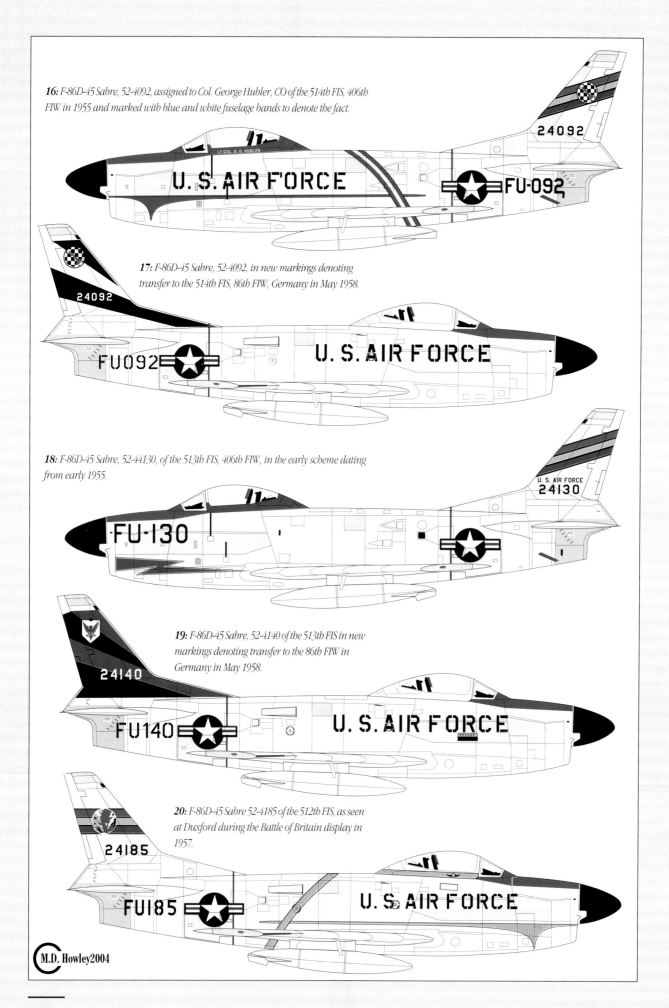

16: *F-86D-45 Sabre, 52-4092, assigned to Col. George Hubler, CO of the 514th FIS, 406th FIW in 1955 and marked with blue and white fuselage bands to denote the fact.*

17: *F-86D-45 Sabre, 52-4092, in new markings denoting transfer to the 514th FIS, 86th FIW, Germany in May 1958.*

18: *F-86D-45 Sabre, 52-44130, of the 513th FIS, 406th FIW, in the early scheme dating from early 1955.*

19: *F-86D-45 Sabre, 52-4140 of the 513th FIS in new markings denoting transfer to the 86th FIW in Germany in May 1958.*

20: *F-86D-45 Sabre 52-4185 of the 512th FIS, as seen at Duxford during the Battle of Britain display in 1957.*

M.D. Howley 2004

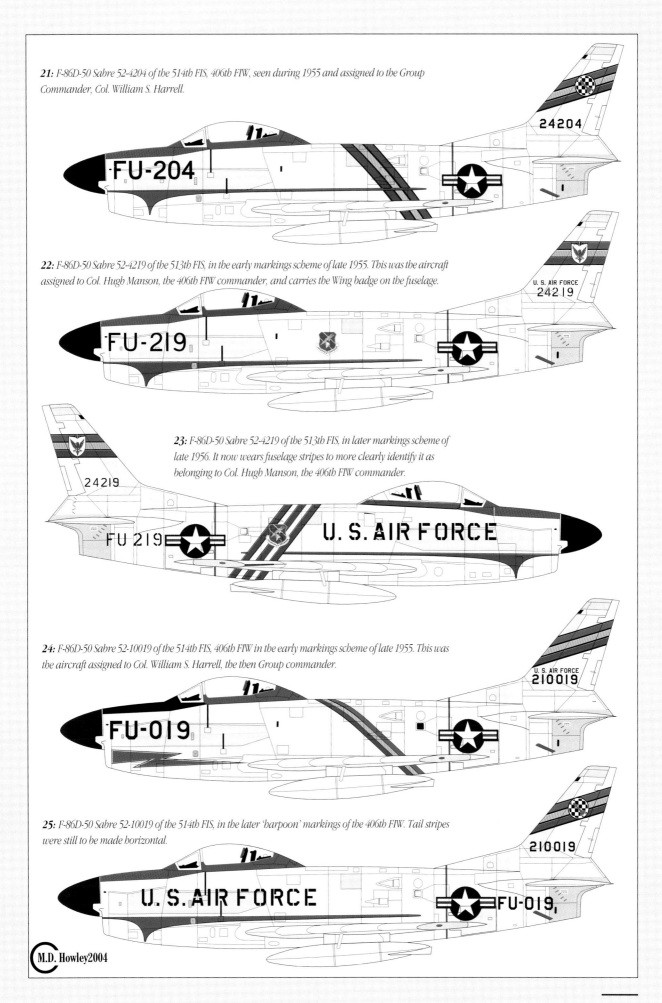

21: *F-86D-50 Sabre 52-4204 of the 514th FIS, 406th FIW, seen during 1955 and assigned to the Group Commander, Col. William S. Harrell.*

22: *F-86D-50 Sabre 52-4219 of the 513th FIS, in the early markings scheme of late 1955. This was the aircraft assigned to Col. Hugh Manson, the 406th FIW commander, and carries the Wing badge on the fuselage.*

23: *F-86D-50 Sabre 52-4219 of the 513th FIS, in later markings scheme of late 1956. It now wears fuselage stripes to more clearly identify it as belonging to Col. Hugh Manson, the 406th FIW commander.*

24: *F-86D-50 Sabre 52-10019 of the 514th FIS, 406th FIW in the early markings scheme of late 1955. This was the aircraft assigned to Col. William S. Harrell, the then Group commander.*

25: *F-86D-50 Sabre 52-10019 of the 514th FIS, in the later 'harpoon' markings of the 406th FIW. Tail stripes were still to be made horizontal.*

M.D. Howley 2004

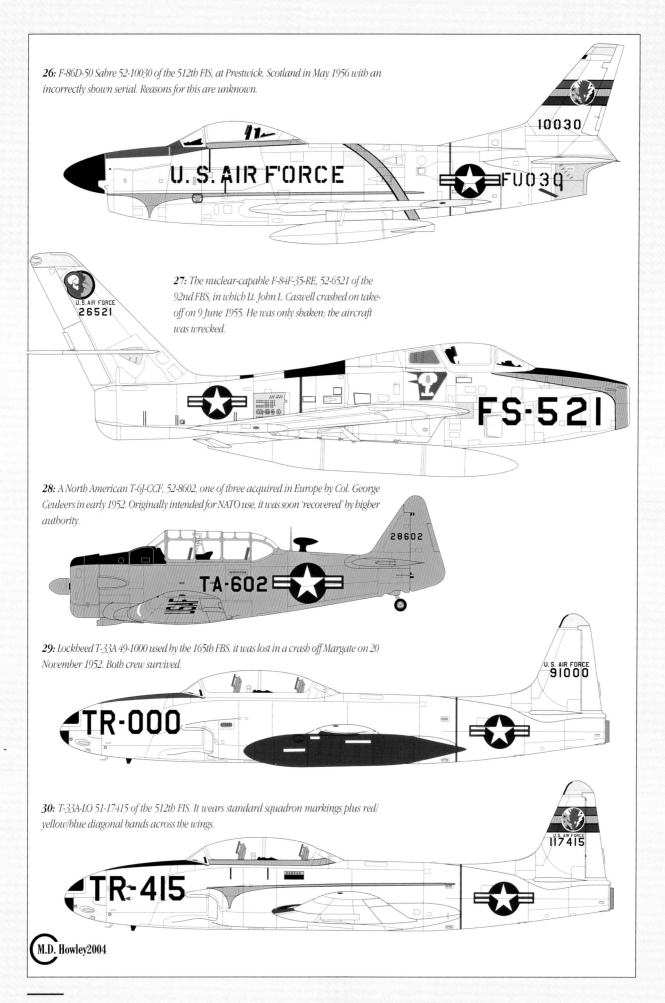

26: *F-86D-50 Sabre 52-10030 of the 512th FIS, at Prestwick, Scotland in May 1956 with an incorrectly shown serial. Reasons for this are unknown.*

27: *The nuclear-capable F-84F-35-RE, 52-6521 of the 92nd FBS, in which Lt. John L. Caswell crashed on take-off on 9 June 1955. He was only shaken; the aircraft was wrecked.*

28: *A North American T-6J-CCF, 52-8602, one of three acquired in Europe by Col. George Ceuleers in early 1952. Originally intended for NATO use, it was soon 'recovered' by higher authority.*

29: *Lockheed T-33A 49-1000 used by the 165th FBS. it was lost in a crash off Margate on 20 November 1952. Both crew survived.*

30: *T-33A-LO 51-17415 of the 512th FIS. It wears standard squadron markings plus red/yellow/blue diagonal bands across the wings.*

M.D. Howley 2004

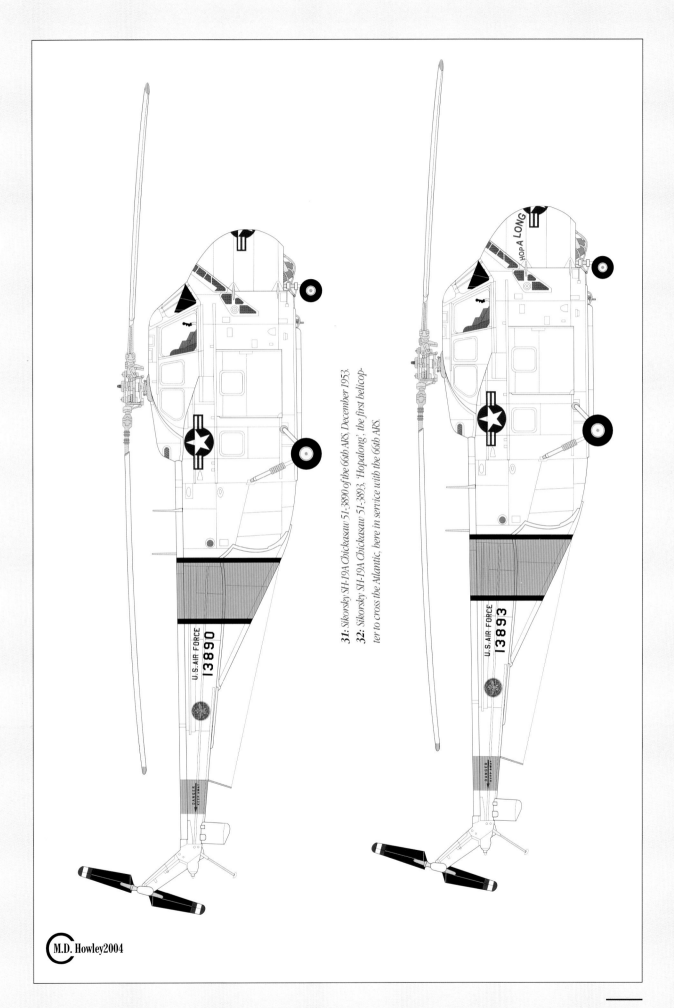

31: Sikorsky SH-19A Chickasaw 51-3890 of the 66th ARS, December 1953.
32: Sikorsky SH-19A Chickasaw 51-3893, 'Hopalong', the first helicopter to cross the Atlantic, here in service with the 66th ARS.

U.S.AIR FORCE 13890

U.S.AIR FORCE 13893

HOP A LONG

DANGER KEEP AWAY

DANGER KEEP AWAY

M.D. Howley 2004

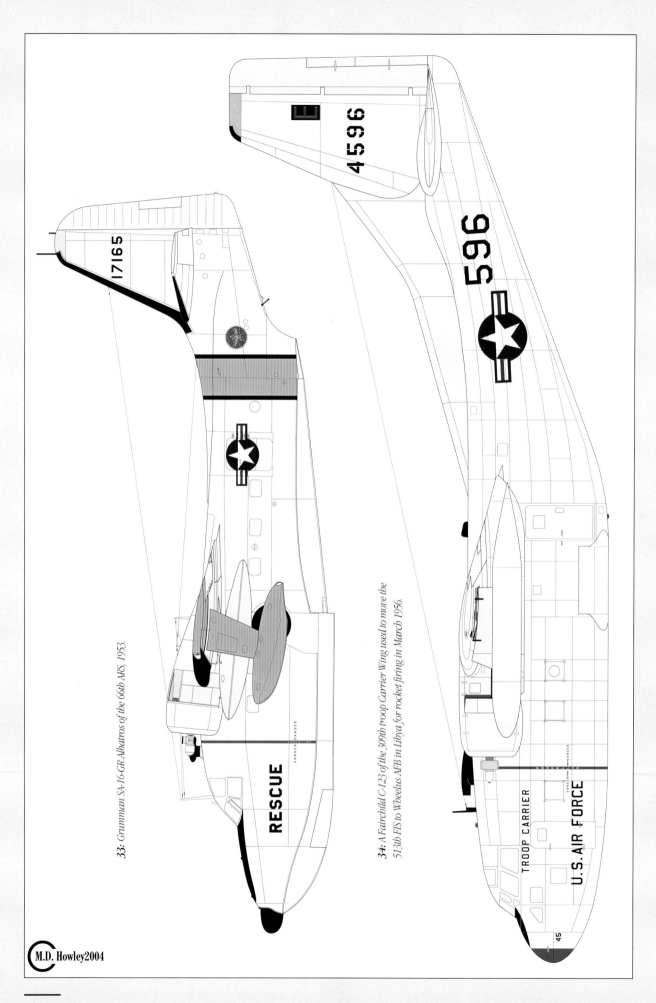

33: *Grumman SA-16-GR Albatros of the 66th ARS, 1953.*

34: *A Fairchild C-123 of the 309th troop Carrier Wing used to move the 513th FIS to Wheelus AFB in Libya for rocket firing in March 1956.*

RESCUE

4596

17165

596

U.S. AIR FORCE

TROOP CARRIER

45

squadron commander. When she came to the door of course she said 'Hi David, where's Joe?' Boy it was tough to tell her. After settling affairs, I accompanied her to Prestwick for the final flight back to the States".

On the day of J.D. Smith's crash, the first three F-86Ds (52-4082, 52-4091, and 52-4101) for the 406th FIW were delivered into Manston by Wing pilots Capt. Tom Willie, Capt. Harry LaRoche and Capt. Richard White. Unlike the F-86Fs, these new fighters had been shipped across the Atlantic on freighters, docking at St Nazaire, France. From the port, the aircraft were transported to the USAF's 7485th Air Depot Wing at the airfield of St. Nazaire, where they were prepared for flight and ferried to the UK. Richard White remembers that corrosion was a problem with these F-86Ds:

"These aircraft were cocooned and shipped as deck cargo to France...many of the aircraft received extensive salt damage on the way over. The seawater got inside the cocoon and stayed on the belly and bottom of the tail section. Some had the metal eaten completely away! A test pilot was assigned to St. Nazaire from our depot at Wright-Patterson Field, Dayton, Ohio. He made all the flights to check serviceability of the planes. We were 'ferry pilots'. We picked them up and flew them to Manston".

In total, 27 F-86D-45 and 43 F-86D-50 aircraft were assigned to the 406th FIW from St Nazaire from October 1954 until the last delivery on 15 February 1955. The first aircraft went to re-equip the 513th FIS, with the 514th FIS receiving aircraft in December.

A later delivery of 17 F-86D-36 aircraft was made via Belfast, Northern Ireland, the aircraft being offloaded from the ship to the nearby airfield for work with Shorts Brothers before being flown to the UK. This batch arrived in Ireland on 11 April 1956 and were assigned to the 406th FIW from 18 April to 1 June that year. Richard White had earlier carried out F-86D conversion at Tyndall AFB, arriving at Manston with a few other F-86D qualified pilots during May 1954:

"I flew the F-86Fs from May until September '54. On September 15, I flew an F-86D again, probably at Ramstein Air Base, Germany in order to be 'current' in the aircraft before I began ferrying them and teaching others to fly them".

This core of experienced pilots then wrote the 406th FIW F-86D ground and flying training programme, which was put into effect during the latter months of 1954. The task of converting the F-86F pilots to the radically different D-model began in earnest and from then on, the 406th FIW would perform all-weather interception with its new machines. Those pilots already at Manston received F-86D simulator training in West Germany prior to an F-86D checkout at Manston. From late 1954, all new pilots posted in to the 406th would undergo F-86D training at Perrin AFB in Texas prior to arrival.

The month of October was rounded off by tragedy with the biggest disaster to befall the men of the 406th FIW. On Sunday 24 October 1954, a C-47 (43-16044) from the Air Base Group disappeared on a return flight from Rome, having left Manston the previous Friday morning. On board were six crew and fifteen passengers, all from the 406th FIW (mainly 514th FIS personnel), who during the 'slow' phase of conversion from F-86F to D had been granted the trip to Italy as a reward for hard work. The aircraft departed Rome at 2.57 pm and had last reported its position over the northern tip of Corsica at 4 pm on Sunday afternoon as the pilot transferred from Rome to Marseilles Air Traffic Control. By 11 pm when the aircraft's fuel would have been exhausted, a large-scale rescue operation was initiated. Despite an international search effort, which included an SA-16 amphibian from the Manston-based 66th ARS, no trace of the aircraft was discovered for nearly a week. The inevitable crash wreckage was finally found on 31 October. The C-47 had slammed into the side of Mount Carbono, north of Nice, France. All personnel on board had perished in the accident.

The loss of so many, mainly maintenance, personnel hit the 514th hard, according to squadron Crew Chief W. Richard Craig:

"After the horrible C-47 crash in Rome, where we lost many Crew Chiefs, Flight Chiefs and Dock Chiefs, we had to shuffle around the remaining people to effect as much utilization as possible. I personally was moved from the flightline to the hangar to work as a Dock Chief performing periodic inspections. By then we were fairly well engrossed with the F-86D. I had a rather extensive maintenance background, which I suppose helped the Dock Chief job. I was only a buck Sergeant and the job called for a Master Sergeant. However, we managed to squeak through rather well".

The long-anticipated move for the 512th FDS finally began on 16 November, the entire squadron flying out to Soesterburg Air Base in the Netherlands with its trusty F-86Fs, landing 26 minutes after leaving Manston. There it would fly alongside the Gloster Meteors of the Dutch Air Force. The requirement to base a squadron of USAF fighters on Dutch soil had seen its roots in an Air Force Plan, submitted to the Dutch Parliament in 1951. This plan foresaw that a revised Dutch Air Force would require nine day fighter squadrons, though a revised arrangement with NATO (named the Paris Plan) saw this number reduced to six day fighter squadrons, though aircraft strength would be increased. The Plan was accepted by the Dutch Parliament in February 1952, but when the Dutch Air Force gained autonomy on 27 March 1953, it soon became apparent that only five day fighter squadrons could equip. As a result, the USAF assisted by offering to base a squadron of F-86Fs in Holland.

Unfortunately, though the move of men and equipment to Holland initially went smoothly, things soon began to go awry. Arriving at Manston in mid-September 1954, 1st Lt. Henry Cowles Bristol took over the slot of Commercial Transportation Officer (CTO), and found that he would therefore be responsible for sorting out the mess that had been brewing prior to his arrival. Upon taking over his post, Cowles was briefed that the 512th's move would take place during late October or early November 1954. The 406th ABG's pair of C-47 aircraft would handle all air freight flights to and from the Continent, supported by the CTO at Manston, plus three airmen in the Air Freight Section, trained as Loadmasters. The Air Freight section at Manston would be responsible for scheduling the C-47s (maximum load of 3,000 lb (1,334kg) per aircraft), selecting cargo by priority, preparing cargo manifests, and arranging the transportation and loading of cargo. As Cowles Bristol recalls, however, implementation of the task was not so straightforward:

"At first, everything went fine, like clockwork. Supplies moved from Manston to the 512th (in Holland) without a hitch during October and November 1954. All priorities got first dibs; the jet engine and F-86 aircraft parts. But in December 1954, bad weather set in over Northern Europe; rainy, cloudy, overcasts, fog and mist all of the time. And guess what? Because of this bad weather, the C-47s could only fly intermittently with their supplies. The weather got worse in February/March 1955. Sometimes the supplies to the 512th didn't get airlifted for two to three weeks. Shipping by British transport (trucks) to ports, thence by freighters across the English Channel was out of the question, in that it would take a minimum of six weeks with absolutely no guarantee any of the supplies would get to Soesterburg".

"The Base Supply warehouse as well as the CTO's warehouse was lipping with supplies. The C-47s were grounded because of the weather. Toilet paper got first priority over jet engine and aircraft parts — over everything. The warcry was: 'Get the 512th toilet paper, and fast'. The 406th Fighter Group Supply Officer was at his wits end".

"Meanwhile, back at the ranch, Manston, there was mass action finger pointing. The 512th were hollering for supplies; the Manston supply officers were hollering at the CTO; the CTO was hollering at the Base Operations Officer; the Base Operations Officer was hollering at the Weather Group; the Weather Group was hollering at God. What a mess. It sounds funny, but it wasn't. The persons I felt so sorry for were the 406th Fighter Group Supply Officer and Major Sid Farrington, the Base Operations Officer".

To remedy the situation, with around 100,000 lbs (44,483kg) of freight in the warehouses at Manston, and two frequently grounded C-47s, each with a meagre capacity to move it, Cowles resorted to the 'back door' approach to solve the problem. Recalling that one of his old commanders, Major Jim Hill, was as-

signed to a C-119 transport Wing at Chateauroux in France, the answer was simple; the C-119 could fly in all weather, and carry a 10,000-lb (4,448kg) load.

"I made a decision to try to get ten C-119s to fly to Manston, load up our 100,000 lbs of cargo and take it to the 512th. I didn't ask anybody if I could do this. I didn't tell anybody I was going to do what I did next. I called this C-119 base in central France. When whoever answered, I asked for Major Jim Hill, the Group Operations Officer. He was there and answered the phone! I asked him if he had any C-119s for hire. He said; 'Who wants to know?' I told him I did. He wanted to know on what authority. I told him mine. One thing led to another, the problem; I needed his help, etc. Hill told me he needed a training mission, and this sounded pretty good to him — we could have ten C-119s, when did we want them? 'As fast as you can get up' was my reply. 'How about the day after tomorrow?' he asked. Hill said that there was one condition. He wanted the planes loaded immediately at Manston, turned around and unloaded immediately at Soesterburg. 'You got it', I said. 'I'm on my way' said Hill".

"The C-119s arrived as promised. They were loaded and unloaded as promised. The 512th got its clean toilet paper and much-needed supplies as promised. The pressure was certainly taken off all concerned at Manston. Looking at all this in retrospect, I know there must have been high-ranking officers who were bound to have been concerned about a 16-jet aircraft fighter squadron almost immobilized and inoperable because of no logistical support. However, nothing was happening until some dumb-ass 28 year-old ROTC First Lieutenant decided enough was enough. I guess it was alright. Nobody said anything to me about it — not even a 'Thank you' — oh well, that's the Military, isn't it?"

Back at Manston, many of the 512th Squadron's maintenance personnel had not been eligible for the move to Holland, however. It had been decided in August to move the unit, but it quickly became apparent that many of the enlisted men did not have the required six months of service left on both enlistment time and rotation date. Many personnel re-enlisted and extended their tour dates, but there were many others who would remain at Manston, and were assigned to one of the sister squadrons. Dick Grace was one such person:

"Since I didn't want to re-enlist and didn't have enough time left to go to Soesterburg, my rotation date was extended two months, and in September, I was transferred to the 514th. I wasn't happy about being extended nor being transferred, but one consoling factor was [that] I wasn't alone, and the other was my promotion to Staff Sergeant finally coming through. While with the 514th, my duties were limited to getting their F-86Fs ready to fly back to the States as the F-86Ds started to arrive. Toward the end of January [1955] I returned to the States and

106: *This 514th FBS T-33 is notable for its sharkmouth nose art; any type of 'unauthorised' artwork on the 406th's aircraft was unusual. 51-4474 was lost in a crash at Manston on 9 April 1958. (via Manston History Club)*

107: *In May 1954, 1/Lt Kenneth Kuhlman of 514th FIS had his canopy shatter returning to Manston from Hahn AB in Germany. Kuhlman can be seen here crouching in the cockpit to keep out of the airstream. The aircraft, 51-13503, was repaired and later flew with the Peruvian Air Force (Jay Blanco)*

108: *Busy scene at Nouasseur AB as 512th FIS ground crews take F-86F 52-5276 through a 50-hour inspection. Aircraft was the mount of 1/Lt William F Vogel. (Richard T Grace)*

109: *Maintenance of 406th FBW/FIW Sabres was often accomplished in hangars near to the squadron location; Hangar 4 on the 'loop' for 512th, and Hangar 3 on the western taxiway for 513th. The 514th used Hangar 1 on the eastern side of the airfield. In this view 1/Lt Harry Schurr of 514th FBS (kneeling) takes a cigarette break before his next mission. (Jay Blanco).*

110: *512th FIS personnel pose for the camera during the summer of 1954. Front row L-R are: 2/Lt Raould Mussenden, Capt James Duncan, 2/Lt Frederick Wallace, Capt David Martin, 1/Lt Donald Oyer, 1/Lt Daniel Daube, 2/Lt Murray Brush, 2/Lt James Pennington, 1/Lt Robert Burns, 2/Lt Herman Griffin and 'Tiger', unk. Rear row L-R: 2/Lt James Toomey, 2/Lt Kenneth Culp, 1/Lt Robert Jondahl, 2/Lt James Henry, unk, Capt Joseph Marling, 2/Lt Thomas Hipps, Maj Frank Haynie, unk, 2/Lt James Orvis, 2/Lt Arthur Longmire, 2/Lt George Nedel, 2/Lt Gordon Bruce. (Kenneth Culp via David Collyer)*

111: *This 512th FBS F-86F is carrying 120-gallon drop tanks on extended inboard ferry pylons. All of the 406th FBW Sabres could carry four drop tanks in ferry configuration, but if two tanks were carried it was more usual to bolt them to the outboard hardpoints. (via Paul Cooper)*

112: *Jay Blanco of the 514th FBS takes time out to pose with his Sabre at a cross-country stop. This aircraft, 51-13490 was being flown by 'JD' Smith when he was killed on 4 October 1954. (Jay Blanco)*

113: *The 512th FDS received a Third Air Force citation for 10,000 accident-free flying hours in September 1954; it painted 1/Lt James Anderson's Sabre in special markings to commemorate the fact. The 512th had been redesignated as a Fighter Day Squadron the previous month; it would depart for Holland in November. (Author's collection).*

114: *514th FBS F-86F 52-5284 being refuelled on the eastern ASP, early 1954. Tall building in background was the parachute drying tower, which was demolished in the early 1990s. (Ernest Panizzoli)*

115: *Capt H.D Stallings prepares to start his Sabre on a cold March morning in 1954. Ground crew member on the wing is plugging in the ground power unit. (Jay Blanco)*

116: *F-86F 51-13371 was the personal mount of 2/Lt Jay Blanco; though his name appeared on the left-hand canopy rail, he did not always fly the aircraft. After service with the 514th, '371 was passed to the Republic of Korea Air Force. In 1985, through the efforts of General 'Boots' Blesse, it returned to the United States and was displayed at the Champlin Fighter Aces Museum in Mesa, Arizona. (Jay Blanco)*

117: *This F-86F was the 514th FIS commander's aircraft and carried a broad blue band around its fuselage to signify the fact. Lt Col James F. Frakes' name appeared on the left-hand canopy rail and that of his crew chief, A/2c S.D. May, on the right. (Dave Roberson)*

118 Above: This extensive mural was painted on the 512th FBS crew room on the 'loop' dispersal at Manston; sadly it no longer survives. At left, Lt Daniel Daube holds 'Tiger', the squadron's bull-dog mascot. (Dick Binga-man)

119: A pair of 514th FIS F-86Fs en route to Rome in Sep-tember 1954. (Dave Roberson)

120: As so often was the case, 406th FIW/FBW Sabre pilots rarely flew their 'assigned' aircraft. In this case, Lt Walt Gutman of 513th FBS took Lt 'Woody' Woodfin's aircraft for a cross-country mission. Gutman's mount was in fact 52-5303, which is nowadays preserved at the Valiant Air Command Museum in Titusville, Florida. (Walt Gutman)

121: *Bob Gottfried in the cockpit at Rome, September 1954. Four 514th FIS F-86Fs had flown to Italy on a cross-country exercise. (Dave Roberson)*

122: *514th FBS pilots 1/Lt Drury Callahan (left) and 1/Lt Tom Gordon (right) walk out for another mission. Callahan was one of the squadron's more experienced Sabre pilots and had already flown a tour on F-86s in Korea. (Jay Blanco)*

123: *Capt Stallings with his Sabre, 1954. Of note are the standard-fit 200-gallon drop tanks and the small 'fence' mounted on the wing upper surface. The 'hard edge' F-86Fs flown by 406th FBW/FIW had a higher stall speed than Sabres fitted with leading-edge slats. The former led to a number of incidents at Manston. (Glenn Stallings)*

124 Above: *These 50th FBW F-86Hs attended Manston's 1957 Armed Forces Day display; aircraft 53-1433 appeared in the static display. The aircraft are parked on the large aircraft servicing platform (ASP) beside the control tower; the runway runs right to tleft in the far distance. (Cowles Bristol)*

125: *Manston's USAF Officers Club seen in the mid-1950s, still bearing the RAF 'Per Ardua Ad Astra' script above the doorway. The buildings had changed little by the 1980s, though by then it had become the RAF Warrant Officers' and Sergeants' Mess. (Milt Torres)*

126: *Maj Larry Blesie taxies back to his parking slot on 3 December 1954 after the first F-86D mission from Manston. Blesie, Operations Officer with 513th FIS, was flying an F-86D-50 serial number 52-10056. As with all F-86Ds that flew from Manston at this time, it was devoid of unit markings. John Hutson ejected from this aircraft en route to Wheelus on 27 February 1957. (via Marty Isham)*

was discharged ending my Air Force career and 38 months at Manston".

The 512th FDS remained at Soesterburg until 8 September 1955, when the squadron designation returned 'on paper' to the UK. All former 512th aircraft and personnel remained in Holland and became the 32nd Fighter Day Squadron, activated on the same day, and attached to the 36th Fighter Day Wing. One final anecdote concerning the 512th's move comes from the then 1st Lt. Dave Roberson of the 514th FBS, who well recalls the unit's departure from Manston:

"When the 512th left we had the 'Dogs', [F-86Ds] but were not yet flying them. As they were leaving, one of the Fs dropped out of formation and flew low over our squadron area. The speed brakes opened and down came a package on a small parachute. We recovered it, and on opening we found a bone and a note which said 'If you can't fly 'em, feed 'em'".

The F-86Fs at Manston were largely returned to the United States via Burtonwood by the start of 1955, and a number later saw service with the Peruvian Air Force. Others were passed on to the air forces of the Republic of Korea, Pakistan, Japan and Nationalist China. Unlike the Thunderjets, the pilots of the 406th sorely missed these aircraft. The F-86F was a true dogfighter, unlike the replacement F-86D which was heavier and less manoeuvrable. Initially pilots had trouble in coming to terms with the apparent step backwards in certain areas of performance. But the F-86D was designed for an entirely different mission: that of bomber interception and destruction. Dave Roberson ferried out one of the last F-86Fs:

"My last flight in the F was on 15 December 1954 to Burtonwood where we were taking the Fs to Scottish Aviation to be rehabbed and shipped out to somewhere. Claud Ward, Joe DeBlock and myself went in a flight of three. I landed number 2 and ended up blowing a tyre on the wet runway and *went out of control. I went right in front of Joe, who landed behind me, and missed him by only a few feet. I luckily ended up going down a taxiway almost 180 degrees from the direction I landed. The landing gear was sort of bent, but I only had hurt pride. The safety type from the Air Force side of the base came over, but we explained that we were delivering the aircraft to Scottish Aviation and didn't think he had jurisdiction. That's all he needed. He left and we never saw him again. The people at Scottish Aviation weren't too happy, but Claud pointed out that they were going to completely overhaul the aircraft, and finally talked them into signing for it".*

The F-86D Sabre

Design of the F-86D began at North American in March 1949 with an all-weather interceptor on the drawing boards. To fulfil its all-weather requirement, the new fighter was equipped with an AN/APG-36 radar dish in the nose, initially controlled by the Hughes E-3 fire control system (FCS), and later the E-4 FCS of increased power. The pilot would carry out most of his interception by viewing a cathode ray tube screen positioned in his lower instrument panel. The nose-mounted radar dictated a repositioned engine air intake, which was re-located below the 18-inch antenna. To assist in ejection, a clamshell canopy was fitted and armament for this bomber hunter would be confined to twenty-four 2.75-inch rockets, fitted in a retractable tray beneath the forward fuselage. To cope with the increased weight of extra internal fuel plus all the radar 'black boxes' and associated equipment, the thrust of the J47 engine was upped by fitting an afterburner, and was redesignated J47 GE-17. One of the major developmental problems for the new fighter was in its electronic fuel control system. There would be no physical link between the pilot's throttle lever and the engine; all fuel metering and throttle variation would be performed by an electronic selector which controlled and correlated engine and afterburner operation.

But what really set the D-model apart from other interceptors was that it was a single-seater. All previous designs, such as the F-82 Twin Mustang and the P-61 Black Widow had been two-seaters with the second crewman dealing with the radar gear. Indeed, the other two contemporary USAF all-weather interceptor designs, the Lockheed F-94 Starfire and the Northrop F-89 Scorpion were also two-seaters. Much was expected of the new Sabre and teething troubles put its service debut back some considerable time.

By the date its first flight in December 1949, the new aircraft had been redesignated F-95A, as there was only a 25% parts commonality with the earlier Sabres. In a political move, the designation reverted

127 Far left: An Erco flight simulator was installed at Manston to train crews on the F-86D. Though basic, it saved a lot of money and accidents; the F-86F by comparison, had no dedicated simulator – each pilot's first solo was also his first flight in the aircraft. (Author's collection's collection)

128: *514th FIS personnel inspect one of their first F-86Ds to arrive – 52-10033 in early January 1955. White dots just visible on the forward fuselage are North American Aviation inspection seals, placed over each inspection panel at the factory. (Drury Callahan)*

129: *This pair of 513th FIS Sabres had only just arrived with the unit and landed at Erding in Germany during early 1955; the aircraft only have red canopy rails as squadron markings. (Gerald Naber)*

130: *Full 'early-style' 406th FIW colours are seen on this 514th FIS F-86D-50. Aircraft was the mount of group commander Col W.S. Harrell. Lightning flash on the nose is mid-blue, echoing the canopy rail treatment. (Milt Torres)*

131: *Manston's Open Day on Armed Forces Day 1955 allowed the British public to see the USAF jets close-up for the first time. Unit markings carried by the aircraft at that time were basic; 52-4304 of 514th FIS has a dark blue canopy rail with pilot's name in white stencil. Slanted tail stripes are (from the top), blue, yellow, and red with 514th badge superimposed. (Larry Brooks)*

132: *Spitfire Mk XVI TB752 was donated to Manston in 1955 and was a landmark for many years. Note the control tower to the rear of this August 1956 view. The aircraft is still on display at Manston, though thankfully indoors these days. (Cowles Bristol)*

133: *Canadian contemporary of the USAF's F-86D, the Avro Canada CF-100 was twin-engined and carried a crew of two. This aircraft, 18365, visited Manston in 1957 and is parked at the Margate end of the ASP. (Cowles Bristol)*

to 'F-86D' in July 1950 as a result of the US Congress requirement to approve budgets for new aircraft types. As the F-86D, the aircraft would be merely an F-86 development and required less strict monetary control. In addition, contractors on the project were restricted to costing outlined in F-86 contracts, whereas an F-95 would require new contracts to be drawn up, no doubt at increased prices. As it was, the fixed price for the first 37 F-86Ds came out at $380,232 each.

Numerous problems, mainly confined to the engine and fire control systems lengthened the test phase of the F-86D's gestation and it was not until 13 July 1952 that the first 'definitive' aircraft with the E-4 FCS was ready for trials. In an effort to show its faith in the F-86D, the USAF set two successive world air speed records in quick succession, at 698.505 mph (1126 km/h) on 18 November 1952 and 715.697 mph (1154 km/h) on 16 July 1953. The capabilities of the aircraft were ably demonstrated when it was revealed that the second record was set with a full rocket load.

In squadron use, the F-86D did present maintenance problems as well as imposing certain limitations on its combat crews. Bill Plunk, a 513th pilot has mixed feelings about the aircraft:

"On the D model at altitude such as 40-45,000 feet [12,195-13,719 m] the slats would pop out in a high turn and would degrade the performance significantly. The airplane at that time was a good flying machine. The big problem, and I might say the only problem with the airplane was its electronic fuel control system. I was a maintenance officer and test pilot at Moody [AFB, Georgia after leaving Manston] and if I had over 50% in-commission, I considered we were doing good. All the problems were either fuel control or radar. I never had the opportunity to fly the F-86H, but from what I have heard, it was one hell of an airplane — kinda like an overgrown [F] 86F. Also I never got to fly in the Canadian '86F, [Mk.5 and 6] which had at least 1,000 more pounds [0.445 kN] of thrust than the USAF version. I can recall being bounced by an RCAF '86 over the UK at 45,000 feet and could do nothing about it — really pissed me off. However, I recovered my ego by bouncing RAF Meteors — nothing's fair!"

Bud Biteman recalls that the F-86Ds were seldom flown 'clean', which did nothing to help the Dog's performance:

"With the exception of Inspection Exercises or specific training missions, we seldom flew our Dawgs without drop tanks. Ours was basically a peacetime training mission, and we attempted to make the most use possible of our time in the air to practice intercepts, which benefited both the pilots and the controllers. If we had flown without tanks, that intercept training time would have been considerably reduced. And even under the most routine weather conditions there on the South Coast,

we were often held down because our 200 foot ceiling minimums could not be guaranteed for the duration of our flights, and there was no legal alternate airfield within our range...in England or on the Continent. The books could attempt to measure and compare scramble, climb, intercept and recover times....all under ideal conditions, which seldom seemed to fit. I recall one exercise where I flew as an 'outside inspector' with the [86th] Wing based at Erding, Germany. We received our scramble, and from our Alert position near the end of the runway, climbing in afterburner almost the whole way, we were not able to intercept our 'enemy' targets, flying at 40,000 feet [12,195 m], until we were both over Paris! The likely conditions for attack from East of the border did little to make us optimistic about our performance in the F-86Ds".

That said, the Dog pilots generally respected their steed. 514th FIS pilot Dave Roberson is quick to defend the F-86D's apparent shortcomings:

"I take exception to the statement that the Dog wasn't suited to the alert mission. You could start it as fast as any other. In fact, with the electronic fuel control you could hit the starter and put the throttle in afterburner position and it would automatically start and accelerate to full power. I think it was well under a minute. The radar may have taken longer to warm up, but you didn't use it until you were in the target's vicinity and it had more than ample time to warm up. There were glitches with the electronic fuel control. As I recall, there was an 'auto' position for take-off. When this switch was 'on', the fuel system would automatically go to emergency fuel as it detected trouble with the electronic system. After take-off, you were supposed to move this switch to the 'normal' position. The problem was that if it had automatically changed to 'emergency', it also drove the 'normal' fuel control to the idle position, so when you moved the switch to 'normal', it felt like a flame-out, in that you were at idle, and it took several seconds for the thing to catch up to the throttle position. Therefore a lot of folks did go ahead and use the 'emergency' fuel [position] for take-off. For its day it was a pretty good system, but did have lots of glitches. For instance, in normal flight, it would sometimes 'lock up', i.e. the power stayed at the last setting regardless of what you did with the throttle. The only way out was to manually switch to 'emergency' fuel. This was always thrilling when you were on someone's wing in the weather".

The F-86Ds delivered to Manston were mainly F-86D-36, -45 and -50 models, the D-36s having gone through Project 'Pullout', an attempt to bring all in-service F-86Ds up to a similar modification standard. Work was centred at North American's Fresno, California plant, with other conversions carried out at the McClellan AFB Sacramento Air Material Area. The pre-D-45 models were fitted with braking parachutes (standard on the F-86D-45), and all models had uncompleted Technical Orders and modifications completed prior to dispatch to operational units. In total 1,128 F-86Ds went through 'Pullout', which was completed in September 1955. For the record, the F-86D-36 model introduced an omni-directional (VOR) set to the aircraft, the D-45 sub-type was the first fitted with a braking chute, and from 52-4136, was fitted with a slightly higher thrust J47 GE-33 engine. The D-50 had modified engine oil drains, brake chute and exhaust assembly. 'Pullout' brought most of these items to all previous models, and Manston's Sabres would be to a similar specification. This was important not only to a pilot, who might find a gauge positioned differently, but also to the maintenance personnel, who could rely on one aircraft being mechanically similar to its neighbour, and that there was the supply back-up to support its operation. These things were all the more important for a unit operating an aircraft at the cutting edge of technology, thousands of miles from its manufacturer. In order to alleviate this problem, there were in addition, many civilian technical representatives based at Manston.

More in-depth maintenance and overhaul of the F-86Ds was carried out at the FIAT company in Turin, Italy. Chuck Metz assures that:

"They did a great job and the ships were better than new when finished. FIAT was a very competent aircraft overhaul facility. We had the utmost confidence in their work. Our only problem with going to Torino was that it was not a USAF facility, and there were none of our people there. The Tower operators did not speak English in many cases, and this led to many strange incidents".

With the lack of new F-86Ds at Manston, and the need for so many personnel to be converted to the type, most flying from the end of 1954 and into the early months of 1955 was carried out on the Wing's T-33 trainers; for example, it would not be until 20 April 1955 — a good four months since his last F-86F flight — that Dave Roberson first flew an F-86D from Manston. His situation was typical.

On 13 December 1954 the first personnel of another F-86D squadron, the 87th FIS, began arriving at RAF Bentwaters, Suffolk from its previous home at Sioux City Municipal Airport, Iowa. Though never actually attached to the 406th FIW, this squadron would maintain close links with the Manston wing, and the first Sabres for the 87th arrived at Bentwaters on 21 December. In a somewhat convoluted arrangement, when the 512th FDS re-numbered as the 32nd FDS on 8 September 1955, the 512th designation was transferred to the 87th FIS, retaining the aircraft, personnel and even the squadron badge of the 87th, whose squadron number was inactivated. Thus, the 'new' 512th at Bentwaters became the third F-86D squadron assigned to 406th FIW. Chuck Metz was a pilot with the 87th FIS (and subsequently, the 512th FIS), and recalls that there was much rivalry between his squadron and the Manston-based Sabre squadrons:

"The 87th was a very old squadron that was active in WWII. Many of our pilots were from the old days in Europe. When I joined the squadron in 1953, it was still flying F-51 Mustangs, and it was some months before we got the F-86D Sabre Jet. Not many of our pilots had been to 86 School, and in fact I was one of the only ones. Everyone else had to learn [the F-86D] the hard way! I had to learn the F-51 the hard way! We had two Medal of Honor holders in the squadron at the time I arrived. They earned their medals in Europe. Our sister squadron commander also had the Medal of Honor for action in the South Pacific. My squadron commander was Mike Quirk, and he went to England with us".

"Since we were already flying F-86s, and had been for some time, it was easy for us to go over as a squadron that could operate 'out of the box', so to speak. We took some spare parts and engines with us, but received new aircraft when we arrived. It took only a couple of months to get all set up and ready to fly, but they wouldn't let us, because of the weather and our lack of experience in England. That was a sort of slap in the face which we all resented greatly. As it turned out, we could not fly because our Wing had not been together, and thus had no organization all set up. We were forced to sit on the ground because the Manston squadrons were not ready [having only just converted to the F-86D]. This was a very poor thing for morale. This single fact probably caused a bad feeling to develop between us and the Wing. When we finally did get to fly, we put 26 aircraft in the air and did a mass fly-by on Manston! We did it in very close formation and very low, just to let them know we were there. I doubt that they appreciated that action. We considered that we were heads above the folks 'down there'. Of course, a lot of this was just good clean competition and I don't think there was anything mean about it. Thus, we always took great delight in tweaking them when we could. We often flew down en-masse, just to show them how many F-86s we could get into the air at one time. Fighter pilots are a different breed, and there has to be a lot of spirit in everything they do, or they won't be worth a darn in action. That is, and always has been the way things are".

The F-86D would require more pilot training than any other USAF aircraft of the time, due to the many operations carried out by its pilot. Fresh F-86D aircrews were trained at the Moody AFB, Georgia, Perrin AFB, Texas and Tyndall AFB, Florida Interceptor Training Schools. The prospective F-86D pilot would begin in the Erco flight simulator, a $150,000 contraption that included a replica of the F-86D cockpit. As the pilot sat in this machine, his progress was monitored by an instructor and a technician seated at a control panel in an adjoining room. From this room, 'targets', and flying situations such as emergency procedures could be fed into the simulation.

The (then) Capt. Duane E. 'Bud' Biteman from 514th FIS, now a retired Lieutenant Colonel, recalls his time at Perrin:

"...I received a call from the Base Adjutant telling me they'd received a wire from Flying Training Command that I was scheduled for the F-86D All-Weather Interceptor School at Perrin AFB, reporting not later than 23 September 1954. My school, a four and one-half month course, was designed to qualify me as an F-86D All-Weather Interceptor pilot, with logical assignment to follow in the Air Defense Command (though things would turn out differently). For the first two weeks we were to be totally involved with ground school, no flying whatsoever. Weather and Instrument Principles; the second month we would fine-tune instrument flying techniques in the air. Only then would we finally check out in the F-86D... the 'Dawg' and learn the latest Air Defense combat techniques".

"With thirty hours in the simulator before climbing into the F-86D for my first flight, I was completely familiar with the single-place machine and all of its systems — even the sounds! It was the first single-seat fighter that I ever checked out (on November 23, 1954) for a first flight with complete familiarity and confidence".

"Upon return to duty following the Christmas holidays, I flew just a few more flights in the '86, beginning a long association with GCI (Ground Controlled Interception) Controllers, as we learned the positioning tactics the ground controllers would use to manoeuvre our flights of attacking fighters onto the 'lead-collision' intercept line, where our short-range airborne radar sets could be locked on allowing the onboard computers to display the track necessary for successful attack".

These attacks consisted of firing rockets at a target towed 6,000 feet behind a converted B-45 bomber. The banner was a mere 6 foot by 30 foot plastic mesh panel with spinning metal discs on it to provide a radar signature. Following the 'daylight' phase came a period of intensive night/adverse weather training, as Bud relates:

"On January 10 the training curriculum put me on the night flying schedule, where I remained for two solid months...straight through to the end of the course, I flew the '86 only at night, practising GCI tactics and intercepts. The 36 hours of night F-86D time acquired during that time eliminated any apprehension I might possibly have retained about flying at night (and a good thing, it was a precursor of things to come...lots of night and solid-weather instrument flying). On February 22 I finally received word of my over-due transfer orders following completion of the course at Perrin and, typically, rather than being sent to the West Coast, as I'd been led to believe by Col. Ike Wintermute, we were to be sent [to] the 406th Fighter Interceptor Wing at RAF station Manston".

Bud arrived at Manston during May 1955 and was assigned to the 514th FIS, where he remained until September 1956, when he became Chief F-86D Standardization Pilot for Third AF at South Ruislip.

The first operational F-86D mission was flown from Manston on 3 December 1954, with 513th FIS Operations Officer Maj. Larry Blesie at the controls. In addition to the training that the new pilots received in the USA, each Sabre 'Dog' driver attended an instrument school at Manston, followed by a squadron check-out prior to taking an F-86D aloft. Ground maintenance personnel also undertook specialist type training. One example was the Radar Technicians training programme, which involved a 10-month course at Lowry AFB, Colorado. Instructors from Chanute AFB, Illinois had arrived at Manston prior to the arrival of the new Sabres and began an intensive maintenance training program. As a result, the Wing managed to convert and come to operational readiness in a very short time. The 'lead-collision' intercept philosophy of the F-86D was also new to the RAF fighter controllers, and these personnel had to be brought up to speed on vectoring the USAF fighters. The main RAF GCI sites which 406th fighters dealt with were at Sandwich, Neatishead and Bawdsey. Richard White, then a Captain, explains the pilot's end of the interception:

"In the F-86D, the pilot had to do the work of the radar operator, as well as the flying. After the pilot, with the help of the ground controller, located the target on his radar scope (up to 30 nautical miles) he closed to within 15 miles, where he could 'lock on' the target, that is, lock his radar on the target for automatic tracking. He then received steering information on his 'scope, and could concentrate on flying the aircraft to follow the steering signals (represented as a dot on the 8-inch screen). At 20 seconds to go, a circle began shrinking on the screen, and the pilot had to increase his precision to keep the dot centred in the circle, while keeping the trigger depressed. If the dot was in the circle when the circle was down to half an inch [diameter], the rockets fired, and when they reached a point 2,000 feet [609 m] in front of the F-86D, the target plane would cross in front on a course 90° to the F-86D".

With 45 seconds to go, 'Phase III' of the fire control system operation came into effect, during which the computer corrected for any movement of the aircraft about the vertical axis; the pilot then just had to attend to the attitude of the aircraft. If the pilot was still flying onto his target, at 2.5 seconds to go, the circuits in the firing section of the computer were readied for the 'target' to be shot down. *"Of course"*, remembers White, *"we did not fire but we still had strict rules to avoid collision on these training missions"*. The twenty-four, 2.75-inch unguided Folding Fin Aircraft Rockets (FFAR), dubbed 'Mighty Mouse', weighed 18 pounds (8 kg) each and could be fired in salvos of six, twelve or twenty-four. As the

134: *Another early 513th FIS F-86D mission completed; 52-4226 taxies down the western taxiway still trailing its brake 'chute. Note 66th ARS Albatross amphibians in background. (Larry Brooks)*

135: *The F-86D lacked an onboard engine fire extinguisher, and so in-flight emergencies often led to ejection. This cartoon was placed in each pilot's F-86D flight manual to explain the situation in graphic terms. (Author's collection)*

136: *These recently-arrived 514th FIS aircraft are still being painted in the unit colours; 52-4204 in the foreground has the blue canopy rail and 1/Lt Jay Blanco's name on it, but no other distinguishing features. (Drury Callahan)*

137: *F-86D 52-4130 gets airborne from Manston's Runway 29. The early 1955 colour scheme consisted of the slanted tail stripes and coloured canopy rail seen on the F-86Fs, but the F-86Ds featured a coloured lightning flash on the nose section. '130 was a 513th FIS machine, delivered to the unit in October 1954. (Drury Callahan via Marty Isham)*

138: *52-4229 of 513th FIS is already looking well-worn despite only a few months' service. When this photo was taken, in March 1955, the red lightning flash on the nose section had all but peeled off. (Drury Callahan)*

139: *When the 'harpoon' nose flash was adopted by 406th FIW, it took some time to standardise markings. 52-10019 still bears the slanted tail bands, which would soon give way to an horizontal arrangement. (JMG Gradidge)*

140: *514th FIS pilots Lt John Michaud (left), Lt Milt McWilliams (centre) and squadron commander Lt Col George Hubler (right) repack a Sabre drag 'chute after landing at Fürstenfeldbruck AB in Germany, late 1955. 52-4204 in background was a colourful aircraft – aside from the standard 514th FIS colours, it carried a red, yellow and blue fuselage stripe. It was assigned to group commander Col William Harrell. (Jay Blanco)*

141: *The 512th FIS took great pride in their aircraft, their T-33s were no exception. 51-17415 wears the standard squadron markings, but also has a diagonal three-colour band running across the wing. ((Pete Hutting)*

142: *406th FIW F-86Ds undergoing maintenance at Manston. Aircraft at rear is 51-6150, an F-86D-36 which had already seen squadron service in the United States. It was assigned to 406th FIW in May 1956. (Dave Keep)*

143: A 514th FIS Sabre unleashes a salvo of Mighty Mouse rockets; the pilot is 'under the hood'. This F-86D has a black underside to reduce the corrosive effects of the rocket efflux. (Milt Torres)

144: When the 406th FIW flew to Wheelus, they usually fired their rockets against flags towed by 7155th Target Tow Sqn TB-29s. Each TB-29 carried two tow reels with 6,500 feet of cable each. The target flags were housed in box-like containers visible under the tail section, and were controlled by a reel operator sitting in the waist position. (Jerome P Burton)

145: SSSR-l5412 was one of three Tupolev Tu 104s that diverted into Manston on 1 October 1956; aboard were members of the Bolshoi Ballet. The three aircraft (-5412, -5414 and -5415) were parked on the south side of the airfield next to the Canterbury-Ramsgate road; this was as far from the USAF aircraft as it was possible to get. (Cowles Bristol)

rockets left the aircraft, they fanned out, to give a 'shot-gun' effect, increasing chances of a kill — each rocket had the explosive power of a 75 mm artillery shell, and travelled at a speed of 2,600 feet per second (792 m/s). Optimum range for the Mighty Mouse was around 4,500 feet (1,372 m), with a theoretical maximum effective range of 9,000 feet (2,743 m).

Late in 1955, Third AF HQ at South Ruislip contacted the Air Ministry to state the need for an air-to-air rocket firing range for the 406th's Sabre Dogs. The range requirements were for year-round use, from 0800 hours to 2400 hours, at 30,000 feet (9,146 m) and below. It was noted that ideally, a range size of 30 x 60 nautical miles (48 x 96 km) would be needed, but that this could be decreased to 20 x 25 miles (32 x 40 km) if the aircraft were allowed to manoeuvre for attack outside the range area. Two sites, both in the North Sea, were suggested:

1.   An area bounded by 52°46N 02°25E, 52°46N 03°17E, 52°12N 03°17E and 52°12N 02°25E, with firing to be carried out from the west to the east.

2.   An area bounded by 53°04N 02°15E, 53°04N 03°05E, 52°04N 03°05E and 52°04N 02°15E, firing also west to east.

In its reply, dated 21 November 1955, the Air Ministry stated that neither location could be approved, due to their proximity to airways Red 1 and Green 2, but suggested either using the Leman Bank range, or re-siting the other proposed ranges to avoid the airways. Further to this, on 9 December, Squadron Leader H. Pears at the Air Ministry proposed an area, bounded by: 52°49N 02°20E, 52°49N 02°52'40"E, 52°09N 02°20"E and 52°09N 02°52'40"E. This area was 20 miles (32 km) out to sea off Lowestoft, and measured 20 by 40 nautical miles (32 x 64 km) in size. As the USAF seemed to be in agreement with this, the Air Ministry applied to other interested parties for approval. On 27 January 1956, Mr. H.N. Taylor at the Ministry of Agriculture, Fisheries and Food responded that he had no problems, followed by Mr. W.J. Madigan at the Ministry of Transport and Civil Aviation on 22 February. Finally, on 9 March, Mr. A. Goddard at the Admiralty agreed that the range as suggested would meet with their approval. On 4 April 1956, the area — named the Smith's Knoll Range the previous month — was approved for use by the 406th FIW, with its eastern extremity extended to 02°53E. This range would see a large amount of use in the coming years.

With the change in mission for the Wing, new squadron badges and colour schemes soon evolved. The 513th FIS dropped its 'flying flea' emblem, and changed to an eagle with lion's head (known as a 'Ligle') painted on a white shield, whilst the 514th FIS chose a chess 'queen' superimposed over a chess board, all bordered by a circle. 1st Lt. George D. Daughtry from the 513th was responsible for the design of its emblem:

"I was the originator of the 513th insignia with artwork/design help from Lieutenant Llewellyn [and Nelson]. This was a new insignia in 1954... It was felt that since the squadron had changed to air-to-air interception, the insignia should be changed. The idea for [the 514th FIS] insignia arose from the fact that the 514th pilots prided themselves on their chess playing ability".

1st Lt. Gerald J. Naber remembers the 513th emblem design process in a slightly different light:

"The new squadron insignia was developed one foggy and rainy afternoon when the squadron C.O. announced that no-one would go home until we had a new insignia. In the scramble for ideas, we rummaged through a few magazines on hand and a large unabridged dictionary. The latter had a full-colour page of national emblems, among them a black bird with large wings that is, or was, the national emblem for Austria. From that, several of us made some adjustments — flared the wings upward, matched it up with a lion's head, added the '513', painted the design red and superimposed the lot on the shape of a shield. The insignia was eventually cleaned up by a good local artist and sent off to Washington to be officially blessed by Headquarters USAF. Much to our surprise it passed all of the necessary wickets".

The 513th's new emblem was officially approved on 28 April 1955. The 514th FIS emblem was designed by Jay Blanco, and chosen from many entries submitted by squadron personnel. Jay's design was officially approved on 1 March 1955. In addition to their squadron crests, the aircraft retained the slanted tail markings seen on the F-86Fs, but in addition to this and the painted canopy rail, a lightning flash extending back from the intake area to the wing root was applied to the F-86Ds. This flash was of the squadron colour, which remained the same as those worn in the F-86F days. Soon the squadron badges began to be painted over the tail stripes, and finally, inspired by the 512th FIS's incorporation back into the 406th FIW during September 1955, the Wing standardised on its 'harpoon' emblem, stretching from the intake down the fuselage, also in the squadron colour. At this time, the diagonal tail stripes were repositioned in a horizontal plane, and the superimposition of the squadron badge was standardised. These markings would remain essentially unchanged until the Sabres left Manston. As well as these markings, a few of the Wing's F-86Ds carried the 406th FIW 'mailed fist' emblem on the mid fuselage. Squadron commander's aircraft usually wore a band around the fuselage in the squadron colour and flight commanders would often have a suitably coloured band painted around each drop tank.

In addition to the 406th FIW colour scheme, some mention should be made here about the 'standard' F-86D markings, such as positioning of 'buzz' numbers, and other USAF identification. As delivered to Manston in late 1954, the F-86Ds wore the NAA-style rounded font letters for the 18-inch buzz ('FU-') number, which was placed on the forward fuselage. The same style of lettering was echoed in the serial number on the vertical tail. A 4-inch high 'U.S. AIR FORCE' was positioned just above the serial number. All these markings were in black.

From roughly the beginning of 1955 (though officially from mid-1953), the 'U.S. AIR FORCE' lettering was moved to the forward fuselage, but this time in 18-inch squared off letters. The buzz number was then re-sited to the rear fuselage, just aft of the 'star and bar'. Other small additions around this time were the yellow 'RESCUE' arrow below the cockpit, with the further addition of a black-painted armament status panel to the lower front fuselage on the left side. Many F-86Ds also received a black, resistant coating to the lower fuselage to protect the skin from the corrosive effects of rocket firing.

Finally, at the beginning of 1956, many aircraft's buzz numbers were re-applied in the rear fuselage location, but this time in 15-inch letters. These markings would remain basically unchanged until the departure of the F-86D from Manston. It should be noted though, that many aircraft retained a mixture of markings (such as retaining the 4-inch 'U.S. AIR FORCE' on the tail at the same time as the 18-inch equivalent on the forward fuselage); the dates given above only equate to the introduction of these marking styles – in many cases it took a long time to repaint every aircraft.

During the early part of 1955, an F-86D simulator was installed at Manston, one of only two in Europe at the time. This equipment took up a whole building and was staffed by six airmen and three factory technicians led by M/Sgt. Bevelly Hart and Capt. James R. Whiting. The $10\frac{1}{2}$ ton simulator was used for up to 55 hours per week, with each prospective F-86D pilot getting 15 to 20 hours of 'time' prior to soloing at Manston.

Even after the completion of his initial solo flight in the F-86D, there were many more hours to be flown before a pilot could be considered to have completed his transition training. And this period of transition training proved no less hazardous than any other flight phase. In the afternoon of Friday 13 April 1955, 1st Lt. Jay Vandertoll left Manston as part of a two-ship F-86D formation from the 514th FIS, with the intention of accomplishing his 8th Transition Mission, which encompassed aerobatic manoeuvres. The flight went entirely to plan until around 3.20 pm, when the two aircraft were out over the North Sea, about 10 miles (16 km) north of Manston. As Vandertoll entered the vertical portion of a loop, he noticed that his forward fire warning light had illuminated. With a healthy altitude of 20,000 ft (6,097m), Lt. Vandertoll immediately brought the J47 engine to idle, at which point the light went out. After a brief sigh of relief, things turned sour when the light came on again, giving Vandertoll no alternative but to shut

the engine down — but this time the warning light stayed on.

At this point, it should be recognised that, (a), no fire extinguisher system is present on the F-86D, and (b), the F-86D Flight Handbook suggests ejection as the only alternative to chopping the throttle and making an unpowered glide to the nearest airfield. As Jay recalls:

"The forward [fire] warning light is very serious because it warns of a fire in the fuel cell areas of the aircraft which most likely will lead to an explosion which will destroy the aircraft and kill the pilot. I considered bailing out at that moment, but I knew that my chances of survival at that time of year in the cold water of the North Sea were slim".

An immediate recovery to Manston was initiated, while the chase pilot 1st Lt. Joseph K. Brown, confirmed that there were no obvious signs of a fire. By this time, the aircraft was down to 7,000 feet (2,134 m) altitude, and with no chance to make a full flameout landing pattern, Jay chose to make a 'dead stick' landing at Manston, as he by now had the airfield in sight. However, it was by no means over yet:

"Another problem I had to face in planning the dead stick landing at Manston was the possibility of total hydraulic failure at the moment of flaring for landing. This would cause the controls to lock and total loss of control close to the ground. With the engine shut down, the emergency hydraulic system was only good for approximately 7 minutes — the life of the main battery driving the emergency pump".

Making an entry onto a wide base leg, the aircraft was coaxed to a smooth landing on the runway's overrun, and rolled to a stop on the runway with no further problems. Neither the pilot nor the aircraft was damaged. Although Jay Vandertoll had previously flown many hours in the F-86F, he had only 8 hours and 55 minutes of F-86D time at this point. His courageous and skilful actions had saved not only his own life, but possibly some on the ground, plus his $300,000 Sabre. For these reasons, he was recommended by his squadron commander, Lt. Col. George O. Hubler, for induction into the 'Thumbs Up Club', which as part of the Wing Flying Safety Program, was devoted to recognising members of 406th FIW who had displayed skill or courage in recovering their aircraft safely from emergency conditions. The recommendation was put forward on 18 April 1955 and approved by Col. Conrad Herlick four days later. In doing so, Jay Vandertoll became only the sixth recipient of a 'Thumbs Up' award.

But life at Manston was not all work, work, work for the USAF personnel. By this time, the local towns of Margate and Ramsgate were full of off-duty GIs from Manston enjoying their leisure time. An unofficial colour bar existed too — Margate was for the whites, Ramsgate the blacks. Despite official public denials of this, the situation existed throughout the

USAF tenancy at Manston. Weekends would see hundreds of girls arriving in Thanet to meet the young Americans, and the hotel at St. Mildreds was the scene of many romantic liaisons. A book could be written solely about the antics at St. Mildreds — if only those involved would allow its publication! Back on base, personnel would live life to the fullest, as Dave Roberson recalls:

"Col. Hubler loved to play volleyball and when things were quiet we had to think of some diversion for him or he had us all out playing. I guess you could call our volleyball games 'fighter pilot volleyball'. No rules, the net was just a demarcation line. Lots of jammed or broken fingers etc. We played a lot of chess at the time, so whenever Hubler walked in someone would try to get him to play chess knowing that otherwise we would be on the volleyball court again".

"I don't know when we got him, but we had a goat for a mascot. He had a blanket with the 514th insignia and his name 'BG Russell' on it. The Russell was for our maintenance officer, Russell Huntley, and of course the BG stands for billy goat. He was kept on a chain between ops and the aircraft. He knew exactly how long the chain was. He would pretend to ignore you, but if you got within striking range he would nail you. He escaped on several occasions and became well known to the local community. He was goatknapped by the 513th on at least one occasion and painted red (their squadron color). We finally gave him to a local farmer. After a while, there was an article in the Isle of Thanet Gazette headlined 'BG Russell Strikes Again'. Apparently he escaped one night and leaped in front of a taxi causing a minor accident".

"I don't recall when it was done, but in the bottom of the 514th latrine, the 513th 'buzzard' (or whatever their insignia was supposed to be) was painted in its full glory. A favorite phrase was 'I think I'll go piss on the 513th'. This may have been done while we were preparing for a visit by Gen. Nathan Twining, Chief of Staff of the Air Force. I know we laid bricks and painted everything in sight. I recall the bitching about it. Especially about the latrine as no one really believed that Twining would come to the 514th, much less use our latrine".

There were none of the usual spring-time gunnery camps at Wheelus in 1955 — the two Manston-based Sabre squadrons were still coming up to operational readiness with their new mounts. When rocketry training did take place, it was performed on the mud flats in the Thames Estuary. However, it seems that the Bentwaters-based 87th FIS did perform limited rocketry training in Libya during August of 1955. It is interesting to note that on more than one occasion, air-to-ground rocketry training was carried out, after a suggestion that the F-86D could be used in the ground attack role. By applying grease pencil aiming marks on the windshield, some Sabre drivers became proficient at this in the short time it was practised. Fortunately the idea did not live too long though.

Something that varied little throughout the USAF stay at Manston was the amount of complaints received from the local civilian population. As early as January 1955, Thanet residents were doubling their complaints due to the increase in noise as a result of the new aircraft being flown out of the base. The uninformed reckoned that the sound of an F-86D was akin to that of a WWII German 'Doodlebug' flying bomb, which of course it wasn't, but the idea was no doubt to inflame peoples' passions. Some consolation could be gained from the knowledge that complaints of noise from the recently opened civil airport at nearby Ramsgate were also flooding in. As usual, Mr Rees-Davies was leading the complaints. In an effort to placate the local populace, as well as to educate them on exactly what 'those Yanks' were doing at Manston, an Open Day was held on Armed Forces Day, Saturday 21st May 1955. At the last Manston Open Day in 1948, 13 people had been killed when an RAF Mosquito crashed whilst performing its display. Fortunately, the 1955 display was accident-free, and included static displays of not only the new USAF machines (the F-86D and F-84F), but also of RAF aircraft such as the Hunter, Canberra and Vampire. Sadly, the show was curtailed by heavy rain, and the event was stopped at 3 pm, while many people were still trying to enter the airfield.

On 26 May, one of the hard-worked T-6s crashed through the perimeter fence on the A253 Canterbury-Ramsgate road, and brought traffic to a standstill for some time, as its wing was blocking the road. No-one was hurt in this landing accident, but the proximity of Manston's runway to this busy thoroughfare would prove to have more serious ramifications in future years, when there were three separate crashes, two of which killed passing motorists.

Initially, many of the 406th pilots were unhappy with the heavyweight F-86D, which brought to an end the dogfighting antics of the F-86F days; indeed, sudden aerobatics could damage the delicate radar equipment of the F-86D. In an effort to dispel some of the discontentment associated with the 'Dog', the North American Aviation Technical Representative, in concert with the squadron commanders, arranged for a visit by the NAA test pilot Gage Mace (and not Bob Hoover, as has been suggested). This would be around September 1955, according to Pete Hutting, who was a groundcrew member with the 513th FIS at the time and watched the display. The 513th Adjutant Clifford Nelson also watched awe-struck as the NAA pilot did things with the Sabre that didn't seem possible:

"Naturally, we all convened on the tarmac in front of the hangars to enjoy the show. [He] soon taxied out to the end of the runway, and we could hear the engine winding up as he held the brakes.

Shortly, he released the brakes, shot forward at full throttle, and after what appeared to be a rather short take-off roll, he lifted the 'Dog' off the ground, and with the nose well up, proceeded directly into a slow roll. He executed the roll very precisely and deliberately, with the gear retracting simultaneously, then climbed out steeply. He gave a virtuoso capability performance, ending with a super 'hot and tight' fighter-type approach and landing. It was a most convincing demonstration".

To cap it all, Mace had picked a normal run-of-the-mill squadron Sabre to perform the display, not some 'tweaked-up' company ship. In the words of Clifford Nelson: *"None of the pilots ever again had any doubts about what the old 'Dog' could do".*

Almost inevitably, the tide of public opinion began to make itself felt on the base. During July, after many more protests, the flying programme was reduced. Now all local traffic would increase its height in the pattern from 1,000 to 1,500 feet (304 to 457 m). In addition, no flying was to be carried out on Saturdays except for test hops, which had to be completed during the morning. No flying or engine ground running of any sort was permitted on Sundays. Night flying was to stop at 1 am, and in an effort to reduce the effects of noise during engine diagnostic and test run-ups, a sound deflecting 'baffle' was to be built. This prominent feature on the Manston skyline remained until the early 1990s when the expansion of the Kent International Airport warranted its removal. At the end of July 1955, the ever-present Member of Parliament W.R. Rees-Davies sent a memo to the Under-Secretary of State for Air, The Honourable George Ward suggesting that Manston be returned to RAF control and quieter aircraft. In the event that this was not possible, Rees-Davies added, he hoped that the less-noisy F-86Fs could return to Manston! As very few F-86F squadrons remained in Europe at this time, the suggestion bordered on the ludicrous and in his terse reply, the Under Secretary stated that there was absolutely no chance of the USAF vacating Manston. Local businesses must have breathed a sigh of relief at this decision, as during an average month, USAF personnel spent over £65,000 in the area, whilst the civilians working on base earned a further £20,000. These were large amounts in 1955.

Two members of the 406th were inducted into Manston's 'Thumbs Up Club' in July 1955. The first was 1st Lt. Art P. Grothouse of the 513th who was on approach to land at Manston when his Sabre's forward fire warning light came on. In an instant, in order to maintain his speed in case of engine failure, Grothouse raised his gear and flew his approach right up to touchdown with his undercarriage raised. At the last moment, the gear was lowered and a safe landing was effected. The second 'member' was 1/Lt Robert G. Rilling, also from 513th FIS, who realised soon after taking off from Manston that his F-86D

had experienced a puncture. Rilling immediately returned to base and popped his 'chute for another 'clean' landing.

August 1955 saw another refurbishment in progress on the airfield as work on strengthening the runway got underway. Earlier in the year, a survey of the airfield had been carried out by Third AF and had suggested re-siting the main runway. These findings were then passed to the Air Ministry. However, in a reply to the Chief Engineer at Third AF HQ dated 26 January, Mr. J.B.F Hawkins, the Deputy Director of Works (Planning) stated: *"The proposal to site a new runway further to the south and use a temporary strip to the north of the existing runway sounds practical, but I am taking no action pending written confirmation of this".* It is more than likely that monetary constraints now played a part, for no further discussion of a new runway seems to have been made. Instead, an ambitious plan for the refurbishment and upgrading of runway, taxiways and hardstands was put forward on 16 February; this called for work to begin during June 1955 and run to July 1956. Two days later, after much discussion between the two parties, a revised plan suggested a start date of mid-August 1955, with completion one year later. Eventually, on 31 March, the final costed draft planned for runway work to commence in mid-August of 1955, to be completed by December the same year with the taxiway and hardstand refurbishment starting off in stages at the same time as the runway work, but running on to completion of the whole project in mid-August 1956. The cost was pegged at £300,000 for the runway, and £830,000 in total.

The execution of the task generally reflected the plan, and during the third week of August 1955, the first of 120 shiploads of granite hardcore arrived at Richborough Wharf, a few miles south of the airfield. As a result of the work, flying from Manston was restricted but by no means curtailed. In any case, very few airfields would have had the available space to house a fighter wing plus the other aircraft and men based at the Thanet airfield. The main part of the runway reconstruction took place during December and the first two months of 1956, Manston re-opening as a Master Diversionary Airfield at 0800 hrs on 30 April 1956. The 'loop' dispersal again received attention in March 1956, with the ASP beside the control tower (added to the contract in December 1955) being completed in July. Final repair work due to the constant use of the runway was carried out over 14 days during August 1956. Civilian contractors were utilised to carry out this work, the majority of the workforce coming from the Thanet area. Sabres from 512th FIS would often drop in to Manston during this period, though at times the odd unscheduled arrival was also necessary. Chuck Metz:

"We [the 512th] had one aircraft that kept flaming out for no reason. The '86D just can't do that, it is physically impossible, but this one did. [The elec-

146: *52-4092 was assigned to 514th FIS squadron commander Lt Col George Hubler and carried a blue/white/blue fuselage band to signify the fact. (Jay Blanco)*

147: *This 406th FIW Sabre mural was painted on the wall of the Officers' Club (now the RAF Sergeants Mess); at weekly beer calls, pilots would often re-paint the aircraft so that their squadron was in the foreground. Fortunately, over the years this mural has been protected and can still be seen. (Author's collection)*

148: *From 1956, the aircraft 'buzz' ('FU-') number was relocated to rear fuselage of 406th FIW F-86Ds as seen here; the font was concurrently changed from a rounded 'NAA'-style to the squared Amarillo type. 52-4219 carried 513th FIS markings, but also had red and white bands painted around the mid fuselage with a 406th FIW badge superimposed. It was Col Hugh Manson's assigned machine. (via Dave Keep)*

149: *A solitary USAF guard stands watch over 1/Lt Edgar Lewis's F-86D, 52-4141. Lewis suffered a tyre burst on landing and his Sabre veered off the runway, hit a car and came to rest in a field just south of the airfield. Sadly the car driver was killed. (Associated Kent Newspapers Ltd.)*

150: *Recovery crews prepare to tow away the Austin A35 car in which George Bagnall was killed. The car was travelling in the direction of Ramsgate when it was hit by the Sabre of 1/Lt Edgar Lewis on 19 November 1956. The Sabre can just be seen at right. (John T Williams)*

151: *A group of contented-looking 513th FIS pilots gather for an informal photograph on the western taxiway; L-R: Lt Ray Medina, Lt Harmon Dungan, Lt Robert Kirk, Capt John Carter, Lt Jesse Stevenson, Lt Richard Montgomery. (Richard Montgomery)*

152: 513th FIS commander Maj Robert E Good (right) saw combat in Europe in WW II and was subsequently awarded the Silver Star, DFC and Air Medal. Good's Sabre was 52-4209, adorned with red and whitre bands on its fuselage. (via Dave Keep)

153: Dave Roberson's F-86D rolls to a stop after displaying at Manston's 1957 Armed Forces Day show. Brake parachute was necessary for landing at most bases in Europe because of their shorter runways. (Dave Roberson)

154: 514th FIS crews walk out to their fighters, L-R: 1/Lt Bill Irving, 2/Lt Dave Roberson, 2/Lt Jay Vandertoll and 1/Lt Bill Eagle. Hangar 1 (eastern ASP) is in the background. (Jay Blanco)

155: *513th FIS maintenance personnel at work on an F-86D in Hangar 3, western taxiway. Like the F-86F, the F-86D's rear fuselage could be detached for engine removal and adjustment. Clamshell afterburner exhaust can be seen here. (via Dave Keep)*

156: *52-10039 of 514th FIS was statically displayed in typical English weather at Sculthorpe on 18 May 1957. Canopy name was that of 1/ Lt R.F Freeman. (JMG Gradidge)*

157: *A smiling group of 514th FIS 'Dog' drivers pose for the camera at Rome in 1957 en route to Wheelus AFB. Standing L-R are: George Bugaski, Capt Earl Bryant, Klenkel, Capt Richard A. Brown, Milt McWilliams, Brown, Milt Torres and Bill Parker. Kneeling are L-R: Rosasco and Walter. (Dave Roberson)*

tronic fuel control system fitted to the F-86D meant that extremely rapid response to throttle settings was possible. Additionally, according to the F-86D Flight Handbook:'Flame outs and compressor stalls due to excessively rapid throttle movements are eliminated because the controls will always respond at the correct rate, regardless of how fast the throttle is moved.'] It caused a lot of problems for us over a year, but no one ever got hurt. Well, Charley Kapsa was out over the North Sea one night, and it did its thing. It was decided that a landing at Manston was the best thing since it was one of those wide, long crash strips. What Charley didn't know was that the runway was under construction on one side. Of course, he landed on that side because he couldn't see in the dark before it was too late. After all, when the engine isn't running, you get committed and you land. No one could ever figure out how he landed in the 8-foot deep stretch of hole that was full of construction equipment, and didn't hit a thing! The real problem was how to remove the ship from the hole".

As a result of the airfield construction, rumours soon spread that the upgrading work was underway so that B-47 bombers could to deploy to the base. However, although the big jets would become a familiar sight smoking over Ramsgate on practice GCA approaches, they were never based at Manston, and the British Air Ministry issued a firm denial to quash the rumour mongers. Reference to Air Ministry files confirms this to be true; Manston was not included in B-47 deployment plans.

In addition to the work being carried out on the airfield, during January 1956, construction of 40 'tobacco' bungalows began on the north side of the base, behind the Astra cinema. Built to an American design, and comprising 18 two-bed, 20 three-bed and 2 six-bedroom dwellings, these prefabricated houses were largely complete by the end of 1956. On Tuesday 20 November, Mr. Winthrop G. Brown from the US Embassy, accompanied by Third AF commander Maj Gen Roscoe C. Wilson performed the opening ceremony for the first completed bungalows.

Pete Hutting, then a lowly Airman, 3rd Class, arrived at the base during 1955, and recalls some of the impressions of his first visit to the UK:

"It all started from the Brooklyn (New York) Army Terminal [followed by] a short stay at Manhattan Beach Air Force Station (ex-Coast Guard and long-closed now, and only being used while McGuire AFB was being enlarged for troop movements). One good thing about 'M.B.' was the elevated subway right outside the main gate that took you to Coney Island, and then on to downtown Manhattan and Times Square. We all wore our uniforms off-base, it got you cheaper fares, show tickets and baseball games (you just paid the tax). In Brooklyn we boarded the USS General Patch. I had a bunk (steel frame with canvas) about number 3 of 5. You could hear the water lapping against the hull; we were

deep down in the hold. If you didn't get on any details, you had time to go up on deck, and the crossing was very smooth. There were guys got seasick just looking over the rail when next to the dock. One Army private got really sick, we put him on a bottom bunk, piled duffel bags around him and there he stayed except for trips to the head (toilet), till we got to England. This was August 1955, that year was a very warm and sunny summer. The ship sailed in to Southampton between small craft, yachts etcetera, all dipping their flags".

"We were sent to a holding base in Dorset at Shaftesbury [7551st Personnel Processing Sqn], which, by the layout, must have been a hospital during WWII. From here the troops were dispatched to the many bases that were active in those days, in our case, Manston. Our troop commander was an old M/Sgt who knew England and particularly London. He asked us if we would like to see London en route to Manston — it was a unanimous 'Yes!' Our transport was one of the buses of the time — a sliding door you opened to get in, cloth/leather seats and a Perspex roof. London at that time still had a lot of bomb damage, especially around St. Paul's, but still it was a thrill for all of us seeing what we had only seen in movies. In 1955, rationing had not long finished, the BBC Light Programme finished at 11 pm, then Radio Luxembourg came on. The hit songs were 'Softly, Softly' by Ruby Murray, Dickie Valentine 'Finger of Suspicion' and 'Lullaby of Birdland', and Rock and Roll was just starting with Bill Haley. There wasn't a lot of traffic on the roads; we all marvelled at the green countryside and the girls on bicycles!"

"At Manston, we were billeted in 8-man tents. We, as 'new' people, and under a Staff sergeant, had to go through an Indoctrination Course, plus FTD [Field Training Detachment] Training on the F-86D. The Indoctrination Course consisted of a familiarisation on the ways and customs of England, history of England, driving in the UK, the money and climate. At least you didn't just get dumped in the country. Being young (19), it was all new to me and I never lost the fascination with England, even after 40 years".

"The FTD was morning classes and work on the flight line (513th) in the afternoon. Our first pass (3-day) we went to London, which coincided with the August Bank Holiday, so London was very crowded. The trains were the steam variety, Southern Rail, 3rd Class, wooden seats and a bit cheaper for us in uniform. We got out at Victoria Station, walked around to all the historical sights, all the usual things servicemen of all countries do. We then started to look for somewhere to stay — needless to say, none was found at a price we could afford, so we ended up back at Victoria Station. We were allowed to sleep in the train going out the next morning by a very kind conductor. Our next foray off-base was to

Margate and our introduction to the delights of the English seaside! Again, going off-base in uniform was an accepted thing. Standards of dress by U.S. Armed Forces were explicit; no Levi jeans, shorts, sneakers, sweatshirts, etc. You were a representative of the United States and you had to look and conduct yourselves properly at all times. Also, there were Air Police (AP) patrols in the town and on the late buses back to the base to ensure proper conduct (and also to ensure all the drunks made it back!). Margate in late summer 1955 was busy and colourful; people then took their holidays at home and not abroad. We met and escorted two young ladies from Nottingham to the amusement park at Dreamland and to the movies there ('My Three Convicts', with Humphrey Bogart, Aldo Ray and Peter Ustinov — I'll never forget it). This led to a passionate — but not enduring — relationship including several trips to Nottingham and an introduction to the British telephone system — red 'phone booths with the 'A' and 'B' button operation that intrigued and frustrated GIs especially in the dark and unlit phone booth!"

"Our normal routine of FTD on the flightline was rather altered by a tragic event in August. A black Air Policeman, Napoleon Green, who was awaiting trial for an assortment of charges, escaped from custody, broke into the armoury and helped himself to arms and ammunition. Tired of waiting to ambush his commanding officer, Green loosed off some shots at the APs in their barracks, sprayed officers, and cars and buses bringing civilians into work. An RAF corporal was shot dead. Green stole a car but was cornered and shot dead at Joss Bay. We saw the carnage left, just missing all the shooting that had taken place not far from our tented area. The main gate was nearby, where Green went through, and the APs [Air Police] in those days on gate duty were not allowed to be armed. The AP on duty could do nothing but take cover and assist the wounded, as his bloodstained khaki testified. Several stray shots had gone into tents, through uniforms that were hanging up, but fortunately no-one was injured".

Sadly, the Napoleon Green shooting on Wednesday 24 August 1955 is often cited by local civilians as the key occurrence while the USAF occupied Manston — indeed, many locals remember little else. A sad indictment for sure. As a postscript, at one of the last USAF reunions at Manston, the men of the 406th held an impromptu 'exorcism' to lay the ghost of Napoleon Green to rest for good.

The USAF was obviously keen to show itself off in a positive light, and one way to do this was to participate in airshows and fly-bys. The Wing's F-84s had done such, and the F-86Fs continued the tradition, one example being the fly-by of four 406th FBW F-86Fs at Plymouth's 1954 Air Day. Drury Callahan flew some of these shows:

"On 17 September 1954, the Wing deployed several F-86F aircraft to various RAF bases where they participated in static displays. I took in one of these displays at RAF Wattisham. The following year, on 15 September 1955, Manston provided 12 F-86D aircraft, which took part in the Battle of Britain fly-by over Whitehall in London. This was the first time an American unit had participated in this fly-by, and I felt privileged to have taken part".

From 1 September, the two Manston-based Sabre squadrons had come under the control of the RAF No.11 Group Metropolitan Sector, the Bentwaters-based 87th FIS having done so a month earlier.

Like Exercise *Dividend* held during July 1954, which qualified the Wing as combat ready on the F-86F, *Beware*, which was initiated on 24th September 1955 marked the 406th's combat qualification on the F-86D. Manston's contribution to this air defence exercise was in providing aircraft to intercept 'targets' in the shape of B-45 and RB-45 Tornados and F-84F Thunderstreaks. It was this exercise that highlighted the difficulty of fitting in the F-86D's 'collision course' tactics with the traditional RAF stern-chase tactics, especially from a GCI point of view. The majority of these problems were resolved during *Beware*, although the RAF was still complaining of a lack of its own all-weather fighters, such as the Gloster Javelin, which made an unofficial debut during the exercise. At a press conference held at RAF Fighter Command HQ soon after *Beware* finished, the Air Officer Commanding-in-Chief, Air Marshal Sir Dermot Boyle declared the exercise an: *"...undoubted success. What we stood up to is tougher than anything they could do to us now, either in quantity or quality".* There were no accidents during the exercise, but the 514th FIS's Dave Roberson had cause to thank his luck:

"I had just completed an attack on a B-47 at 40,000+ when I had a loud explosion in the engine. All the fire lights came on and the engine spooled down. I thought about bailing out, but I realized that I was over the North Sea and the water was cold. Anyway, I did an air start and the thing came back on line. However, if I tried to go above 85%, the aircraft would start shaking and the fire warning light would come on. As I had so much altitude and with the power, I could get, I returned to Manston OK. I can't recall just what the maintenance people found, but I think some of the blades had separated in one stage of the engine and I think there was a hole in the side of the aircraft. Anyway, my flight commander, Al Mauldin, happened to be in the area at the time and was quite impressed with how cool I was. I told him that it was only because I didn't have time to get on the radio, or he wouldn't have been so impressed".

From September 1955 until October 1956, many 406th personnel were involved in ferrying 59 F-86K fighters from Short Brothers and Harland's airfield at Belfast to the Royal Norwegian Air Force at Gardermoen Air Base, near Oslo. The F-86K was a simplified version of the F-86D, and was designed for use by NATO air forces, replacing the rocket armament of the 'D' with four 20-mm cannon. Many of these aircraft were built by North American and shipped across the Atlantic to Belfast for delivery. Bill Plunk from 513th FIS remembers these missions:

"In 1955 or early '56, a friend of mine (since deceased) and myself ferried two F-86K models from Ireland to Oslo, Norway — landing on a snow-covered runway. As I recall we spent about five days in Copenhagen because of 'inclement weather'. It was a nice five days".

Chuck Metz from the 512th adds:

"We flew them from Belfast to Norway, via Holland and Denmark. The aircraft were assembled in Belfast, but those flown by our pilots were brought to Bentwaters for a good inspection prior to the trip. We didn't trust the assembly process, and we did trust our maintenance people. Most trips were not eventful, but I had one that was a real corker, and it took me several weeks to get home. I did not ever get the ship to Norway. I sold it to the Danish Air Force, and as far as I know, it may never have flown again. The whole trip was a comedy of happenings, and it might have ended in my death, but for good luck and caution on my part".

The F-86K eventually equipped the European air forces of Norway, Holland, France, Italy and West Germany.

On 8 November 1955, Lt. Gen. William H. Tunner, Commander in Chief of USAFE, visited Manston to present Col. Manson with a plaque in recognition of 10,000 hours of safe flying. It had been over a year since the Wing had suffered the loss of an aircraft. In March 1956, the 406th FIW was again named as Safest Unit in Third AF and retained its plaque. Col. Hugh B. Manson had taken over as 406th FIW commanding officer in July 1955.

During the November-December period, location shooting commenced on the film *Not For Money*, being shot mainly at Pinewood Studios. Revolving around the story of a defecting female Soviet pilot who lands her 'MiG' in Germany at the height of the Cold War, the film starred Katherine Hepburn, Bob Hope and James Robertson Justice. The stars were never involved in the Manston scenes, and those parts of the film shot at the base amounted to less than five minutes in the final 'cut'. However, director Ralph Thomas enlisted pilots and aircraft of 514th FIS to fly the 'intercept' scenes, and used a C-119 with the rear cargo doors removed for capturing the aerial shots. The finished film showed some nice views of F-86Ds intercepting the 'MiG' (actually a 92nd FBS F-84F with red stars applied in the relevant locations), though little else of interest crops up in this unremarkable movie which bears some similarity to Howard

Hughes' earlier film *Jet Pilot*. Renamed *The Iron Petticoat* prior to release, Manston's contribution to the history of the silver screen was released in 1956.

The Manston Sabre squadrons flew out to Wheelus for rocketry practice on 4 April 1956 — the first time with F-86Ds. The 513th FIS was the first squadron to depart, spares and equipment leaving aboard C-119C/F transports of USAFE's 322nd Air Division. At least one newly arrived C-123 transport was utilised on this rotation, however, coming from the 309th Troop Carrier Wing at Dreux AB, France. Following one month of training, the 513th was replaced at Wheelus by the 514th FIS in May 1956. The Bentwaters-based 512th FIS had previously flown out on 2 March for its 1956 TDY. Each squadron was detached to Wheelus for thirty days, deploying via Marseilles and Rome. It usually took 12-15 C-119s to transport spares, personnel and ground equipment out to Libya, and these flights were efficiently utilised so that the outgoing flights would pick up the equipment and personnel of the squadron rotating home to Manston.

Once at Wheelus, when rocketry missions were flown, there was always another aircraft flying 'wing', whose crew alerted the 'hot' pilot of any important information. At Wheelus, this task was usually undertaken by the 406th's own T-33s, but sometimes the resident 7272nd Aircraft Gunnery Group's F-86Fs performed the job. Leading the 7272nd was the legendary Robin Olds, WWII Mustang ace, who later became C.O. of an F-4 Wing in Vietnam. The then 1st Lt. Milton Torres had Olds fly his wing during a gunnery sortie and remembers him and his select band of friends very wellL:

"He [Olds] flew chase for me while I was flying rocketry in Libya. His wife was the movie star Ella Raines. While we were in Libya [circa 1956] they were shooting Legend of the Lost *in the desert with Sophia Loren and John Wayne. Somehow they were invited to the Officers Club at Wheelus AB through social efforts on Ella Raines' behalf. John Wayne showed up with Robin at the bar, whereupon he [Wayne] bought the bar for all the fighter pilots. That was back in the days when he smoked profusely, and drank more than he did in the movies. He was quite a man!"*

Dave Roberson of 514th FIS attended every detachment to Wheelus up to the end of 1957, and remembers that one such mission nearly ended in disaster for him:

"The drill was that each element consisted of two '86Ds with two T-33s chasing as safety. Normally the back seat was occupied by an enlisted crew chief or other non-rated. After chasing the 86s through their four passes (we fired six [rockets] on each pass) the T-33s had enough fuel to join the next pair of '86s and chase them. Somewhere along the line we decided the join-up of the T-33s on the second element was taking too much time and came up with the

idea of one of the '86s in the second element serving as safety for the other for their first pass. In the meantime, the T-33s were to join up on the B-29 tow ship while the first pass was made, and then peel off and join the '86s for the remaining runs. I happened to be the pilot of one of the T-33s the first time we tried this".

"After chasing the first element, we started to join on the B-29 as the next fighter element was on their run. John Michaud was the 'hot' ship and Walt Smith was chasing him. I was having a hard time getting joined up on the '29 as I had never been close to anything that big. Anyway, Michaud called his 'contact' [radar contact['Reno" [target and tow separation] 'Judy' [lock on] and '20 seconds'. Walt Smith gave him the clearance to fire. For some reason, I was looking out to my right. I felt the shock waves and saw the rockets come by. Without prior experience, I didn't think too much of it until a voice (Smith I think) said, 'You fired on the T-bird'. The crew chief in the back seat asked me what was going on and I told him. He immediately threw up".

"Later, the [gun camera] film showed the rocket package going 6 feet high and 30 feet behind. I don't recall how close the nearest rocket was. I guess I was lucky, as I had flown the same 86 [52-10063] earlier in the day and gotten four hits out of four passes. I wanted to keep the film, but the squadron commander, Col. Hubler, made us destroy them".

But it was not just the military personnel who deployed to Wheelus — the company technical reps also followed the Wing south to render assistance as necessary. Larry Brooks was the Lear Incorporated representative, dealing with the autopilot and yaw damper fitted to the F-86D. Larry flew directly to Libya from the United States during the Wing's TDY:

"Some of the 406th was at Wheelus when I left the US on a MATS flight, so I flew directly to USAF HQ in Germany and then on to Libya. In an attempt to secure the base, a high concrete and rock wall surrounded this large facility, in addition to broken bottles embedded in the top layer. T-33s with a reel of steel cable and a target sleeve were used for rocketry practice [though not by the F-86Ds]. Upon return to base, the tow pilot would drop the tow cable alongside the runway and inside the wall — except that many times the end was hanging over the wall. The locals learned to grab the end as soon as it stopped and run like mad. The solution was to keep a Jeep warmed up to hook the cable on, and then floorboard it. The bodies would really fly!"

Dave Roberson recalls another occasion when the local Africans tried to steal a Sabre tail unit:

"There was an incident involving the 431st [Fighter Interceptor] Squadron, whose area adjoined the wall on the end of the base. West, I think. A local had crawled over the fence and attached a cable to an '86 aft section and had tied it to a donkey on the other side of the wall and was attempt-

ing to pull it across. The security personnel discovered what was going on, but as the locals were across the wall, they couldn't shoot them or anything. Finally, someone came up with some cable cutters and snipped the cable".

It was during 513th FIS's deployment that 'B' Flight leader 1st Lt. John C. Hutson made a name for himself as a sharp-shooter, and in doing so, he helped his squadron break two records. Commanded by Maj. Robert E. Good, the 513th FIS set a new USAF outright record for actual hits and a new USAFE record for assessed hits. Firing at 15,000 feet above the Mediterranean at targets towed by B-29 bombers, squadron pilots racked up 120 hits, to beat the previous record of 112 hits held by the 317th FIS from McChord AFB in Washington State. The 513th FIS broke the USAFE record by scoring 201 hits, breaking the 512th's record of 134, with John Hutson claiming 13 hits, the highest individual score. The Bentwaters-based 512th FIS would claim the record again in March of 1957, when they increased the number of hits to an incredible 365.

July 1956 marked the Wing's victory in the rocketry phase of the annual Fighter Weapons Meet contest held at Wheelus for USAFE F-86D units. During the contest, a team pilot had to score 1,000 points on his first pass (height: 9,000 feet/2,743 m), score 800 on the second (25,000 feet/7,622 m) and 600 points on the final pass (35,000 feet/10,670 m). Again, the pilot never actually saw the target during this phase, being entirely controlled by the fighter controller and his F-86D's radar scope.

Members of the team were selected from the two top scorers in each squadron during previous gunnery camps at Wheelus Air Base's USAFE Weapons Center. The members of the 406th team were: Col. William S. Harrell, Director of Operations 406th FIW (team leader), Capt. Charles W. Teater (512th), Capt. Jacob Eicher (514th), 1st Lt. John C. Hutson (513th), 1st Lt. David M. Roberson (514th) and 1st Lt. Bill Moss, Jr. (512th), the last two being reserves in deference to seniority. In addition, there were two RAF fighter controllers on the team; Flight Lieutenant Stanley Kehoe from Neatishead and Flying Officer R.H.G. Kitcatt from Sandwich GCI. The competition was between the 406th FIW from Manston, 86th FIW from Landstuhl, Germany and the 431st FIS stationed actually at Wheelus. The 431st had won the USAFE competition in 1955, but may well have had an advantage, being in such close proximity to the rocketry training regime. The 406th team arrived at Wheelus on 11 June and departed for the UK on 12 July. 406th pilots scored 11,000 points, against the 10,800 of their nearest rival, with John Hutson of the 513th FIS again the highest individual scorer with 5,000 points, reflecting his prowess displayed during the previous stint in Libya.

By winning this competition, the 406th FIW won the right to represent USAFE at the Air Force Rock

158: Entrance sign at Wheelus; home to the USAFE Weapons Center. Wheelus finally closed in 1970 when it was turned over to the Libyan government. (Jerome P Burton)

159 Below: When the squadrons moved to Wheelus for rocket firing, it was usual to use C-119 transports in conjunction with C-47s from the 406th ABG. When the 513th FIS deployed in March 1956, at least one Fairchild C-123 from the 309th Troop Carrier Wing at Dreux in France was used. (Cowles Bristol)

160: The remains of T-33A 51-4469 in the scrap area at Wheelus. The trainer crashed on 31 May 1956 during the 514th FIS rocketry camp there. Back-seater Tony Luppino, intelligence officer with the 514th was badly burned, but survived. (Milt Torres)

161: *514th FIS personnel take a breather at Marseilles during the squadron's 1956 deployment to Wheelus. L-R: Sgt Collier (ground crew), Capt 'Chet' Lane and Lt Montgomery. (Dave Roberson)*

162: *Lt Montgomery takes a drink during a stop at Marignane, France during May 1956. The F-86Ds in background all have the black anti-corrosion paint on their bellies. (Dave Roberson)*

163: *A trio of 514th FIS F-86Ds at Marseilles during the 1956 deployment to Wheelus. Aircraft L-R are 52-4148, 52-4141 and 52-4167. '141 crashed at Manston in November 1956 and was scrapped. (Dave Roberson)*

164: *Dave Roberson poses with a 'Mighty Mouse' rocket at Yuma, October 1956; diminutive size of round is evident. Rockets were stored in the trolley seen here and dispensed to individual aircraft on the flightline. (Dave Roberson)*

165: *406th FIW ground crews look indifferent as they pose to record the wing's victory at the 1956 Wheelus meet. Officer in front row with prominent 513th FIS badge is Capt Richard Brown, the squadron armament system officer. (Bill Moss)*

166 Below: *Weather-beaten 52-4101 was actually a 513th FIS machine, though unusually it lacks the squadron tail badge or the usual 'harpoon' fuselage flash. It was displayed at Greenham Common in May 1956. (MAP)*

167: *This immaculate 514th FIS F-86D-36 has yellow flight commander's bands around the drop tanks. As with all F-86Ds flown by the 406th FIW, 51-6188 had seen previous service in the United States; the F-86D-45 and -50 aircraft flown from Manston were, by contrast, all brand-new. (JMG Gradidge)*

168 Below: *1/Lt Glenn Mackey's 52-4053 of the 513th FIS in the static display at Upper Heyford on 19 May 1956. Like so many of the 406th's F-86D-45 and -50 aircraft, it was scrapped in 1961. (Author's collection)*

169: *This spare J47 engine is being loaded for shipment from Manston aboard a C-119 transport, bound for Wheelus AB in Libya. This movement supported the 513th FIS deployment in April 1956. (Cowles Bristol)*

etry Meet at Yuma AFB, Arizona in October. From their return to the UK in mid-July until then, the team members practised rocket firing on the Smith's Knoll firing range. Targets were provided by bomb-shaped Delmar frangible targets, towed 5,000 feet (1,524m) behind Wing T-33s. The target weighed 14 pounds and disintegrated when hit by a Mighty Mouse rocket.

From Wednesday 1 August, further flying restrictions came into force to appease local residents. No local flying was permitted from 1 pm on Saturday to 8 am the following Monday. In addition, night flying could now only be carried out from Monday to Thursday, and morning flying during the week was permitted only after 8 am.

August saw more diversions and a wide variety of types too. On Sunday 29th, a Dutch KLM airliner bound for London landed with its port engine unserviceable. The passengers were taken on to London by bus. Later the same day, a USAF C-47 transport on the run from West Germany landed with a broken radio. Finally, on 30 August, a glider piloted by the well-known Hawker test pilot A.W. 'Bill' Bedford was forced to land in high winds. The aircraft had been on a 310-mile (500km) flight from the Royal Aircraft Establishment at Farnborough in Hampshire.

For Battle of Britain Day 1956, the 406th FIW had a special treat for the British public. Aircraft from the Wing would perform flypasts over various locations in the south of England, but before this could be accomplished, there was one hurdle to overcome. Battle of Britain Day was traditionally commemorated on a Saturday, and the flying restrictions recently imposed would prevent the aircraft departing from Manston. Luckily, the Mayor of Ramsgate, realising that common sense should prevail, agreed that the flying scheduled for 15 September should go ahead despite the noise ban. On the day, 8 F-86Ds took off in two diamond four formations, a quarter of an hour apart to overfly RAF camps in the south. The first group of four overflew West Malling, Biggin Hill, Hendon, Benson, Halton and Debden before returning to Manston in the afternoon. The second formation overflew the coastal resort of Newhaven before passing over Thorney Island and West Malling.

Meanwhile, 12 Sabres left Manston at 10.39 am for a flypast over Whitehall, London. As they passed over the Capital, the aircraft took up formation in three diamonds of four aircraft each, before returning to base at 11.15 am. The whole exercise was a great success from a public relations point of view.

The annual test of the UK air defence system — Exercise *Stronghold* — was played out again during the last weeks of September 1956. The Suez Crisis led to the preceding Bomber Command Exercise *All Square* being cancelled, and the numbers of aircraft available for *Stronghold* were greatly reduced. The exercise would encompass two phases:

Phase 1: 21 to 23 September, sponsored by Fighter Command

Phase 2: 26 to 28 September, sponsored by SACEUR (Supreme Allied Commander Europe)

Phase 2 of the exercise was subtitled Exercise *Whipsaw*, and would see raids pressed home from Europe by USAFE's tactical nuclear fighter-bombers, the F-86H and F-84F. These strikes would be flown in daylight.

Assigned to Metropolitan Sector, the 406th FIW declared 25 aircraft ready from its two Manston-based squadrons, with the 512th being assigned to Eastern Sector. No other USAF aircraft were involved with the defence of the UK. Raiding aircraft included B-45, B-47, B-57 Canberra, F-100, F-84, F-86, Hunter, Meteor, Vampire, Varsity, Attacker and Sea Hawk — the latter two operated by the Fleet Air Arm. In addition, radar countermeasures sorties were flown against the UK by RAF Lincoln bombers and FAA Avengers. From the first raid, *Stronghold* got off to a bad start. Instead of the planned 600 aircraft attacking the UK at dawn on Friday 21st, (the largest raid) only 130 took part, and further raids were reduced by a similar amount. At the end of Phase 1, only 1,800 sorties from a planned total of 3,000 had been launched, these raiders simulating Il-28, MiG-15/17 and 'Type 39' (*Badger*) aircraft of the Warsaw Pact. Bad weather hampered the Phase 2 attacks, and any raids that were successful were considered too light to stretch the defences.

During *Stronghold*, however, only 24% of daytime raids were intercepted before they reached the coast, compared with 31% for *Beware* in 1955. But by this time, the RAF was ready to field not only the Hunter day fighter, but also the Meteor, Canberra and Javelin night/all-weather fighters. Clearly, the requirement for USAF all-weather fighters in the UK was coming to an end.

An unusual event on 1 October 1956 saw the 406th come to alert status as no less than three Russian Aeroflot Tupolev 104s diverted in from a foggy Heathrow. On board were 170 people, among them members of the Bolshoi Ballet and even though their intentions were benign, the arrival of these aircraft must have brought into question the viability of Manston to play the dual roles of diversionary airfield and front-line fighter station. In the frenzy of activity, many USAF personnel thought that World War III had broken out, as Milt Torres explains:

"I was in the commissary, in flight suit when the three Tu-104s landed at Manston. I had just placed about 3 or 4 items in my basket when an announcement came over the loudspeaker; 'This is a Red Alert, I repeat, this is a Red Alert! This is not a practice alert! All members of combat crews report to your respective units immediately!' I left the basket and ran to my car, and immediately went to my squadron (514th). I reported in and was issued an aircraft and told to check in on squadron comm. channel prior to starting my engine. I did just that. As I

was strapping into the aircraft, I looked up, and directly in front of me was a Russian Tu-104 landing. I will never forget my sensations or my thoughts when this occurred. I thought to myself 'My god, they're invading by air and landing on our runway!' I checked in and as I was talking to the squadron, yet another landed. The squadron told me to stand down and return to operations. My thoughts again were that we had yielded without firing a shot. Then the entire field was assholes and elbows running to cover the 'shapes' that the [92nd FBS] F-84Fs were carrying [nuclear bombs] and to surround the aircraft that had just landed. As I was getting out of the plane I saw yet another Tu-104 landing".

It still seems strange that, at the height of the Cold War, Russian aircraft could land at a front-line USAF fighter base. Nonetheless, their American hosts entertained the passengers, and all of the Russian aircraft departed the next day.

On Thursday 11 October, the Deputy C.O. of the 406th FIW, Col. Herman F. Smith told a meeting of Thanet ratepayers that one jet squadron would be departing Manston for an indefinite period *"..before the next holiday season"*. Whether this was a delaying tactic to pour oil on troubled waters or just an honest piece of misinformation, no squadrons departed Manston during this period, other than to complete the very finite (30-day) rocketry camps in Libya. Another P.R. exercise was carried out on Wednesday 24th, when local dignitaries were invited to the base and given joy rides in the 406th's T-33s. The Mayor of Margate, Alderman J.G. Read, was taken up for a 40-minute trip which took him on a typical traffic pattern to show how everything was being done to reduce noise. The 406th's Commanding Officer, Col. Hugh Manson flew the Mayor of Ramsgate, The Reverend Harcourt Samuel on a very special mission. From Manston, their T-33 routed to Boulogne, France, along the coast to Calais, where the aircraft was pointed out into The Channel, making landfall at Dungeness. Once over the English coast, they flew on to Maidstone, London, along the Thames Estuary, back to Foreness on the Thanet coast, and into Manston, buzzing the Mayor's house at 1,700 feet along the way. These trips were very successful as far as they went, but the respective Mayors would have an uphill struggle in swaying public opinion.

The Secretary of State for Air, Mr. Nigel Birch met a deputation from the Ramsgate Council at the Air Ministry in London on Tuesday 30 October. Birch informed the party that the UK government considered Manston to be an essential link in the country's air defences, and it was not considered feasible to close the airfield. The Secretary of State also disclosed that there were plans to extend Manston's runway to the west, which, allied to a reduction in GCA practices and more night flying during winter months, would alleviate noise problems during the lucrative summer period, when tourists flocked to the coastal

resorts of Thanet. However, the revelation that a runway extension was under consideration enraged residents of Minster village (situated to the southwest of the airfield), and it seemed that any solution to the noise problem would be at someone's inconvenience. By mid-1957, plans for the runway extension were well advanced, with work to commence in September. Alas, later in the year things began to move quickly, and it soon appeared that the much-debated extension work was not going to be required.

The one event on Manston's calendar that everyone had waited for — the USAF Gunnery Meet at Yuma — finally took place in October 1956. Rather than risk the ferry flight of a 'team' of Sabres across the Atlantic, it was planned to allot the team Sabres once the personnel arrived in the US. In addition to the six pilots and two controllers, 33 other Wing personnel were dispatched to the United States to add their practical and moral support. 1st Lt. Richard J. 'Monty' Montgomery was a 513th pilot assigned to fly one of the 406th's T-33s on the east-west crossing:

"We were to assemble at Suffolk County AFB, New York to pick up F-86Ds and to practice before going on to Yuma. Capt. Bob Rilling and I were assigned the task of getting the Delmar target operational. This was a bomb-looking target stored under the left wing of the T-33 in a basket. Then it was reeled out to about a mile and the F-86s fired rockets at it on a 90-degree attack path. Bob and I must have lost 20 targets before we ironed out the problems in launching and recovering the target".

"Anyway, we flew our two modified T-33s back across the Atlantic Ocean by way of Prestwick, Iceland, Greenland, Goose Bay and on to Suffolk County. I was in the lead T-33 with Col. Harrell (wearing 'poopy suits' — sea survival suits — his knee-length with the suit would have been chancy for his knees if we had to bail out) so that is why I was in the front seat. On our wing was the second T-33 with Capt. Teater and Lt Moss. Going into BW1 [Bluie West One, alias Narsarssuak, Greenland] was a bit chancy. The weather was terrible on arrival. We made a penetration over the ocean and the base put up an SA-16 rescue ship at the mouth of the fjord. One has to fly up the fjord 44 miles to the airstrip. As we were going through 1,000 feet over the water, I commented that the weather was awful and Col. Harrell said 'We have to press on, son.' (There wasn't any fun riding in the back seat with a young Lieutenant flying in bad weather.) I saw the SA-16 about 50 feet above the ocean shooting flares, so put our wing man in trail and slowed down to make a thrilling join-up on his wing as he accelerated to about 170 knots. We flew his wing to the airdrome where the Base was anxiously seeing if we would make it. The Base Commander was there to greet us and mentioned that we had filed in below required weather minimums. We referred him to Col. Harrell

and departed for the bar with their famous glacier ice from the fjord. We stayed there four or five days before proceeding".

The Team collected its 'new' Sabres from Eastern Air Defense Force squadrons at Suffolk County AFB, where they stayed for two weeks, getting in some rocketry practice before setting out for Arizona. Each pilot on the team was assigned an aircraft, so there were six F-86Ds on the 406th's rocketry team. The Yuma meet at Vincent AFB was to be the first USAF use of the NADAR system; a magnetic tape recorder-reproducer system designed to assist in scoring. Developed by North American's Autonetics Division, NADAR was placed in the warm-up condition when the aircraft's E-4 Fire Control System was turned on. When the Sabre pilot established a radar 'lock-on' to a target, the NADAR's magnetic tape began recording the display signals on the pilot's radar scope. On completion of a sortie, the tape magazine was removed from the plane (The NADAR equipment was located in the Sabre's no.2 right hand equipment bay, just below the windshield) and could then be viewed by the judges, led by Capt. Charles A. Earnhardt. NADAR would later become standard on F-89H Scorpion, F-94C Starfire and F-102A Delta Dagger aircraft for scoring purposes.

Three other teams, all flying the F-86D took part in the competition; Eastern Air Defense Force, Air Training Command and Far East Air Force. Despite its best efforts, the 406th/USAFE team was beaten by the Eastern Air Defense Force team from the 94th FIS, who scored 13,000 points, and also won the tie for individual scoring. The USAFE team clocked up 9,000 points overall, with John Hutson again the top hitter with 4,000 points. The 406th had not won the competition, but against such fierce opposition, the team did USAFE proud. The Sabres were left at Yuma and then ferried to the North American plant in California for overhaul.

There were two crashes at Manston in November, neither caused by the actions of the pilot. Thankfully, F-86D accidents at Manston were few, the all-weather fighter being remarkably safe to fly considering its complexity. The first incident involved 1st Lt. Robert 'Zeb' Zbornak from 513th FIS, who parted company with his Sabre, 52-4216, near the village of Tille in France. This is how Zeb remembers it:

"On November 1, 1956, I ejected from an F-86D over France on a night flight out of Manston. In October 1956, I [had] received orders to transfer mid-November to an F-100 Wing at Peru, Indiana. On November 1st I was attempting to acquire the minimum flying time for pay purposes (The USAF required four hours flying time minimum, to pay Flying Pay for any month). I flew one sortie during the day. At dusk that evening, I took off in a flight of three F-86Ds for a night mission. I was to fly as 'target' for the other two fighters to practice 90-degree intercept passes — controlled by ground radar. To

make a long story short, there were mitigating circumstances which led up to my ejecting from the aircraft:

1. Weather was to clear up by landing time; instead, it deteriorated to heavy rain squalls. There was a jetstream at altitude.

2. GCA lost aircraft blips in the heavy rain, forcing them to come around again, taking up valuable time.

3. North Foreland Radio Station, our only navigational aid, started failing at intervals, giving false station passage signals.

4. I had the highest altitude so I was the last aircraft to descend; remaining at altitude until minimum fuel was indicated.

5. The jetstream blew my aircraft considerably south of the normal descending turn to low altitude.

6. As I started my descending penetration turn, an alternator failed, temporarily locking up the hydraulic flight controls as well as the flight instruments.

7. GCA picked up another aircraft, an SA-16 returning from Holland, thought it was me and directed me accordingly".

"My fuel level became critical at low altitude, forcing me to climb to altitude and call Mayday. I was gliding toward Laon, France, following steering directions from their tower when my engine flamed out. I ejected and my aircraft landed in a field and slid into a hedgerow. The fuselage sheared from the wing".

The second crash occurred at 5.10 pm on the night of 19 November 1956. As 1st Lt. Edgar Lewis of 514th FIS put his 'Dog' down on the tarmac, the right mainwheel tyre burst and the aircraft careered off Runway 11 towards the main Canterbury-Ramsgate road. Unfortunately, just as Lt. Lewis crashed through the perimeter fence, a car was travelling along the road at the precise point where 14,000 pounds of Sabre, travelling at barely abated speed crossed it. The driver, George Bagnall, was killed instantly. The roof was ripped from his car by the force of the impact. Local man Peter Balmer was cycling along the road at the time of the accident and saw the resultant carnage:

"I looked to my left and it [the F-86D] seemed to be coming straight for me. The searchlight [actually the nose-mounted landing light] on the front of the aircraft seemed to be on. The aircraft crossed the road and hit the car broadside on. I thought the tank under the wing hit it. The plane crossed the road about 20 yards in front of me and the car went backwards across the road, against the fence".

It had been Lewis's first night flight out of Manston (he was also the first coloured pilot to fly with the 514th), and fortunately he was unhurt, but the inevitable outcome was that local arguments for the cessation of USAF operations at Manston were strengthened. The Sabre, 52-4141 was dismantled and taken to the Burtonwood depot, where it was scrapped.

1957 began with plans for the closure of public roads around the Manston base, in an effort to increase security. On 24 January, Mr. E.W.H. Vallis of the Kent County Council (KCC) reported the findings of a KCC Roads Committee meeting that had discussed the road closures. An Air Ministry representative at the meeting had made it clear that any costs arising from the construction of new roads to replace those closed would come from the US purse. In turn, representatives of the USAF were reportedly aghast at the £300,000 estimate for such work. Such expenditure would require US Congress to sanction any further decisions, and the plans were — for the time being at least – put on hold.

The annual trip to Libya began on 3 January 1957, when 514th FIS deployed for its weapon training. The 513th deployed during the last week of February, and its Wheelus deployment was marked by an 'eventful' flight out from the UK which cost the squadron two F-86Ds, but thankfully not their pilots. For the 513th's deployment, a comprehensive general briefing was carried out on Monday 25 February. Immediately prior to departure from Manston on the morning of Wednesday 27th, the Squadron received an up-to-date weather briefing, then departed in pairs on the first leg to Marignane Airport near Marseilles on the southern coast of France. 1st Lt. John C. Hutson, flying in 52-10056, was the flight leader, with nearly 700 hours in Sabres, with 1st Lt. Bob Platenburg in 52-4245 flying his wing. The pair arrived in France around lunchtime, and waited for their aircraft to be fuelled.

Before leaving Marignane, all Sabre crews were given further updated weather reports for the next leg of the journey; to Pratica di Mare aerodrome, south of Rome. These reports were given by the Squadron Commander, Maj. Bob Good, and also by the Operations Officer, USAF Weather Officer and by Air Rescue Service personnel, the latter following the formation to provide assistance. At 2.13 pm in the afternoon, John Hutson and Bob Platenburg set off for Rome. Hutson had planned their course to route via Bastia on the northeast tip of Corsica, and Ostia beacon, their landfall on mainland Italy. Twenty-nine minutes after departure, the aircraft — the fifteenth and sixteenth Sabres to depart the base in pairs — were overhead Bastia, two minutes ahead of schedule, and Hutson received a good radio compass signal from the station there. It was at this point, however, that Platenburg discovered that the low frequency equipment in his Sabre was not working. This was not considered a problem, and the pair checked their position visually, and set course for the Italian coast.

Soon after leaving Corsica, an undercast appeared, and the two F-86Ds were set on a course of 120 degrees to intercept a hole in the cloud, to the north of Rome, which had been reported by earlier flights of the detachment. At this point, John Hutson attempted to contact Rome Control and tune his ra-dio compass into the Ostia Radio Beacon, but without success. Bob Platenburg fared even worse, and could obtain no signals at all, and heard nothing but static on his radio compass. Things were now looking bleak, and both pilots flew to their ETA (3.02 pm), plus five minutes, before turning briefly southeast, and then to 310 degrees, on a reciprocal bearing. There was no sign of the hole in the cloud that had been reported earlier, and with fuel dwindling, the pair had no option but to select their emergency IFF (Identification Friend or Foe).

Lt. Hutson subsequently requested Direction Finding (DF) information from Pratica di Mare tower, then Rome/Ciampino, but these attempts were unsuccessful, and the pilots listened in desperation as the Italian controllers offered them landing instructions. Fortunately, a USAF SC-47 rescue plane had been in the area and received one of Hutson's messages; radio contact was established 20 minutes after the pair had reached their ETA. Subsequent steering information from the rescue plane was however declared unreliable after its crew discovered that their AN/ARA-25 radar equipment was behaving erratically. With no steering information and fading UHF transmissions to the rescue plane, Hutson was by now heading south, with Platenburg close in after the weather had begun to worsen.

Realising that he was lost, and with 600 lbs of fuel remaining, the flight leader decided to fly north and began a letdown in the hope of sighting an airfield. Through breaks in the cloud, the pair discovered that they were not over land, but water. Fortunately, upon breaking out of the weather at 6,000 feet, they sighted land ahead, which turned out to be Ustica, a small island in the Tyrrhenian Sea, more than 200 miles south of Rome, and about 40 miles north of Sicily. Looking to his rear, John Hutson just made out the mountains of Sicily, and adjusted course to head for them. Initially Bob Platenburg, by now without radio contact with his element leader, thought that Hutson had not seen the island ahead of them, and delayed following until he too saw the Sicilian coast. Both pilots then searched the area unobscured by clouds, but could find no landing area.

Hutson then instructed Platenburg to eject. Bob turned his aircraft out to sea, set his autopilot, and pulled the handle. Five minutes later, Hutson stop-cocked his engine and ejected also. Platenburg sustained a back injury, but was otherwise OK, his Sabre was last seen heading out to sea. Hutson was unhurt; his 'Dog' came down on a hillside near Castellamare. Both pilots were picked up by locals and taken to the nearby town of Alcamo, where they managed to telephone Pratica di Mare and let it be known that they were generally none the worse for their experience.

The accident received a brief mention in the Thanet Gazette the following Friday, which included the somewhat naive statement that Hutson and Platenburg had ejected when *"...the Sabrejets they*

170 Above: *Right-hand side view of 52-4053 shows that its crew chief was A/1c B. Ferguson. 'FU053' buzz number had only recently been relocated from the nose to rear fuselage. (JMG Gradidge)*

171: *Two British RAF policemen inspect 52-4124 of 514th FIS at Biggin Hill on 14 September 1957. The aircraft carries a blue fuselage band. (MAP)*

172: *This 514th FIS Sabre is parked alongside its British counterpart, the Gloster Javelin at Aldergrove in 1957. The advent of the Javelin meant that Manston's all-weather interceptors were no longer needed. The writing was on the wall. 51-6185 later flew with the Yugoslav Air Force. (Author's collection)*

173: *52-10030 of the 512th FIS was seen displayed at Prestwick, Scotland in May 1956 with this strange serial number presentation, missing the year prefix '2'. (MAP)*

174: *By the time 52-10030 appeared at Turnhouse's 1957 Battle of Britain display, its serial number presentation had been further shortened for reasons unknown. Part of the fuselage 'harpoon' design had also been stripped off. (MAP)*

175: *With F-84Fs ranged in the background, 52-4082 taxies in at Shepherds Grove in 1957. Non-standard font of the tail number is unusual. Note that with the engine running (and with hydraulic pressure built up), the undercarriage doors are shut; soon after shut-down they would droop open. (Author's collection*

176: *It is unusual to see F-86Ds without drop tanks – the thirst of their afterburning J47 engine meant that maximum fuel was carried for anything other than local missions. 52-4148 was taxiing for a display at North Luffenham in September 1957. (JMG Gradidge)*

177 Above: *An afterburning J47 engine being loaded onto a C-119 transport on Manston's western taxiway in April 1956. The aircraft were present to transport equipment to support the 406th deployment to Wheelus at that time. (Cowles Bristol).*

178: *Rarely photographed, 406th Air Base Group's C-47 aircraft were unsung workhorses of the wing. They often flew personnel and cargo to Wheelus and visited other bases too. 43-16004 was seen at Blackbushe in 1956. (MAP)*

179 Above: *This panoramic shot was taken from the vicinity of Manston's control tower in April 1956 and shows French-based USAF C-119 transports parked where the 513th's F-86Ds would normally be. Note the Spitfire station guard at right, just in front of the USAF automotive repair shop buildings. (Cowles Bristol)*

180: *C-119s parked at the top (southern) end of the western taxiway. A 66th ARS Albatross amphibian can just be seen at right. The C-119s would help to transport equipment to the squadrons at Wheelus, and once the firing stopped, would bring it all back to Manston. (Cowles Bristol)*

181: *A youthful 1/Lt Dave Roberson with F-86D 52-4063. Roberson was the most junior pilot in the 406th FIW Rocket Team and thus was reserve for the Yuma meet. (Dave Roberson)*

were flying developed trouble simultaneously over the Mediterranean on Wednesday night".

The detachment to Wheelus fortunately ran without further hitch, and when the 513th FIS returned to Manston on 30 March, its pilots had broken the previous record by scoring 337 hits on the targets (comprising 177 actual hits and 160 assessed hits) after 84 hours and 39 minutes on the range. The squadron's high scorers were 1st. Lts. Ramon 'Ray' Medina and John Hutson, both with 15 points each. The 496th FIS, based at Hahn AB in Germany had previously held the short-lived rocketry record. Sadly, although the 1957 Rocketry Meet was again held in the United States, pilots from the USAFE team were selected from the highest hitters in the Continent, and none were chosen from Manston.

The continuing noise problems again reared their head in March, when it was revealed in a local newspaper that Ramsgate resident Mrs. R.H. Butcher had written to the Minister of Transport and Civil Aviation. Mrs Butcher had invited the minister to stay at her home and hear the noise from Manston. Though the offer was politely declined, the publicity from this revelation led a USAF officer to visit residents of King Arthur Road in Ramsgate, to inform them of measures being taken to reduce the effects of noise. The anonymous officer stated that F-86Ds would be moved to another area of the base for 'revving up'.

In reply, one angry resident stated that he had written to the US Ambassador concerning the noise problem, and in reply been told to either sell his house or rent it to an American! In all fairness,

though, it was unrealistic to imagine that noise could be reduced much further. The so-called 'revving up' of Sabres was a necessary part of a normal engine start, and it was only possible to apply any sort of restriction to aircraft undergoing post-maintenance ground runs on their J47 engines. To further reduce the effects of the noise from this activity, the purpose-built sound deflector promised during July 1955 had finally been constructed on one of the dispersal pans in the central airfield area. This enabled ground runs to be carried out so that any jet noise fell on the generally less-populated area to the south west of the base.

Sadly, even on the ground, the F-86D could be a dangerous beast. Twenty-year old A/2c Joseph A. McMurray, an electrical mechanic with the 514th FIS was killed on the afternoon of Thursday 7 March. He had been working in the forward fuselage inverter bay near the nose of an F-86D during an engine run and was sucked into the Sabre's low-slung intake. Though the airman was rushed to the base hospital, he was pronounced dead on arrival. A well-known hazard of early jet operations, and especially those involving the Sabre, the dangers of ground crew being sucked into the engine intake led to the introduction of an F-86D 'Danger Areas' poster soon after the aircraft arrived in service. In addition, technical manuals stressed that coarse mesh intake screens should be fitted to the engine intake prior to any ground run. These screens had a two-fold benefit; not only were ground personnel protected from the hazard, the engine was also protected from sucking

182 Above: With buzz numbers painted on their noses, these 513th FIS Sabres were flying a mission from Manston in late 1955. 52-4219 nearest the camera was the wing commander's aircraft and had the 406th FIW badge painted on its fuselage. This aircraft later sported red and white bands around its fuselage. (Al Kemnitz)

up ground-borne foreign objects. At low temperatures, however, ice could form on the mesh of the intake screen, causing engine flameouts or compressor damage when the ice broke off; the screens were rarely fitted. McMurray was thankfully the only airman to be injured in this way at Manston.

The detachments to Wheelus were completed in the spring — the 512th FIS departing the UK on 26 April 1957 for four weeks of rocketry training in the sands of Libya. During this deployment, the 512th, under the command of Lt. Col. John J. Ruettgers, set a new USAFE record for rocket hits. That the record was broken after only three of the four-week deployment had passed, is even more remarkable. The 512th's top scorers comprised; Lt. Col. Ruettgers, Lt. John Garnish, Lt. Ken Whittemore, Lt. Charles Metz and Lt. Dave Johnson. On his first pass, Lt. Francis shot the target banner clean off its cable, while his squadron commander repeated the feat in scoring hit number 365 to beat the 513th's existing record set in March by 28 hits. As with the earlier TDY deployments to Wheelus, RAF GCI Controllers from the RAF Eastern Sector of Fighter Command, headed this time by Flight Lieutenant Ronald S. Williams, accompanied the USAF personnel. The squadron's aircraft returned to the UK on 18 May, arriving back at Woodbridge during the Station's Armed Forces Day display, along with the accompanying C-119s and T-33.

In recognition of its achievements, the 512th FIS was awarded the prestigious Hughes Trophy, which was presented to Lt. Col. Ruettgers at a banquet held in Washington the following July 29. The Trophy was awarded annually by the Hughes Aircraft Company to the top fighter squadron nominated by HQ USAF. One aspect of the nomination was a squadron's ability to use the Hughes fire control system. The 512th retained this trophy in perpetuity.

One of the 512th's top scorers, Chuck Metz, remembers that the Hughes Trophy represented the culmination of a long slog to the top for the 512th:

"...we went to Wheelus and shot a higher score than had ever been done by any F-86D squadron in USAF. It was quite a thing for us, especially since the first gunnery practice in the States [in 1953], resulted in a 'Maggies Drawers' for us, the then 87th FIS. 'Maggies Drawers' means that you missed the target completely, and boy, did we! Well, it all ended up well with the Hughes Trophy in our hands. We had one hell of a party at Bentwaters when we returned from Wheelus. Even our non-drinkers got blasted at that one. Well, why not? we came from the bottom of the heap to the top in just 4 years. I doubt that any F-86D squadron ever equalled our record gunnery score. We beat the theoretical maximum possible score of hits by better than a hundred percent".

Though not based at Manston, the squadron's glory reflected on the excellence of the Wing in general, though long-time Sabre Dog pilot Richard White recalls of the 512th's Sabres: *"Their aircraft were the*

best maintained I have ever flown".

Easter Monday 1957 dawned in typical fashion — overcast and with a cloudbase at around 3,000 ft (914m). 1st. Lts. Milt McWilliams and Greg Turner of the 514th FIS had been tasked to fly a T-33 practice instrument flight, Turner in the back seat as the pupil, and McWilliams in the front as pilot. The mission would be a radio navigation round robin profile. Departure was delayed by maintenance work on the aircraft, but despite this it was decided to press on and fly the mission.

The two-seat jet, 51-8756, took off from Manston just after sunset on the afternoon of 22 April 1957 and following contact with GCI at Bawdsey, proceeded to fly along the south coast. Milt McWilliams takes up the story:

"We flew to Portsmouth and were just turning toward our next checkpoint when we started having problems. We lost our UHF radio first, then our ADF (direction finder) and VOR radios. Unable to contact anyone, or navigate by radio over the undercast, we began flying a triangular pattern to the left and turned our IFF to emergency. The IFF was one of the items they had fixed before we took off. We had been airborne about 50 minutes and had completed two left hand triangular patterns when we had the generator fail, and were left with about 50 gallons of fuel left in the tip tanks and a full fuselage tank".

The weather in the interim had not let up at all, and the crew now realised that they were hopelessly lost, though they reckoned their position to be somewhere to the west of the Isle of Wight. With this in mind, Lt. Turner in the front seat set a north-easterly course to take them back inland.

"Greg and I talked back and forth without the intercom and decided we should let down below the undercast which was forecast to be about 2,000 feet [608 m] above sea level. We felt there shouldn't be any obstructions in our area above 1,000 feet [304 m]. We had about 45 minutes of fuel left when we made our decision. Our plan was to find a landmark and return to Manston or find an airfield enroute. We descended using dead reckoning and our magnetic compass. We broke out of the clouds at about 2,200 feet [670 m] and were heading towards the east when we saw an airfield beacon flashing a 2-letter code. Our decision was to land. We lowered the gear and flew past what appeared to be a control tower. We knew Easter Monday was a holiday for the RAF and as such figured that the people in the tower had the night off. I set up a pattern for landing, and while the runway looked short and there were no field lights on, I continued the pattern for landing. On final approach, there were large chimneys (later identified as cooling towers) obstructing the final approach. I managed to clear the towers and landed about 200 feet down the runway. The runway was littered with loose stones,

chunks of cement and potholes. There was a roadway at the far end of the runway full of headlights. One of our main gear tires blew out just as we stopped. We were on the ground and safe, but didn't know quite where we were. Lt Turner got out and put the gear pins in to prevent the gear from collapsing, and we shut the aircraft down".

The airfield turned out to be Harwell, unused by aircraft since 1946, but now the home of the Atomic Energy Research Establishment (AERE), and thus a very sensitive place to land without prior invitation.

"After about ten minutes, a Land Rover pulled up and a bloke approached us enquiring what the 'bloody hell' we were doing. We identified ourselves and explained our predicament. Our flight had lasted one hour and 20 minutes. I asked the bloke if he could take me to where I could call in by phone and explain what had happened. He informed us that we had landed at Harwell, one of two prohibited flying areas in all of England at that time, the other being Buckingham Palace. Lt. Turner stayed with the plane and I rode to security headquarters in the Land Rover. I tried calling the Flight Service Center, but could not get an answer. Then I tried to call Manston collect, but the Officer of the Day (OD) would not accept a collect call. I then called Lt. Col. Hubler collect and explained what had happened. He said he would notify everyone and get back to me. A little later he called and told me to find a place to stay for the night".

"Harwell security suggested taking us to an RAF station close by [either Abingdon or Gaydon]. We agreed, and after securing the aircraft, we accepted the offer of a ride to an RAF base full of V-bombers. We were taken to the Officers Mess. We arrived in the midst of a huge party and were welcomed by the Wing Commander, who listened to our story and replied that he was going to fly to Oakridge, Tennessee, in the morning in his V-bombers in retaliation. We laughed, joked, drank and ate well into the night. Lt. Turner and I finally collapsed into bed about 2 am".

"We were up by 7 am, and the staff duty officer assisted us in contacting Manston and Col. Hubler's office. The Colonel questioned us about the condition of the runway, aircraft and ourselves. He stated that he was dispatching a C-47 with the maintenance officer and mechanics to repair the aircraft, and some JATO bottles so we could fly the plane off the runway and back to Manston. Turner and I looked at each other and mentioned to the Colonel that neither of us knew anything about JATO assisted take-offs and wouldn't it be better to take the wings off, load the aircraft onto a flatbed and take it to a better field. Col. Hubler told me that he wasn't ready to do that, and after my refusal to fly the aircraft out of there, he would send someone with JATO experience to fly it out".

Capt. Chester H. 'Chet' Lane from the 514th, who had experience with the JATO (jet assisted take off) system fitted to the B-47 bomber, volunteered to fly the aircraft out. The boffins at Harwell initially refused to let this go ahead unless the USAF accepted full responsibility for any subsequent actions. As the only alternative would have been a rather embarrassing aircraft dismantling operation, the USAF officialdom quickly agreed to this,

"Major Don Adams and the mechanics arrived by bus from Upper Heyford with Chet Lane. While they repaired the aircraft, Major Adams, Chet, Turner and I talked about the takeoff. Chet and the rest of us walked the runway to check after the AERE had cleared the runway and filled in the holes. Chet had a full load of internal fuel and about 30 to 50 gallons in the tip tanks (each)".

Lane then started the T-33's 4,600-lb (20.46 kN) thrust J33 engine, and taxied to the end of the runway. Running up to full power against the brakes, Lane soon had the T-33 rolling, and punched in the JATO at about 60 knots. From this point, however, things began to go wrong in quick succession.

"The aircraft broke ground almost immediately in an extremely nose-high attitude and started to veer off the runway. There was a fence about eight feet high and it was lined with people in long white lab coats from Harwell, and the police had stopped the traffic on the road. There was a circus atmosphere for the jet takeoff from Harwell. The aircraft's left wing struck the ground, and it left the runway heading for the fence. The long white lab coats began scurrying away from the fence and it looked like a flock of geese taking off. Chet had shut down the engine, but the JATO bottles pushed the plane to within about 50 feet of a huge hole in the ground, full of construction workers".

When the aircraft finally slid to a halt on its belly, Greg Turner and Milt McWilliams were first on the scene. They managed to open the canopy and make safe the ejection seats by fitting the safety pins. Chet Lane was found to be unconscious, and was pulled out of the aircraft and taken away in an ambulance. After only a short spell in Harwell's medical care, he was pronounced fully fit. Although fire trucks had arrived at the scene of the crash, no fire had started. The aircraft had come to rest next to a reactor base that was in the course of construction. Impact with this feature would have had dire consequences.

"Late that day, Colonel Hubler arrived by staff car from Upper Heyford, where he had flown to get to the crash site. He was really pissed, and let me know in no uncertain terms that he was going to have my ass. Turner and I rode back to Upper Heyford on the bus and took the C-47 back to Manston. It was Tuesday, and we were grateful to be back and safe. Two and a half weeks later, I got married and went on leave".

'756 had its wings removed and was trucked away

to Upper Heyford for repair. The aircraft was then returned to the 514th FIS at Manston for further service. She was later passed on to the 20th Fighter Bomber Wing, and in the 1960s to the Dutch Air Force.

Late April again saw the noise problem being aired in the media. As a prelude to this, the Secretary of State for Air, Mr. George Ward stated on Tuesday 23 April that, in addition to summer flying restrictions along the lines of those brought in for the previous year (to run from 1 August to 15 September 1957), there would be an additional period of restrictions during the Whitsun holiday. In his communication with Thanet Member of Parliament Mr. Rees-Davies, Ward stated that there would be no normal flying training carried out from the evening of 7 June until the morning of 11 June. It seems that Rees-Davies was finally becoming receptive to these concessions, and when he chaired the ITA's television programme *Member's Mail* at the end of April, which covered the noise problem, he conceded that it was *"One of the penalties of the age of speed"*. That other staunch opponent of the Manston base, Lady Carson, appeared on the programme and was also conciliatory, revealing that, despite having a 92nd FBS F-84F crash through her garden wall, the USAF had been very helpful, and had built the wall up again. Finally, to complete a rather radical turn-around of local opinion, Mr. George Brown, president of the Margate Chamber of Commerce stated that it would be regrettable if the USAF left Manston, due to the loss of trade, and went on to praise the gallant efforts of the 66th Air Rescue Squadron.

During May of 1957, the 406th was called to readiness for deployment to Turkey following the Suez Crisis. It was planned that the Wing would block the anticipated support of Egypt by Russia, but in the event, Manston's help was not required. In a continuing programme of the USAF grasping as many PR opportunities as possible, on Monday 13 May members of the newly formed Thanet Advisory Committee on Jet Noise were flown in a C-47 from

Manston. The idea of the flight was to demonstrate normal traffic patterns, with a few simulated GCA approaches thrown in to demonstrate the problems being faced by Sabre pilots juggling noise constraints and safe landing speeds as they turned finals to land. Among those present was the Mayor of Ramsgate the Rev. Harcourt Samuel, Mayor of Margate the Rev. J.G. Read, and the chairman of Broadstairs and St. Peters Urban Council, Councillor H.E. Seccombe. Numerous other local government dignitaries took the opportunity to get a bird's eye view of the noise problem. All were advised to expect disruption during the period of 25 to 29 May, as the 406th FIW would be participating in an RAF Fighter Command exercise.

On Saturday 18 May 1957, Manston held another open house on US Armed Forces Day, and this event was a much more successful event than its 1956 equivalent. One of the 'star' items on display was an F-100A Super Sabre. The first of the 'Century Series' fighters, the supersonic F-100 had arrived in USAFE during 1955. In addition to the resident aircraft on static display, the RAF brought along one of its new Valiant V-bombers, the flying display featuring a mock H-19 helicopter rescue and a formation JATO take-off by the Thunderstreaks of the 92nd FBS. Despite these attractions, however, as few as 1,000 spectators turned out to witness the event.

The Sabres of 406th FIW made a rare public appearance in the air for the RAF's Battle of Britain Day on 14th September 1957. A flight of four aircraft (52-4009, 52-4224 and 52-4226 and one other — all believed to have been from the 513th FIS) performed flypasts for the airshows at Tangmere, Horsham St. Faith and Duxford. At the latter, 52-4185 also put in a solo display after departing from static display. However, if the F-86Ds of the 406th were rare performers in the air, they did at least make regular appearances on the ground at airshows during the 1950s.

During the first week in September, rumour had begun to spread that a USAF pull-out from Manston was imminent. Indeed, the 6 September issue of the

183: *Aftermath of Capt 'Chet' Lane's aborted takeoff from the disused airfield at Harwell. Buildings in background were used for nuclear research and the aircraft's presence caused some embarrassment. 51-8756 was repaired and flew again. (Chriss Dadds/UKAEA)*

184: *The 406th FIW 1956 Rocket Team at Wheelus prior to the Yuma meet. Pilots came from all squadrons within the wing. L-R: 1/Lt David M. Rober-son (514th FIS), 1/Lt Bill Moss (512th FIS), Capt Jacob M. Eicher (514th FIS), Col William S. Harrell (director of operations, 406th FIW), Capt Charles W. Teater (512th FIS), 1/Lt John C. Hutson (513th FIS). (Bill Moss)*

185 Below: *Sometimes 406th FIW Sabres had to be dismantled for transport by road to repair organizations; 52-10028 being loaded for delivery to Burtonwood. (Cowles)*

186: *Pilots and ground crew responsible for developing and flying 'Delmar' targets for the 1956 Rocket Team pilots. The targets were flown behind T-33 jets; the only 406th FIW aircraft to fly out to Yuma for the meet. Front row L-R: unk, unk 514th member, Lt John Michaud (514th FIS), Lt Richard Montgomery (513th FIS), Lt William Vinopal (512th FIS), Capt Robert Rilling (513th FIS), SSgt Charles Pierce (513th FIS), unk. Sadly, the rear row of ground personnel are unknown. (Bill Moss)*

187: *These 406th FIW personnel accompanied the Rocket Team to Yuma; they posed in their specially-made pale blue uniform prior to departure. L-R front row: SSgt Ferrell, A/1c Walsh, A/1c Loesch, TSgt Young, TSgt Yetman, SSgt Bomkamp. Rear Row L-R: A/1c Campbell, unk, A/2c Hammond, SSgt Hendrix, A/2c Tatoe, A/1c Grunder, TSgt Maynard, A/1c Owen, unk, unk. Capt Sweigard, the 512th Maintenance Officer is sitting at front centre; he oversaw the whole maintenance operation at Yuma. (Bill Moss)*

188: *The 406th FIW Rocketry Team aircraft at Yuma, October 1956. All of the team's Sabres were F-86D-60s, on loan from units on the East Coast. (Dave Roberson)*

189: *This is the full 406th FIW Rocket Team in front of one of their F-86D-60s at Yuma in 1956. Back Row L-R: Capt Charles W. Teater, Col William S. Harrell, 1/Lt John C. Hutson, Capt Jacob M. Eicher. Front row L-R: 1/Lt Bill Moss, Flying Officer R.H.G. Kitcatt, Flight Lieutenant Stanley Keboe, 1/Lt David M. Roberson. The RAF officers wear powder blue fatigues, specifically made for the 406th FIW ground crew at Yuma. (Bill Moss)*

190: *As the band marches past, Col Hugh Manson (in centre of the dais) prepares to salute his departing troops. The closing ceremony was held on Saturday 29 March 1958. 513th FIS Sabre in background (52-4138) is today owned by an individual in St. Louis, Missouri and is awaiting restoration. (Associated Kent Newspapers Ltd.)*

191: *Two flights of F-86Ds and a flight of F-84Fs brought Manston's closing parade to a close. Within two months all USAF flying at the base had ceased. (via David Collyer)*

192: *With assignment to the 86th FIW in Germany, 514th FIS Sabres gained this colour scheme. Tail flashes were black and white, though the 514th FIS badge remained the same. (via Jack Friell)*

local newspaper, *The Isle of Thanet Gazette*, revealed under the headline '*Americans Off Next April?*' that it had asked both British and American officials to deny the rumours, but that neither had done so. These rumours were lent considerable credence one week later, when the European edition of the USAF's *Air Force Times* presented a similar point of view. It would be some time before the facts were finally verified, but the writing was undoubtedly on the wall. The arrival in service of sufficient numbers of RAF all-weather fighters made the Thanet base an unnecessary luxury. The real nail in the coffin, however, was the continuing noise problem. As the then Col. Hugh B. Manson, Commanding Officer of 406th FIW related some 38 years later:

"The noise of the jets was the straw that finally broke the camel's back. Seaside concerts on certain air traffic days were impossible to hold (or hear); in bad weather the GCA brought the landing aircraft almost straight down the high street in Ramsgate — and if you had to add power to complete your approach or go around, the noise was horrendous. And some of the locals made a problem of the black military personnel".

On 21 September 1957, Col. Manson had spoken to a Canterbury Farmers Club meeting, declaring that: *"The noise is terrible. I've lived with it for seven years, and it's nearly driving me mad".*

From Thursday 19 September until Sunday 22, 406th FIW took part in its last big exercise whilst at the Kent base. Exercise *Counterpunch* was another of the air defence exercises carried out yearly, and again involved aircraft from all NATO air forces. As the USAF's only fighter interceptors in Europe (the F-100s being either tactical fighters or fighter bombers), the F-86Ds, and especially those from the 406th FIW at Manston and Woodbridge bore the brunt of bomber attacks during this exercise.

January 1958 brought the news that many had feared but expected — the USAF was to depart from Manston. In a press release of 21 January, Third AF at South Ruislip revealed that an average of £125,000 revenue to the local area would be lost each month, and in addition, up to 1,000 properties would become vacant. This was tempered by stating that the empty homes would house poor local families. Finally, it was thought that all of the 420 locals who worked at the base would lose their jobs. Closure was set for June 1958. In desperation, Thanet MP Mr. Rees-Davies approached Air Minister George Ward to gain assurances as to the future use of the base — none were forthcoming.

It was thus decided that the three jet squadrons at Manston would be reassigned to continental Europe. The 406th's Sabre squadrons were split up, with the 512th moving from Bentwaters to Sembach, West Germany, the 513th to Phalsbourg, France and the 514th to Ramstein in Germany. Pete Hutting recalls that the allocation of the 406th's squadrons to the new bases was carried out in a far from scientific manner:

"Some time in late 1957 or early 1958, Colonel Ruettgers [CO of the 512th FIS] flew in '110 [F-86D 52-10110, his personal aircraft, to which Hutting was Crew Chief] to Manston, to find out where the 512th was to go. I can remember him getting back to Woodbridge, where we were because of the runway being closed at Bentwaters, and being met by several officers. He told us we were going to Sembach, the 514th were going to Ramstein, and after the toss of a coin, the 513th were to go to Phalsbourg in France. I think he was quite pleased with himself that he had won the toss".

The Manston Sabre squadrons began their last 406th FIW deployments to Wheelus AB during early 1958 for their live gunnery camps, the 513th from 9 January, followed by the 514th from February to early March. On Tuesday 14 January, during the 513th's deployment its top sharpshooter, the newly promoted Capt. John C. Hutson was killed. Dick Montgomery, a fellow 513th pilot and close friend of Hutson was on his way to Libya when the accident happened:

"We had deployed again for rocketry. I had broken down in Rome (there are worse places) and after four or five days I was flying across the Med. to Wheelus. While letting down enroute, I recognized John's voice taking off. We had a challenging rat-race of a call back then of 'Check Six'. John responded to my call by giving me my new date of rank as Captain (I hadn't known). Well, John had a serious maintenance problem and was returning on the secondary flight control system and very low on fuel. He flamed out turning base leg in the landing pattern, stalled and crashed. That was a dark day for the 513th and his family".

John Hutson, flying F-86D 51-6167, had departed Wheelus as number two in a pair with 1st Lt. Tom Blevins leading. As 'X-Ray' flight, the pair climbed on military power to 20,000 feet to await join-up by 'Yankee' Flight, comprising Lts. Barnes and Strand. After joining up, the four-ship completed a series of manoeuvres, before becoming separated, Hutson joining with Barnes, and Blevins and Strand forming their own pair. John Hutson then sighted another flight of F-86Ds ahead, and cut in afterburner for around five minutes to catch up. This pair — Maj. Faison and Lt. McMath, were also on a local flight from Wheelus, as 'Whisky' flight. Blevins and Strand subsequently joined up and Major Faison requested a fuel check from his flight members, insisting that anyone with less than 1,500 lbs remaining to announce as such. Hutson replied that he had between 1,250 and 1,300 pounds, and was cautioned to watch his fuel.

The flight then overflew Wheelus Air Base, before the formation broke up, with Hutson and Strand continuing over the Tripoli area, to a point south east of the Base for a join up to land. It was now, at approximately 6.05 in the evening, and roughly 45 minutes after take-off, that Hutson radioed that he was down to 600 lbs of fuel and operating on his alternate flight control system. Wheelus advised of a possible go-around, due to a casualty evacuation C-47 in difficulty on finals, and asked if Hutson was declaring an emergency, to which the reply was negative. Completing his go-around, Hutson was advised that the C-47 was still on final, to which John replied, *"I have to land this time"*. Hutson by now had declared an emergency, and was cleared to land, while the C-47 was advised to pull up and abort.

The C-47 had not commenced his go-around by the time Hutson's Sabre turned finals, about a quarter of a mile from the runway, and this was quite rightly queried by the Sabre pilot; Hutson was advised to use his own discretion as to whether it was safe to land. In truth, however, there was no option. The fuel in Hutson's F-86D was fast being gobbled up by its thirsty J47, and another go-around would be pushing things too far.

But with the slow transport looming large in his windshield, Hutson was left with nowhere to go. At approximately 100 feet, the Sabre was hauled around once again, climbing to 300 feet, while Hutson radioed to the effect that his Sabre's engine was about to flame out. Somehow, Hutson managed to coax the Dog onto the base leg, but there his luck and his fuel ran out. With a dead engine and very little forward speed the aircraft plummeted to earth like a stone from 150 feet. The aircraft hit the ground in a nose-down attitude, left wing low. John Hutson was killed instantly.

Whatever the cause, 513th and indeed the entire Wing had lost one of its finest pilots, who was surely destined for much greater things. John Hutson was only 28 when he died. Ironically, it was Hutson who, along with Bob Platenburg, had ejected from his Sabre during the previous year's Wheelus deployment.

The 514th FIS deployed to Wheelus in February. Paul Byrum flew his first rocketry missions with the squadron at Wheelus in 1958:

"Relations with the natives were always strained, and most of our people remained on the base for the whole month we were there. There was a competitive aspect to firing. The squadrons vied with each other for the most 'hits', as did the pilots within each squadron. On my first trip to Wheelus, I was about the junior officer in the squadron but succeeded in becoming the 'high hitter'. A lot of this was due to luck. There was a tremendous difference between each airplane in the radar and fire control computer. This equipment was all vacuum tubes and very unreliable. Airplanes were assigned at random, and I was lucky in drawing good birds. We fired at a radar-reflective sleeve and scored with stereo movie cameras. You didn't have to actually hit the sleeve to score (although I did many times), but if your rockets could be framed by an overlay or transparent drawing of a B-29 imposed over the sleeve, credit for a hit was given. Two stereo cameras mounted on the wings resolved the range as well as placement".

The 514th FIS returned to Manston on 4 March and immediately began preparing for its last move. The final days of USAF occupation at Manston were rather frantic, and continued to be tragic. On Thursday 23 January, an RAF Varsity navigation trainer crashed at Manston, killing three. Landing at night, the twin-engined Varsity was the last of four similar aircraft that had diverted into Manston from Thorney Island in bad weather. Three Canberra jet bombers had also diverted into the airfield earlier. As the Varsity came into land, one wing apparently hit a snow bank, and the machine broke up, bursting into flames in the process. Twenty-eight year old Sgt. Donald Bessant was killed instantly, and two other crew members, Flight Lieutenant Douglas Malpas and Flight Sergeant Frank Lomax died later in Margate Hospital.

The first of many farewell dinners for the USAF began on Monday 10 March, with an event at the Beresford Hotel in Birchington, organised by the Birchington and District Chamber of Commerce, with guests of honour Col. and Mrs. Manson. The Birchington farewell was especially poignant as many personnel had settled in the area. In his speech, Lt. Col. P.B. Moore revealed that as many as 185 of the 922 families at Manston — up to 20% — were living in Birchington. A saddened Mr. B.S. Bellingham, president of the Chamber of Commerce, in turn toasted *"Our American friends"*.

Manston's closing-down parade was scheduled for Saturday 29 March 1958, nearly eight years after the first USAF aircraft had arrived at the base. In typical English weather, as many as 5,000 visitors viewed the attendant display from the ASP beside the tower. Against a backdrop of F-86D, two F-84Fs, a T-33 and a C-47, Col. Manson brought proceedings to a close as an honour guard marched past with the USAF's 751st Band. The ceremony was accompanied by a short display and a flypast of 12 Sabres, four from each squadron, with four F-84Fs from the 92nd FBS bringing up the rear. Ironically, one of the many guests at the parade was Member of Parliament W. Rees-Davies, in many ways the architect of the USAF pull out. Amongst the other notable dignitaries at the ceremony were Air Vice Marshal V.S. Bowling and Air Chief Marshal Sir Hugh Saunders from the RAF, with USAF Third AF being represented by its deputy commander, Brigadier General J. Stanley Holtoner.

In his closing speech, Col. Manson stated:

"A wise man once said — if something cannot be said simply, it is not worth saying. We have worked hard and we have done well. It is my privilege on this last parade to pay the last tributes to the commanders and the staff. My thanks to each and every one of you; good luck wherever you go and may God bless you".

Fate, however, had one more tragic card to deal the USAF at Manston, for although the final parade had taken place, flying carried on at the base for more than two months. On Wednesday 9 April, shortly before four in the afternoon, a 406th FIW T-33 trainer (s/n 51-4474) veered off the runway on landing, and shot across the Canterbury-Ramsgate road. As with the similar F-86D accident in 1956, the aircraft hit a car, but this time the four occupants, all members of the Booth family from Broadstairs — the father, mother and two young children — were all killed. The aircraft came to rest in a cabbage field 200 yards from the road, with the pilot, Capt. Herman Hines, still inside. He was lucky to escape unhurt, but was taken to the base hospital for a routine check-up. Hines had been carrying out a 'target' mission for F-86Ds.

At an enquiry held in Ramsgate on the following Friday, the USAF expert witness, Capt. Chester Lane stated that subsequent investigation had revealed that one of the T-33's tip tanks was empty, while the other had up to 100 gallons of fuel in it. This, allied to a crosswind on landing were assessed as contributory factors to the crash. No reason was given for the fuel imbalance. Captain Hines later stated that the left wing tip had hit the ground on landing, adding, *"The aircraft started to veer to the left, and I applied power to take the aircraft round. It kept going left, I could not correct it".*

Although the 'official' closure of the base had been carried out, flying continued, but at a much reduced level. Squadrons prepared to move out, and many cargo flights were scheduled. The first squadron to leave was the 513th, which officially departed on 25 April 1958, reassigning to the 86th FIW in France on the same day. On 15 May, the 514th FIS departed for assignment to the 86th, and the 406th FIW was inactivated concurrently. Manston would never again see the sheer numbers of aircraft which had been based there with the USAF, and Thanet would take years to recover from their loss — indeed, some say that the area has never recovered. With handover to the Air Ministry on 30th June, the base reverted to largely civilian use.

193: *Besides the USAF pilots and maintenance personnel that accompanied the Rocket Team to Yuma, two RAF personnel also went along. They were Flt Lt Stanley Kehoe (right) from Neatishead and Flying Officer R.H.G. Kitcatt (left) from Sandwich GCI; both were fighter controllers. (Bill Moss)*

406th FBW/FIW Commanding Officers

Col. Philip P. Ardery:
10 July 1952 to 13 October 1952
Col. George F. Ceuleers:
13 October 1952 to 26 October 1952
Col. Conrad J. Herlick:
26 October 1952 to 15 June 1955
Col. William S. Harrell:
15 June 1955 to 8 July 1955
Col. Hugh B. Manson:
8 July 1955 to 15 May 1958

512th FBS/FIS
Maj. William E. Preble:
10 July 1952 to circa 1953
Maj. (later Lt. Col.) Frank M. Haynie:
circa 1953 to 8 September 1955
Lt. Col. Michael J. Quirk:
8 September 1955 to circa 1956 (Formerly CO of 87th FIS)
Lt. Col. John J. Ruettgers:
circa 1956 to 1 July 1959 (inactivation)

513th FBS/FIS
(Capt. Alma Flake?): 10 July 1952 to circa 1953
Maj. Jack. B. Owen: circa 1953 to June 1955
Maj. Robert E. Good: June 1955 to June 1957
Maj. Ed Faison: June 1957 to end of period at Manston

514th FBS/FIS
Maj. James Covington:
10 July 1952 to circa 1953
Lt. Col. John R. Bennett:
circa 1953 to February 1954
Lt. Col. James F. Frakes:
February 1954 to July 1954
Lt. Col. George O. Hubler:
July 1954 to circa 1957
Lt. Col. Joe Zeller:
circa 1957 to end of period at Manston

194: *This element of 514th FIS Sabres is returning to Manston from Wheelus in May 1956. Aircraft at right is 52-4141, which was written off after a crash at Manston on 19 November that year. At left is 52-10130, which carries a blue squadron commander's fuselage stripe. Note also the different locations of the tail bands. (Milt Torres)*

195: *During early 1955, most 406th FIW Sabres began to be painted in these colours, comprising squadron-coloured canopy rails and lightning flash on the forward fuselage. Red/yellow/blue tail bands were standard for all wing aircraft, but 52-10019 also carries the Group commander's fuselage stripes in the same colour. (Drury Callahan)*

196: *52-10110 was the personal mount of 512th FIS squadron commander John Ruettgers. Colourful yellow fuselage bands make this a bright-looking machine: it is the subject of plastic kits by both Hasegawa and Monogram. Crew chief for '110 was Pete Hutting. (Author's collection*

THE 92ND FIGHTER-BOMBER SQUADRON

Into a new era

The 92nd Fighter Interceptor Squadron, one of three squadrons forming 81st Fighter Interceptor Wing, had been based at RAF Shepherds Grove in Suffolk since September 1951. The unit was initially equipped with the F-86A Sabre day fighter, and the two sister squadrons within the Wing, the 91st and 116th FIS, were based at RAF Bentwaters. The 81st FIW would fly the Sabre for three years.

During April of 1954, the whole Wing began to practice Low Altitude Bombing System (LABS) training from the back seat of assigned T-33 trainers, in preparation for the arrival of its new mount — the Republic F-84F Thunderstreak. At the same time, the Wing designation changed from that of Fighter Interceptor to Fighter Bomber Wing (FBW), and it was assigned to the support of NATO through fighter and bombardment operations. Ground School for both pilots and ground crew soon commenced, in order to bring all Wing members up to operational status as quickly as possible, and the Wing in effect became one large training establishment. To cater for the gradual shift from the fighter interceptor to fighter-bomber mission, Wing pilots attended base weapons instruction under Capt. William A. Tilford of the Wing Special Weapons Office. As Bomb Commanders, these pilots would require refresher training every three months; the impending nuclear capability of the Wing was taken very seriously indeed.

The F-84F Thunderstreak

The F-84F Thunderstreak started life on Republic's drawing boards as a swept-wing Thunderjet, and was proposed to the USAF as early as 1947, to counter North American's success with the XP-86 Sabre. The prototype Thunderstreak (the name change dictated by the great difference between the 'F' and previous F-84s) was a converted F-84E, with swept wings and tailplane, powered by an experimental Allison XJ35-A-25 engine. It first flew on 3 June 1950 from Edwards AFB, California, piloted by Republic test pilot 'Bud' Haas. F-84Fs in the production batch would be powered by a 7,100-lb (31.58 kN) thrust Wright J65, the license-produced version of the British Bristol-Siddeley Sapphire engine. In addition, these aircraft featured an entirely new fuselage, with an 'up and over' opening cockpit canopy.

Production difficulties delayed the introduction of the F-84F into USAF service from a planned date of December 1951 until January 1954, when the first aircraft arrived with the 506th Strategic Fighter Wing at Dow AFB, Maine. In USAF service, the F-84F would be employed more as a bomber than a fighter, however. The Thunderstreak was designed from an early stage to carry the Mk. 7 thermonuclear weapon, a 2,000 lb (890 kg) bomb with a 1 kiloton yield. The Mk. 7 measured 15 ft 5 in in length and had a diameter of 30½ inches. Only one nuclear weapon could be carried per aircraft, and this was always loaded on a specially configured pylon fitted inboard under the left wing. The right wing carried a standard 450 gallon fuel tank. For practice bombing missions, a small training bomb dispenser was often fitted to the 'nuke' pylon. To enable pilots to get used to the carriage of the special store, an inert Mk. 7, (often referred to as a 'shape') could be fitted. This item had the same weight and external appearance as the real thing.

To give the F-84F some 'fighter' weaponry, six .50-calibre machine guns were fitted, four in the nose and one in each wing leading edge. Each gun was supplied with 300 rounds of ammunition, enough for 15 seconds of gunnery. The Thunderstreak used the then standard AN/APG-30 radar ranging unit, coupled to an A-4 gunsight. This gunsight could also be used for precision bomb delivery, the 'F' having provision for 6,000 lbs (2,669 kg) of bombs, using inboard pylons plus a second set of pylons outboard of the main landing gear. In the nuclear role however, the aircraft would have these pylons fitted with a 230 gallon tank each. With three fuel tanks and a nuclear weapon, the aircraft had a range approaching 2,000 miles (3,200 km). In addition, the Thunderstreak could be refuelled in flight, via a receptacle concealed beneath a door in the upper surface of the left wing.

A fully laden F-84F could weigh as much as 27,000 lbs. (12,010kg) at take-off, and to help the aircraft into the air, four 1,000-lb thrust JATO (Jet Assisted Take-Off) rocket bottles could be mounted beneath the machine. Ignited during the take-off run, the JATO bottles burned for 14 seconds, and could not be shut off once they had been lit. During a JATO takeoff, the pilot felt more like a passenger, and the bottles were jettisoned once away from populated areas. Thus, a fully laden F-84F could reduce its take-off run from 7,000 feet to 5,000 feet (2,134 to 1,524 m) if JATO was used.

From a maintenance point of view, weapon crews received training in the loading of Special Weapons (nuclear), with the aid of a mock-up held by the 91st FBS. Maintenance personnel from the 79th FBS at RAF Wethersfield provided on-the-job training, and although this squadron was operating nuclear-capable straight-wing F-84Gs at the time, the personnel from 81st FBW gained much experience in the loading of offensive weaponry. To complete the training, the F-84F Mobile Training Detachment (MTD) arrived on 15 September 1954, and by the end of the year, all Wing pilots and maintenance personnel had completed the MTD course. In addition to the majority of Wing pilots that would convert from F-86A to F-84F, further experienced F-84F pilots were posted in to replace Sabre drivers who were returning to the USA.

The Wing finally began to receive its first Thunderstreaks on 4 October 1954, when ten aircraft arrived from St. Nazaire in France. In a similar fashion to the deployment of F-86Ds to the 406th FIW in the UK, the F-84s were shipped across the Atlantic by aircraft carrier. Further aircraft were off-loaded at Lisbon, Portugal, and the last F-84F to bring the Wing to full strength arrived on 5 May 1955. The remaining F-86As were flown to Belfast in Northern Ireland and put aboard carriers for return to the US.

As part of a USAFE policy of not putting all of its eggs in one basket, it was decided that wherever possible, squadrons would be dispersed to ensure that an entire Wing could not be wiped out by a single enemy strike. Thus, it was decided to redeploy the 92nd FBS to RAF Station Manston, 150 miles south-east of Shepherds Grove, beginning on 28 March 1955, where the squadron would come under the 'on paper' control of the resident 406th Fighter Interceptor Wing.

Sixteen F-84Fs of 92nd FBS, under the command of Lt. Col. James A. Carlyle, were relocated to Manston during a single day — 30 March 1955. The relocation of the remainder of the squadron was completed by 10 April, and left the other two squadrons of the Wing back in Suffolk. The move had other benefits in addition to those described above, as 92nd FBS Flight Commander and Nuclear Weapons Officer Jack E. Austin explains:

"The 92nd moved to Manston for several reasons:

1. *A shorter distance to Russian targets.*
2. *(Better) Nuclear storage facilities.*
3. *Longer/wider runway.*
4. *Personnel to be closer to the base and some decent housing.*
5. *Customs available.*
6. *Instrument landing facilities.*
7. *Create less noise — take-off over the ocean to drop JATO bottles".*

Ironically, it would be the last point which would lead to the somewhat premature departure of the squadron from its Kent base. The noise problem had such an effect on local feeling in later years that there would remain little option but to move back to the less-populated areas of East Anglia. At Manston, practice take-offs by F-84Fs with dummy nuclear loads usually led aircraft over the busy seaside resort of Ramsgate. And with a maximum take-off weight in the region of 27,000 lbs (12,010 kg), the F-84F often required rocket assistance, remembers Jack Austin:

"Nuclear take-off required 4 bottles of JATO when loaded with internal fuel, two 230 gallon drop tanks, one 450 gallon drop tank and a 1,850 lb [823 kg] nuclear weapon. JATO was fired for only 15-20 seconds after which the heavy steel rack and 4 spent JATO bottles had to be jettisoned — thus the ocean drop".

At Manston, 92nd FBS took up residence in the

198: *The 92nd FBS used this Rolls-Royce hearse as a crew bus at Manston; Rolls were apparently less than amused at the idea. Note the early Volkswagen Beetles (Jay May)*

199 Below: *Typical of the 92nd FBS scheme worn by the unit's F-84Fs in 1956, 52-6516 was Bob Brinker's aircraft. It wore the name of his crew chief, A/2c Aubrey on the right-hand canopy rail. (Bob Brinker)*

200: *the massive width of Manston's main runway can be seen in this shot, taken at its eastern end. The canister on the outboard pylon carried eight 3-lb practice bombs which had similar flight characteristics to the nuclear store. (Bob Brinker)*

201: *Looking north towards the 'loop' dispersal on 10 September 1955. Red-roofed hangar on the dispersal is still there today. (Bob Brinker).*

202: *To commemorate the Wing's victory at the 1956 USAFE Weapons Meet, 92nd FBS painted F-84F-45 52-6812 in this colour scheme. Red, blue and yellow tail markings denoted the three squadrons in the wing and the words 'USAFE CHAMPS' were painted in pale blue on either side of the wing badge. Yellow fuselage band is bordered by thin black and pale blue lines. (Jay May)*

203: *52-6521 in happier times; this was the machine lost in John Caswell's crash near Cliffsend on 9 June 1955. (MAP).*

'loop' dispersal on the north west side of the airfield, on the large area of land which stretches toward the north Thanet coast and the village of Birchington. The loop area had previously been home to the 512th FDS's F-86F Sabres. Because of the squadron's ability to carry 'Special Stores' (nuclear weapons), security was always high, and the aircraft often carried 'shapes' (inert special stores) during practice missions; a dedicated Air Police Section was assigned to the squadron. At the northeastern end of the airfield, a revetment-style facility was set up for the storage of nuclear weapons. It is the proud boast of many a former 92nd FBS pilot or maintenance man that, throughout the squadron's 3-year tour at Manston, none of the civilian population ever had an inkling that there were 'nukes' at Manston.

The squadron did have a torrid time with the Thunderstreak however. The qualification of squadron pilots in the early part of its tenure at Manston was held up by severe airframe corrosion affecting the aircraft. Insufficient preservation during the long voyage across the Atlantic, plus the poor English weather was put down as the cause. A general lack of spares only served to exacerbate these problems. And then there were accidents.

Thursday 9 June 1955 marked the first of a fair few incidents to befall the unit whilst it was at Manston. As 1st Lt. John L. Caswell, Jr got into his take-off roll on Runway 11 (in the direction of Ramsgate), his aircraft veered sharply to the right, crossed the Ramsgate-Canterbury road, and came to rest after careening off a house in Canterbury Road West, Cliffsend. Though shaken, Caswell was unhurt and was helped from the wreck of 52-6521 by local people working in the fields around the base. He was transferred to the Base Hospital by 66th ARS H-19 helicopter. USAF investigators surveying the scene soon appreciated Caswell's lucky escape — the F-84 had ended its bumpy ride mere yards from the WWII FIDO oil storage tanks. The cause of the crash was relatively simple; Caswell's aircraft had been equipped with one 450-gallon fuel tank on the right inner wing pylon, the left (special store) pylon being left vacant. During take-off, this configuration was known to produce an asymmetric loading, which was normally compensated for by the pilot applying aileron. It seems that Lt Caswell was caught out by the (at the time), unusual and unfamiliar external stores load.

Typical of the many missions flown by the 81st FBW were those on NATO exercises *Shock Absorber* and *Carte Blanche* in June 1955, and *Red Well*, held during July. The idea behind the latter exercise was to maintain the proficiency of Wing personnel, and this type of exercise was often organized at Wing level. *Red Well* required each Bomb Commander to carry out a navigation and dive-bombing mission, while *Brown Cow*, beginning in August 1955, brought 92nd FBS, as well as the other squadrons within the Wing,

to a tactical alert. *Brown Cow* was held in two phases, with the first running from 24 to 26 August, phase two following on 1 September, and running for the subsequent four days. These small exercises would be typical for the Wing's operation of the Thunderstreak, with bombing being carried out on the Dengie Flats range off the Essex coast.

On 24 September, the annual UK air defence exercise *Beware* was initiated, with 92nd FBS Thunderstreaks assigned to provide 'attacking' forces for the scenario. Alongside the F-86D-equipped squadrons at Manston, this would be its first major exercise aboard the new aircraft. Raids were flown singly, and generally originated over Europe, as Bob Brinker recalls;

"I went out over France, then 'penetrated' the UK somewhere around 20,000 feet [6,097 m] — coming in over the South Coast west of London. I saw two Hawker Hunters and ducked in between two cloud layers. They never saw me. East of London an '86D intercepted me, but I saw him, turned into him and got away (I think). The '84F was a little faster than the 86D even without afterburner, so one pass was all they'd get".

On 25 October 1955, Maj. William E. Charlson was flying 52-6743 out over the North Sea when his generator failed 20 miles (32 km) northeast of Great Yarmouth. Charlson had a full load, consisting of two 230 gallon tanks, a 450 gallon tank and an M-21 shape. He immediately tried to jettison his load, and though this was partially successful, he still had the 450 gallon tank hung up; such a load would make the aircraft difficult to land for sure. It was not until the aircraft was 20 miles southeast of Great Yarmouth that the tank finally swung loose, and Charlson managed to recover for a safe landing. This incident was initially regarded as an unauthorised bomb release!

The 92nd FBS had begun its twice-yearly 30-day visits to Nouasseur AB on 14 November 1955; the unit deployed to French Morocco for gunnery and bombing practice. All squadrons within the 81st FBW deployed individually for this mission, the 92nd flying its F-84Fs down over the Bay of Biscay to air refuel. During one of these practice camps at Nouasseur, the squadron lost a T-33 trainer (53-5827) in a take-off accident, which was caused by an improperly installed fuel line. This led to the jet's J33 engine flaming out, the pilot, Lt. Kenneth Nelle and his passenger, Capt. Roberts escaped with nothing more than dented pride. During the previous February the 92nd FBS had completed its only TDY to Nouasseur while based at Shepherds Grove. It was on this detachment that 1st Lt. Bill Carney was killed when his Thunderstreak exploded during a practice dive-bombing run on the range to the south east of the base. Striking similarities between this accident, the only fatal F-84F crash to befall the squadron, and another which occurred whilst the squadron was at Manston are described by Herbert H. Stone:

"At Nouasseur, 1st Lt. George Burke was on a low-level bomb run and as he pulled up to execute his bomb release manoeuvre, his engine blew up and he ejected. The unmanned F-84 struck a mud hut and killed a young jackass. Uncle Sam paid dearly for the mud hut and the jackass. George was Jewish and I was concerned for his safety among the Arabs. He reported that he was treated well, but did not flash his Star of David!"

It appears that the Thunderstreak's J65 engine was to blame for a fair few crashes. This powerplant had caused numerous problems during the F-84F test programme, and at one point, the retrofitting of aircraft with the General Electric J73 engine had been considered. It was also recognised that the LABS manoeuvre had caused numerous crashes under instrument conditions, and a policy of gaining permission from Squadron Commander or Operations Officer prior to flying such a mission came into force.

When the 92nd Fighter Bomber Squadron arrived at Manston in 1955, its aircraft bore very plain markings which consisted merely of the standard USAF F-84F colour scheme — not even the famed 'skull' squadron emblem was applied. By 1956, however, the Squadron had begun to apply a very colourful design to its aircraft. Initially, the F-84s gained yellow noses, this colour curving upwards and rearwards to the windshield, bordered in black. The Wing badge was painted just aft of the canopy on the fuselage side. By late 1956, the squadron badge was being applied to the tail fin, but within a year or so, the tails of the 92nd FBS's Thunderstreaks began to be painted in the form of a yellow diamond on the upper portion, with yellow wing-tips completing the scheme. By early 1958, the 92nd's F-84Fs sported black lightning flashes on the tail and wing tip areas, whilst under the tail, the jet-pipe area was also painted yellow, with two small lightning flashes superimposed. In addition, the cockpit canopy and the forward spine also received paint in the squadron colour. Wing and squadron badges were then often carried slightly to the rear of the cockpit. The nose treatment was typical of the Wing's other two squadrons (though the squadron colours varied), but instead of the tail 'diamond', the 78th FBS employed a red (squadron colour) sun-burst design on the vertical tail, the 91st FBS Thunderstreaks being applied with a more conservative horizontal blue band.

Late November 1955 brought 92nd FBS its brief moment of glory — one of its aircraft played the role of a 'MiG' in the film *The Iron Petticoat*. The film told the story of a defecting Russian pilot (played by Katherine Hepburn), who is intercepted 'Somewhere over Germany' by USAF fighters. These intercept scenes were shot around Manston. After being intercepted by 514th FIS F-86Ds, the 92nd FBS 'MiG', with black stripes judiciously applied to obliterate any telltale USAF 'star 'n' bar' insignia and with overpainted red stars, was brought in over Ramsgate, forced to land at Manston, and escorted up to the ASP. The F-84F scenes were flown by Capt. Lloyd Sjulstad, and when released in 1956, the movie was generally well received; it is still worth looking at, if only to marvel at Manston's three minutes of fame. The other stars of the film were Bob Hope and James Robertson Justice, but none of these leading actors came to Manston for the filming, the majority of *The Iron Petticoat* being shot on the Pinewood Studios set.

In mid-1955, the early F-84F-35 aircraft had begun to be supplemented and replaced with later specification dash-45 aircraft from Chateauroux AB in France. The main difference between the two models was the introduction of spoilers on the inboard section of the -45's wing, which supplemented the roll output of the ailerons. As these later model aircraft arrived, the dash-35's held by the squadron were flown out to Lisbon and returned to the Zone of Interior (ZI) by sea. The pilots were then picked up by a C-47, flown to Chateauroux to pick up the 'new' F-84Fs, and flew them back to Manston. Such missions were flown on 8 September 1955 (six aircraft), and 10 November 1955 (two aircraft). Each of these sorties usually took something less than five days, and on the second mission noted above, rather than pick up replacement aircraft, the two pilots involved (1st Lt. Robert Brinker and 1st Lt. Max B. Irvin) were ferried straight to Nouasseur AB for weapon training. By early 1956, all remaining F-84Fs would begin to be passed through 3110th Maintenance Group at Burtonwood for a 2,000 man-hour modification programme. The modifications involved the fitting of Lear F-5 automatic pilot, brake parachute and identification (IFF) radio equipment.

From 11 February 1956, the 92nd FBS again deployed to North Africa for weapon training. All went to plan until the return flight to the UK recalls Robert Brinker:

"When we returned from Nouasseur in March of 1956, I was flying wing to Major Charlson who was lead plane. His radio was acting up, so I was trying to contact Col. Willsie at Manston (over central France). It was late, and the tower told me the field was closed due to weather. I told Maj. Charlson and we all (8 or 10 planes as I remember) landed at Chateauroux. Apparently Col. Willsie was trying to reach me — he was going to have us come in anyway — all the wives were out at the field to welcome us".

"We came in the next night in the worst weather (fog and low ceiling) I ever landed in — thank heavens for a good GCA unit! When he taxied in and stopped, Bob Drown handed out the gear locking pins — hung them over the side of the cockpit, and thought the crew chief was pulling on them. He let go, then they went in the sucker door and destroyed the engine. He forgot to extend the bird screens at 2,000 feet or so where we were supposed to. He wore his wings upside down for a few days, but nothing

more was said about it".

The second crash at Manston to involve a 92nd FBS F-84F proved a disaster for the base's fragile relations with the local community. On the morning of Thursday 14 June 1956, Lt Thomas B. Adams firewalled his Thunderstreak's 7,800 lb (34.7 kN) thrust J65 engine and released his brakes to take off from Manston's Runway 29. At least, he would have done, had not a tyre problem with his aircraft, 52-7096, interfered with his mission. Still into his take-off run, Adams' right tyre threw a tread, ripping out the brake hydraulic lines, and giving him no means of stopping. The F-84 shot to the right, off the runway, over the road which passed to the north of the airfield, hit a passing car and embedded itself in the wall of Cleve Court, a house off the north west end of the runway. Adams came to rest less than a quarter of a mile from his squadron dispersal, and luckily was able to extract himself from his smoking aircraft. Likewise, the startled driver of the car was unhurt, and probably had a good line in stories in the pub that night. The aircraft's tyre failure was inexcusable as, according to Jack Austin, *"We had been forced to use French 're-cap' (remould) tyres on the F-84Fs".* There was one other person who was thanking his good luck that night, as Herbert H. Stone explains:

"At the time of Tom's accident, runway construction was underway at Manston. A construction worker was sleeping off a hangover behind Lady Carson's wall and was rudely awakened by Tom and his F-84. Out of the dust and debris, Tom and the construction worker emerged; running like the devil was in hot pursuit. The construction [worker] looked back at Tom and asked 'Where did you come from?' Tom answered 'Poughkeepsie, New York, where did you come from?'".

Unfortunately, as if the crash wasn't bad enough, worse was to follow. Cleve Court was home to Lady Carson, one of the most vehement anti-noise, anti-Manston campaigners on the Isle of Thanet. The USAF agreed to make good the hole in her wall, and the aircraft was swiftly removed, but another nail had been banged in the coffin... More than forty years later, it is still possible to make out the line of replacement bricks in the wall of Cleve Court, and imagine the events on that momentous day in 1956.

On the evening of Wednesday 15 August 1956, the squadron lost its fifth Thunderstreak when 1st Lt. William H. Byrd bailed out of his stricken aircraft 10 miles off North Foreland. Herbert Stone was flying with Byrd at the time:

"I was Flight Leader when Lt. Byrd bailed out off North Foreland. The cause of the accident was simple — we were 'rat racing' and Lt. Byrd got into a very unusual attitude at a very low altitude and could not recover. He did the only thing he could have done under the circumstances".

Byrd was later picked up by the Norwegian tanker *France Stove* and transferred to the Margate pilot boat, returning to operational duties soon after.

By mid-1956, the 92nd FBS possessed 24 aircraft, supported by a like number of pilots, headed by Squadron Commander, Lt. Col. Richard B. Willsie, who had replaced Jim Carlyle during June 1955. In addition, Operations Officer Maj. William E. Charlson, Executive Officer Capt. William S. Leidy, Maintenance Officer 1st Lt. Daniel Fontenot, Personnel Officer 1st Lt. Fred C. Sivia and Squadron Adjutant 1st Lt. William A. Staempfli completed the command line-up. Technical Representatives Noel Allen, Lou Cannagallo, Edward Lynch and Charles Swab backed up the maintenance effort. Finally, just over two hundred non-commissioned personnel provided the backbone of the squadron, mainly in support of the maintenance operation.

Throughout 1956, practice alerts became routine, and Squadron pilots were examined quarterly on their assigned targets, and intelligence relating to them. Targets would be changed regularly, and within 48 hours, a pilot was expected to be fully conversant with all aspects of his new assignment. These 'targets' invariably related to Poland, East Germany and Czechoslovakia, for which escape and evasion techniques were also briefed. 1st Lt. Sam Adams remembers the qualification of pilots as Bomb Commanders to be a particularly lengthy affair:

"To be qualified, you had to score a number of specified bomb hits within a target circle by dive bombing, toss bombing and LABS [Low Altitude Bombing System]. [we] were assigned specific targets for a period of time, usually 30 to 60 days. You would then be assigned a new target for another period of time. When you got a new target, you would make out or develop a mission profile including route to target, route of return to base, visual ground check-points (you assumed no radio or navigational aids would be working), flight altitudes, air speeds, etc. The missions were to be flown solo (individually). As I recall, I had 5 different targets over time, in what is now the Czech Republic".

Sam Adams had been with the 92nd since their F-86A days, and left the Squadron in late August of 1956. He subsequently returned to the United States and was discharged from the USAF to continue his education. Sam was later alerted for recall to active duty during the Suez Crisis, but as with so many others, his services were not called upon. Jack Austin, another pilot from the Manston days, recalls his memories of the period:

"At Manston, each F-84 pilot had at all times 2 or more specific targets, [we] had intelligence photos, maps, etc. We studied the target folders, made up a kit for each target. Higher Headquarters would come to Manston about every 3 months and all the pilot Bomb Commanders were tested about target info, aircraft guise, terrain, target routes, etc. If you didn't score an 'excellent', you were demoted from Bomb Commander status and received additional

training. Every so often, we (Squadron or whole Wing) were called to alert for an ORI (Operational Readiness Inspection) — a mock war. [We would] perhaps move all aircraft and equipment and personnel to another base, set up a field operation, and fly mock combat missions to friendly targets within NATO boundaries, divert to other bases, etc. There were a few 'interesting' happenings as our 'targets' were usually near Russian [occupied] territory. These missions were flown often times in very poor weather, without navigation aids. Some aircraft strayed into Russian territory and were intercepted by MiGs".

Compared to the fighter pilots based at Manston, the lives of the 92nd FBS Combat Crews were far more complex, and regular alerts were pulled to verify the effectiveness of the training being undertaken by the squadron. On top of this workload the Wing took part in the annual UK defence exercise *Stronghold*, staged from 21 to 30 September 1956. However, the crisis in the Middle East intervened, and far fewer aircraft were available for the exercise, which went ahead nonetheless. The 81st FBW provided three waves of Thunderstreaks in simulated attacks on the UK from 22 to 24 September. UK-based F-84Fs flew a total of 37 daylight attacks during Phase 1 of *Stronghold*, followed by a further 60 attacks in Phase 2. They were backed up by B-45s and TDY B-47s, which flew both day and night missions. The F-84F raids were flown in formations of 2 or 4, compared to Exercise *Beware* of the previous year, when they had flown singly. Sadly, these attack missions were considered of little use in the scenario, as they were neither intensive nor susceptible to analysis.

In September 1956, members of the 81st FBW won the USAFE Weapons Meet at Wheelus AB in Libya, the same year that the 406th FIW's F-86D Sabres won the rocketry title. As a result, five pilots, led by Wing Director of Operations Col. Walter I. Moore, Jr travelled to Nellis AFB in Nevada, along with eight Thunderstreaks, to take part in the USAF Wide Gunnery Meet. At the end of the competition, the unit had placed first in the Special Weapons Delivery category, beating five other top USAF teams, including F-84F outfits from the 506th Strategic Fighter Wing and the 3600th Combat Crew Training Wing. Pilots involved in this feat were Captains R.F. Kingston and Dee McCarter, 1st Lt. Richard Blazso and 1st Lt. Kenneth Nellermoe. The first three all came from 78th FBS, with Nellermoe being 92nd FBS's sole representative on the Team. In addition, 24 maintenance personnel accompanied the aircraft to Nellis, and to their great credit, during the course of the competition, there were no aircraft or armament aborts. The achievement at Nellis added to the award of USAFE's Tactical Proficiency Trophy to the Wing earlier in the year. This award was for the first six months of the year, and followed an Operational Readiness Inspection, when the visiting examiners

proclaimed the 81st FBW as the best Wing they had ever inspected. The 81st weapons team returned from the USA during November.

Late 1956 marked the outbreak of two international crises: the nationalisation of the Suez Canal, and the Hungarian uprising of October. In line with many other USAF units, the 92nd FBS stood 24-hour quick reaction alert to counter a possible Soviet attack on Europe. During this period, half of the squadron was at immediate readiness on duty at all times. Jack Austin:

"During the Hungarian and Suez Crises in 1956, we were on alert 24 hours a day. We were loaded with Mk. 7 atomic bombs; 1 per aircraft. The pilots were considered expendable; [they] were headed for all different targets. The aircraft would go individually to different targets from Manston. The pilot had a generally quiet, lonely life in the air at that time. We were using converted B-29 bombers for air refuelling — later they upgraded to KC-97 aircraft tankers which were a little faster".

It should be pointed out that the official USAF line was that the pilots were not expendable, but more than a few of the 92nd FBS Thunderstreak pilots have expressed their doubts over this. In particular, Robert Brinker confirms that:

"My targets were also in Czechoslovakia. In my intelligence file (where our planned routes, fuel control, etc. were) I had three return routes. Case 1, with 'X' pounds of fuel left, I'd head back to Manston. Case 2, with 'Y' pounds, I head to North Africa. Case 3, with 'Z' left — fly over Switzerland and bail out. With a LABS delivery, we were a sitting duck on top of the Immleman manoeuvre. My targets were airfields. With the 'toss bomb', which we were just starting when I left Manston [1956], escape was much more likely. Much more precision was required, however, to get the bomb on the target".

As risk of hostilities resulting from the Suez and Hungarian Crises decreased, personnel were stood down and 'normal service' was resumed during early December. It was noted during the latter half of the year that USAF HQ was honouring its promise to allot experienced pilots to the Wing, with two Captains posted in to 92nd FBS having combat experience in addition to jet fighter 'time'. Four Lieutenants newly-arrived with the 92nd all had F-84F experience as well as special weapons training prior to their assignment. These new pilots initially reported to 81st FBW Headquarters at RAF Bentwaters, where they attended a concentrated course concerned with flying in the UK, in addition to covering Wing Organization and Policy and Special Weapons. Following completion of this course, instrumentation, night flying and standardization check rides were flown in the T-33, prior to the well integrated pilot being assigned to the 92nd FBS. Unfortunately, due to a lack of bombing range availability, only one of the six pilots newly-assigned to the 92nd was able to qualify as a Bomb Commander

204: 52-7044 was displayed at Manston's 1955 Armed Forces Day open day. It carried the early 92nd FBS colour scheme of yellow nose flash and squadron badge on the tail fin. This aircraft, an F-84F-35, was exchanged for a later-standard aircraft in November 1955. (Larry Brooks)

205: The 92nd FBS possessed a number of T-33s whilst at Manston; 49-1001 was the oldest it used and had no ejection seats. Plain colour scheme is typical of 1955 period. (Bob Brinker)

206: T-33 51-17428 was despatched to Madrid during March 1956 to pick up Col Willsie; he had gone u/s there with generator failure. The T-33 took Willsie to Nouasseur where the squadron had deployed for live weapons training. This jet carries the later-style yellow tail and nose flashes of 92nd FBS. (Bob Brinker)

207 Above: *Aerial view of Manston from the south in 1955 with Margate at the top right. 'Y'-shaped fighter hardstandings are clearly visible alongside the taxiways. (Larry Brooks)*

208: *The Mk.7 nuclear weapon or its training 'shape' are rarely seen; 52-5812 carries a training round on its inner pylon. The nuclear pylon differed from the drop tank version in being contoured to accept the 1 kiloton weapon. Note 406th ABGp Dakota outside Hangar 4 in background. (Jack Adams)*

209: *When the 92nd FBS deployed to Nouasseur AB for bombing practice, its aircraft often carried practice bomb dispensers on the inner pylons. The squadron later modified the outer pylons to carry these dispensers, which meant that a pilot had to be more accurate in his weapon delivery technique. (Jack Adams)*

by the end of the year, giving the squadron 20 fully-qualified combat crews.

1957 represented a change for the worse as far as the Thunderstreak squadron at Manston was concerned. In a marked turnaround from previous policy, ten F-84F pilots were posted in to Manston during the first half of the year, but none had previous Thunderstreak time, and their experience was limited. The squadron estimated that it would take up to six months to bring them up to speed. This in addition to a 300-hour-a-month flying allocation meant that sorties had to be restricted to 1 hour duration to ensure all aircraft could be flown at least every third day. When, at the end of June, four very experienced and qualified Bomb Commanders left the Squadron, in addition to a rise to a 475-hour flying month, resources became severely stretched. At this stage, six pilots remained to be qualified, and that the unit survived such an upheaval to remain combat-ready is a credit to the flexibility of the personnel involved.

The 92nd FBS had been involved in all the annual United Kingdom Defence Exercises up to, and including *Vigilant*, held from 25 May 1957. This latter scenario saw three waves of Thunderstreaks from the Wing penetrating British defences at low level, and largely under the radar 'screen', in a similar vein to the previous year's effort. Very few interceptions were made, and Wing staff believed that the whole exercise was somewhat unrealistic as a result of speed and height restrictions imposed on participating forces. It was recommended that in future, participating aircraft should be allowed to drop their tanks and attack in a more realistic manner, but common sense prevailed, and the unknowing inhabitants of Eastern England did not have to dodge 450 gallon tanks during subsequent tests of the UK defence system.

1957 brought to light numerous difficulties in the isolated operation of the 92nd's Thunderstreaks. In reporting to the Sabre-equipped 406th FIW, the squadron could no longer rely upon the resources being available to support its operation away from base during an alert. This problem was never solved during the unit's tenure at Manston, and a return to Bentwaters was surely on the cards. In addition, three further 92nd FBS pilots were whisked away from mid-1957 on special assignments. Firstly, Lt. Charles Taylor was sent to Iran to become a check pilot on its F-84G introduction programme from 5 May until 28 October. Further to this, 1st. Lts. Tom Adams and Paul Baker were detached to the Pakistan Air Force from 20 November for a month's worth of flying simulated attacks against the Pakistan Navy in T-33 jets. A/1c Eldin Stroberg was also deployed on the latter mission.

With the closing down of Manston for USAF operations in 1958, the 92nd FBS was reassigned to RAF Bentwaters, home of its parent 81st FBW. The squadron finally left the Kent airfield on 30 April 1958, and began re-equipping with the McDonnell F-101A and C Voodoo from 4 December, in turn becoming a Tactical Fighter Squadron. Forty-eight of the Wing's surviving Thunderstreaks subsequently went through IRAN (Inspect and Repair as Necessary) maintenance prior to their allotment to West Germany's Luftwaffe.

81st FBW Commanders - Manston Era

Col. Gladwyn E. Pinkston: ? to October 1954
Col. H.N. Holt: October 1954 to 10 June 1955
Col. McElroy: 10 June 1955 to 1957
Col. Lester Krause: 1957 to 8 July 1957
Col. H.L. Crouch: 8 July 1957 to end of Manston era

92nd FBS Squadron Commanders - Manston Era

Lt. Col. James H. Carlyle: start of detachment to June 1955
Lt. Col. Richard B. Willsie: June 1955 to end of detachment

210: 1/Lt Tom Adams' Thunderstreak lies in the Lady Carson's garden, 14 June 1956. Adams was fortunate to escape uninjured as his aircraft had passed right through a high garden wall before coming to rest. Lack of squadron markings at this time is noteworthy. (Associated Kent Newspapers Ltd.)

211: *Recovered from the crash site, 52-7096 makes its way back along the runway to the 'loop' dispersal. The aircraft was not deemed repairable. (John T Williams)*

212: *Ground clearance of the F-84F's drop tanks was less than six inches, so that even small bumps could cause them to scrape the ground. This pilot has run off the side of the 'loop' taxiway and beached his aircraft, though the drop tank has probably minimised any further damage. 52-6800 was one of the later F-84F-45 aircraft delivered to 92nd FBS from mid-1955 (Sam Adams)*

213: *1/Lt John Caswell's crash of 9 June 1955 was the first of a number that involved aircraft on takeoff from Manston. The village of Cliffs-end can be seen in the background; a minor disaster had been narrowly averted. (Associated Kent Newspapers Ltd.)*

214: *During 1956 the squadron markings for 92nd FBS Thunderstreaks changed; the 'FS-' buzz number was relocated to the tail section and other markings were also relocated; notably the squadron badge, which moved to the mid-fuselage position. This allowed the bold yellow tail design to be applied, along with a black lightning flash. 52-6877 was Lt Col Willsie's aircraft and bore his name in Old English script on the canopy rail. (Jay May)*

215 Below: *This fine shot shows 1/Lt Sam Adams in the cockpit of his F-84F, 61-6452. The aircraft was an early-standard F-84F-35 and was exchanged for a 'dash-45' model in 1956. Unusual 'up and over' canopy actuation mechanism was unique to the later F-84 series. (Sam Adams)*

THE AIR RESCUE SQUADRONS
Water, wings and rotors

216 Above: *One of a number of public relations missions performed by 66th ARS was this flight to drop 'Father Christmas' (actually A/2c Kenneth Hughes) onto the North Goodwin lightship on 17 December 1953. The mission was not successful and a further attempt to drop Santa onto the boat Salvor (foreground) also failed due to strong winds. Gifts for the North Goodwin eventually reached the ship on 21 December. The helicopter used for the flight was SH-19A 51-3890, which served at Manston from August 1952 to December 1956. (Sunbeam photo)*

It was during the Second World War that USAAF planners realised the need for a formal rescue service, in the main to provide cover on air supply routes and to escort fighters and bombers on long-range missions. It was not long before dedicated air-sea rescue squadrons were formed to perform this mission. After WWII, Continental US-based units were formed into an unofficial air rescue organization until May 1946 when the Air Rescue Service came into being, under the control of the Air Transport Command (later Military Air Transport Service).

In Europe, only one Air Rescue Service unit had served the continent post-war, and this unit — the 7th Rescue Squadron — was based at Wiesbaden AB, West Germany. In accordance with ARS tradition, the 7th RS had its Flights dispersed around the area of operations; and the 7th's area was considerable. 'A' Flight was based at Wiesbaden, with Flight 'B' at Lajes in the Azores, 'C' at Wheelus AB in Libya and Flight 'D' at Dharan in Saudi Arabia. Rescue Squadrons had become Air Rescue Squadrons (ARS) from August 1950.

The 7th ARS regularly visited Manston in the early years of its USAF occupation. Indeed, even prior to the arrival of the USAF flying units, the aircraft of the 7th ARS had occasion to drop into Manston for rescue missions over the North Sea and English Channel. On the afternoon of 7 June 1950, an RB-29A reconnaissance aircraft from the 5th Strategic Reconnaissance Wing on TDY at Sculthorpe, left the base on a post-maintenance air test. The flight would take the aircraft out over the North Sea where the turret-mounted machine guns would be tested with live ammunition. During the flight however, disaster struck when gunfire from the forward upper turret hit the number 4 engine. The turrets were supposed to have been fitted with a contour-follower ring which would make it impossible to hit any part of the aircraft's structure; it later transpired that the follower ring had been omitted during maintenance.

With only three engines functioning and the aircraft losing height steadily, the RB-29 commander, Capt. Walsh, ordered his crew to bail out; eight jumped, leaving three aboard the aircraft, which ditched in the North Sea 20 miles (32km) east of Cromer. An intensive search was immediately put into action, and SB-17s and H-5 helicopters from the 7th ARS were involved, the former flying out of Manston. By the end of the search, only four survivors had been rescued, and the need for a permanently based ARS unit in the UK was strengthened.

Just over a month later, it was aircraft from the 7th ARS Flight at Wiesbaden which escorted the 20th FBG's Thunderjets across the last leg of their transatlantic deployment to Manston. In addition, C-82s often passed through in addition to the SB-17Hs and (from August 1950) SB-29s. The then Corporal Richard B. Saich was a radio operator on many of these flights:

"At various times I crewed SB-17s, SB-29s and C-82s in and out of Manston. I recall one instance when the flight engineer and I 'ground flew' a C-82 all through one night during a severe storm. We had tied planks on top of the wings to act as spoilers and reduce the lift and kept turning the aircraft into wind while holding the controls to avoid damaging the control surfaces. We were successful but exhausted when morning came. Another time we flew into Manston in an SB-17 which blew a cylinder off the top of number 3 engine. Our C-82 flew in a new engine and toolbox. The RAF provided a crane and the flight crew changed the engine".

"Early on in my Manston experience, there was no USAF organization at Manston. After a while, the F-84s arrived (with our help). We flew out and took positions between Newfoundland and Iceland and between Iceland and the UK and transmitted low frequency homing signals for the fighters to navigate by. When they came within range, we also used our search radar to help pinpoint their positions".

Late 1950 witnessed many visits by aircraft from the 7th ARS. At the beginning of December, for instance, SB-17 44-83730 was ferried through Manston and on to Prestwick to assist in the 20th FBG's return to the United States. By the beginning of 1951, with the impending arrival of the 31st FEW's Thunderjets at Manston, both SB-17 and SB-29 aircraft were deployed through Prestwick and Keflavik to support Fox Able 10. SB-29s then began to make regular short-term TDY visits to Manston to provide rescue cover.

In order to provide rescue facilities for the ever-increasing amount of USAF aircraft in the UK, however, the 9th ARS was finally organised on 12 February 1951 at South Ruislip in Middlesex. On the 27th of the month, the new squadron moved to its permanent base at Bushy Park, from where it could control the detached flights; the 9th ARS reported ultimately to the 7th Air Division. Arriving at Manston with its ex-7th ARS SB-29s and C-82As on 12 April 1951, 'A' Flight of the 9th ARS was supplemented by four SA-16 Albatross amphibians, which arrived from 30 June. The C-82As were used in the support role, but were generally unreliable and were later retired. 'B' Flight was soon formed at Sculthorpe in Norfolk, with further detachments of the 9th ARS at Burtonwood in Lancashire ('C' Flight) and at Wiesbaden AB in Germany ('D' Flight — replacing 7th ARS's 'A' Flight). The 7th ARS's area of operation

was relocated and would now encompass the Middle East and North Africa.

It was not long before operational missions were flown from Manston, and even prior to this, the odd incident punctuated the early days of the unit. On 16 May 1951, SB-29 44-84030 ran off the runway, damaging the FIDO installation. On 25 June, another 9th ARS SB-29 made an emergency landing due to a hydraulic system failure. No damage was incurred this time, and a safe landing was made. These SB-29s had been flown from the USA during 1950, as Richard Saich recalls:

"On 25 June 1950, the North Korean Army invaded South Korea, and on July 4, 1950 I arrived at Tinker AFB, Oklahoma, along with a total of four flight crews to attend B-29 Ground School. This training had lasted 30 days and then we transferred to Montgomery, Alabama for flight training. Upon completion of flight training, we travelled to Mobile, Alabama where we picked up four B-29s, which had been pulled from storage and modified to SB-29 type, complete with Edo droppable lifeboats. My crew flew aircraft no.4030 from Mobile via the Azores to Wiesbaden, Germany, being the first B-29 to arrive at Wiesbaden. This was either late August or early September 1950 [actually 29 August 1950]. We were followed shortly by the other three aircraft and were soon flying long-range search missions out of Wiesbaden".

"On March 6th 1951, Flight D, 9th ARS was formed, replacing Flight A, 7th ARS at Wiesbaden. We received two SA-16 aircraft, and expected two more, while still retaining the SB-17s, SB-29s, C-82s and [H-5] helicopters. Flight A, 9th ARS was scheduled to move to Manston, taking the SB-29s. Initially I was assigned to the new organization, along with the SB-29s, and I was processed for transfer to Manston on 23 March 1951. However, my friend, Cpl. Harry A. Sullivan, who had attended B-29 schools and flew as assistant radio operator/gunner on my crew was not scheduled for transfer. Harry wanted to marry a German woman, but could not do so as long as he was stationed in Germany. I offered to trade assignments with Cpl. Sullivan and this was approved, so Harry went to Manston and I stayed at Wiesbaden. I don't know the actual dates, but the SB-29s did not spend much time at Manston, as they were transferred to Sculthorpe".

The arrival at the end of June 1951 of the first SA-16 amphibians for Flight 'A' signalled the beginning of a new era. The SB-29 'Dumbo' previously in use by the Flight was really better suited to long-range rescue missions, where it could drop a 30-foot (9m) A-3 motorised lifeboat by parachute. The boat suspended from the bomb bay of the SB-29 was the largest ever dropped from an aircraft. Allied to a long loiter time over the 'target', the SB-29 could also illuminate the search area with on-board flares. The SA-

217: *Aside from the aircraft operated by the Air Rescue Flight, B-29s were rare visitors to Manston. This KB-29P tanker was parked on the ASP for technical work to be carried out. It came from 420th Air Refuelling Squadron at Sculthorpe. (Larry Brooks)*

218: *This very rare photo shows one of the 9th ARS B-29s landing at Manston in early 1951; insignia red arctic markings can be seen on the tail section. 9th ARS reportedly operated a number of 'standard' B-29s, which did not have the liferaft fitted; this appears to be one of those machines. (Al Farnes)*

219: *Many of the World War II-era buildings used by the USAF crews at Manston are still in existence today; this is the airmen's dining hall (building 11) in April 1953. It is still used for this purpose nowadays. (Gale Nelson)*

220: *9th ARS Albatross amphibians often used JATO bottles to shorten their takeoff run from Manston. The bottles were not needed when the main runway was used, but in this case the aircraft is using the 2,600 ft grass runway, orientated 06/24. 51-040 was later passed to the Royal Norwegian Air Force. (John T Williams)*

221: *This postcard was produced by Manston's 9th ARS detachment to celebrate Christmas 1952. The aircraft depicted is 50-176, one of the unit's first two SA-16s. (Scotty McHenry)*

222: *Sikorsky SH-19B 53-4458 performed at the May 1957 Armed Forces Day display. The helicopter later picked up a 'volunteer' from the ground to display its rescue capabilities. (Cowles Bristol).*

16, however, which could actually land on the water to pick up survivors, was a wholly new proposition. The Albatross initially supplemented the SB-29s at Manston, but very soon replaced them altogether. By September 1951, the SB-29s had been reassigned to 'B' Flight at Sculthorpe, which could better utilise their long-range capabilities over the North Sea. At the same time, one of the C-82A Packets also passed to 'B' Flight.

The prototype SA-16 had first flown on 1 October 1947, the USAF receiving the first of 305 aircraft just under two years later. Powered by two Wright R-1820-76 radial engines developing 1,425 hp each, the SA-16B Albatross could stay airborne for 20 hours — a great asset for a search and rescue aircraft. The SA-16B variant differed from the earlier SA-16A in having a 70 inch wing extension outboard of the engine nacelle, plus a further 39 inches added to the wing tip. To compensate for this, the vertical fin of the 'B' version was increased in area. Both variants of Albatross were used at Manston, and in addition, many of the SA-16As were retrofitted to -B configuration.

As an aid to 'difficult' take-offs, the aircraft could be fitted with JATO (Jet Assisted Take Off) bottles, providing a 14-second rocket boost from the four boosters fitted in pairs on each side of the fuselage aft of the wing. In Search and Rescue mode, the SA-16 would carry a crew of six (pilot, co-pilot, radio operator, flight mechanic and paramedic), with accommodation for four litters (stretchers). The rugged Albatross survived many hazardous missions from Manston, and on more than one occasion, an SA-16 pilot returning from a long mission would discover a gale blowing across Manston's runway. With a tired crew not relishing a night away from home, the pilot would put his amphibian down by landing across the runway. As 9th ARS Albatross pilot Scottie McHenry would recall saying to the Tower: *"The runway I am using is 750 feet long, and 9,000 feet wide!"*

The summer of 1951 saw the first regular use of the aircraft for their intended mission. On 7 July, the flight was alerted to assist in the collision of two ships off Selsey Bill, but the mission was aborted prior to take-off. On the same day, an SA-16 was scrambled to search for a missing Swiss Cessna Crane, HB-CAP off Cap Gris Nez, to no avail. It was later discovered that the aircraft had landed safely in France, and the search was called off. 14 August 1951 saw an SA-16 and two Thunderjets detailed to search the sea 75 miles southwest of Calais, but on this occasion, the search details were so vague that nothing could be found.

In the early morning of 18 January 1952, the flight dispatched two Albatross amphibians, 51-003 and 50-177 to assist the SS *Pamir*, a German-registered four-masted sailing barque with 49 young cadets aboard. The *Pamir* was in difficulty 29 miles east north-east of Margate. Aboard one of the SA-16s was Captain Scottie H. McHenry, an experienced rescue flyer, who had co-piloted B-24 bombers with the 466th Bomb Group out

of Attlebridge, Norfolk during World War Two. Recalled to active duty for two years on 10 March 1951 as a result of the Korean War, McHenry had arrived at Manston during September of the same year. His memories of the *Pamir* mission are still strong today:

"On January 18, 1952, our Rescue Operations received a distress call. The Pamir *four-mast sailing vessel was experiencing very rough seas and gale-force winds. She had a broken rudder, was adrift and requested a position 'fix'. I was co-pilot on Kenneth Speith's crew. We scrambled from Manston in those gale-force winds to use our radar to locate the Pamir. The [weather] ceilings were about two hundred feet, visibility about a half mile, but we found her! We prepared a message drop, and gave them their geographical co-ordinates. Just as the container was dropped, Ken made a sharp left turn, and the crew were able to see the* Pamir *crew members pick up the message drop container — their crew gave friendly waves to us as Ken rocked his wings in response. Our crew saw their crew experiencing fearful sea conditions. [Assisted by the Margate lifeboat, the* Pamir *managed to resume her voyage.] We returned and landed at Manston. My records show our flight time as two hours and ten minutes for that mission".*

"In January of 1953, my family and I were leaving Southampton on a ship to return to the United States. Two things I remember — we sailed right by the Pamir, *and also, Vic Ruffer (my replacement pilot) gave us fine demonstrations of the Albatross performing take-offs and landings! I was disappointed months later to learn that the beautiful* Pamir, *and all of its crew were lost in the Atlantic Ocean [on 21 September 1957]. A terrible hurricane caught up with her".*

On 18 April 1952, an SA-16 flew to the Wash area, off the north coast of East Anglia, to search for the pilots of two Royal Canadian Air Force Sabres, who had baled out after a mid-air collision. The two aircraft came from 410 Squadron at North Luffenham. An RAF Lincoln bomber dropped a lifeboat, but it was subsequently discovered that both crewmen had perished. On 3 May 1952, after the report of a C-47 crash near Ostend, an SA-16 was again scrambled. The rescue aircraft conducted a search, but the outcome is not known. These sorties were often false alarms, involving either witnesses misinterpreting bangs and splashes at sea (often attributable to sonic booms in the former case), or were a result of an aircraft being 'lost' by air traffic controllers. In many cases, these 'lost' aircraft would turn up at an alternate airfield, having suffered radio failure. Nonetheless, such scrambles were still necessary until the safety — or otherwise — of the crews could be ascertained.

The Albatrosses were busy again on 11 May 1952 when one of the big amphibians was sent to search for two boats in distress near the Isle of Sheppey. The SA-16 assisted as the boats, whose occupants were alive and well, were towed to harbour by an RAF launch.

Just over a week later, on 20 May 1952, two parachutes were seen descending into the sea off Great Yarmouth on the east coast, and concurrently a Mayday call was received from an aircraft 'Escort 25' on the emergency channel. It soon became clear that two RAF Meteor NF. 11 jets from 141 Squadron at RAF Coltishall had collided during a tail chase. One aircraft, WD613, managed to limp back to base, where it required Category 3 repairs. The other aircraft, WD607, piloted by Sergeant Frank Jarrett, was unable to stay aloft and the Meteor's crew was forced to bail out. Jarrett remembers looking at the severed tail of his aircraft as he followed it spinning down into the North Sea from 35,000 feet (10,670m). 141 Squadron had only just received its first Meteor NF. 11s, and Jarrett and his navigator, Sergeant R. Hirst, were the innocent victims of some over-zealous mock dog fighting. Within minutes of the crash, an SA-16 from Manston was airborne to search for the hapless occupants of the Meteor. What followed was one of the epic air-sea rescues of all time.

Captain Scottie H. McHenry was standing alert that day and takes up the story:

"I was at the Air Rescue desk on duty on May 20, 1952 when Manston Tower informed me that two RAF Meteors had bumped together over the North Sea, that the crew had bailed out and that the other jet was attempting to return to land. Our assistance was requested and I told them we would scramble a crew to assist the downed airmen. I called our Commander, Maj. Jim Nelson, who was at lunch at the Officers Club. He instructed me to depart as soon as possible. We were airborne seven minutes later, and set course to search for the downed RAF pilot[3]. When we arrived, many 'land-type' aircraft were circling over the pilot, and there were no surface vessels anywhere near. My co-pilot and I evaluated sea conditions and saw a very rough sea condition below that was a bit scary, especially when only a successful landing could save the downed pilot, who was in about forty-five degree water without protection except for his Mae West".

The crew of Scottie's SA-16 comprised: 2nd Lt. Ben Howell - co-pilot; 2nd Lt. Joseph Glasgow - navigator; T/Sgt. Jerry Ferragiro - flight engineer; A/2c John Richardson and A/2c J.J. Scotty, Jr - both medics; and finally Pfc Louis Stamp, the radio operator. By this time, Jarrett had been in the water for around 30 minutes, about the time it normally takes to kill a man in seas of this temperature. Obviously, time was now of great importance.

"After we decided to attempt landing, we made a low approach at seventy knots, and flew low over the water, hoping to have the swell patterns in phase to provide a smoother condition to land in. Just as I saw this pattern, I closed the throttles and instantly made contact with the sea — it was a very rough contact! The Albatross was thrown upward away

[3] Frank Jarrett's navigator, Sergeant 'Ginger' Hirst, appears to have been hurt during bailout, and drowned. His body was washed up on the German coast near Hamburg several months later.

from the sea; my co-pilot said 'Reverse?' I said 'Roger!' and gave the engines max. power in reverse and she landed! We quickly checked all of the bilges for water with the great hope that there would be none, and all were dry. We quickly noticed that the right wing flap was damaged and that we must not attempt to take off".

This proved to be of minor importance for the moment. With the aircraft wallowing in 12 feet (3.7m) swells, the crew not only had difficulty in controlling the aircraft, but could not easily see Sergeant Jarrett.

"We made radio contact with the aircraft flying overhead, they gave us directions to help us taxi near the pilot. Due to the high seas and their deep depressions we were having difficulty keeping our pilot visible. Those positions we received from overhead were essential, and greatly appreciated! We picked up our pilot on the very first pass! I had the help of a very wonderful crew that day. We all worked together to rescue Sgt. Jarrett, who was first seen in that very cold water, holding his hand upward. He was so cold that he was unable to make any body movement. We brought him on the aircraft and laid him on a couch. The medics instantly took steps to warm his body. We removed our jackets and covered him frequently to help warm his body. After about two hours, he was able to make 'grunting' sounds. Later, he was able to speak faintly. We all believed he would make it through to health".

The damage incurred during the landing left the crew of the Albatross with no option but to try to taxi back to dry land.

"We had 48 nautical miles left to taxi back to land with our patient. Seas were so rough that it was necessary to taxi back with the landing gear lowered to help prevent the Albatross from weathervaning to the opposite direction. When that did happen, a swell would pass under one wing and float, causing the other wing-tip and float to go under the water. Also, the propeller on the lower wing would make contact with the water! We were asked if we would like assistance from a lifeboat that was coming to intercept us. I replied that I would appreciate any assistance they could provide!"

"The Gorleston Lifeboat approached us near land, in shallow waters. We cut both engines and saw a lifeboat crewman aim a long gun toward our aircraft, and instantly saw a small rocket propel a small rope right over our Albatross. Perfect shot! The [flight] engineer drew the small rope into our bow compartment until the very large rope was in the hands of our engineer. He firmly tied the rope to the buoy cable, which was secured to the Albatross. We soon learned that we would need to run our engines to make towing possible, and to reduce the possibility of damaging the Albatross in those very rough seas. I certainly appreciated the help of the Gorleston Lifeboat crew".

"Soon, the rough seas caused such a strain on

the rope that it broke. The Gorleston Lifeboat crew bravely manoeuvred their boat so that their crewman could hand the rope to our engineer! Our engines were running, [and] at the instant we received the rope, the boat captain and I reversed propeller thrust to quickly increase separation distance of our craft. We were able to proceed for a short time until the rope broke again. The lifeboat then cruised near, all the way to the harbour".

"We arrived at the [Gorleston] harbour after dark. I hoped both engines would keep running at least for a little while, [as] both were needed to maintain perfect direction control while taxiing within that narrow harbour, which was lined by many people on either side. We were able to taxi in safely and beach the aircraft. Help was waiting for Sgt. Jarrett. We were given generous thanks and appreciation for each crew member and for that rugged Albatross that had survived the rough landing".

The SA-16 had taken nearly eight hours to taxi into shore. She was soon repaired and returned to Manston, where she continued to fly rescue missions. Jarrett spent a few days in Coltishall's Station Sick Quarters, followed by some sick leave, but returned to work and was detached to 19 Squadron during June. But the story did not stop there, as Scottie explains:

"A few weeks later, my crew was invited to meet Sgt. Jarrett again, and celebrate the occasion at a wonderful banquet, attended by Air Marshal Sir Basil E. Embry, KBE, CB, DSO, DFC, AFC. The day after the banquet, Sgt. Jarrett piloted his Meteor to give each of my crew members our very first jet rides. I was awarded the Distinguished Flying Cross. I wish I could give each member of the Gorleston Lifeboat a special award for their great seamanship and courage. I will always be thankful for how they helped us in a very difficult time!"

Scottie noted one further point relating to the rescue; the navigator, Joseph Glasgow, had not made any landings at sea before this mission; he had been borrowed from an SB-29 unit to make up for a lack of navigators at Manston. As a postscript, soon after the rescue mission, as so often happens, Scottie and Frank Jarrett lost contact. Many years later, a chance remark by Scottie to the author started the latter on a trail that eventually led to Frank Jarrett, now living near Cirencester in Gloucestershire. Within days, Frank and Scottie (from his home in Missouri) were talking by telephone to each other for the first time in over 40 years. Finally, in June 1993, Frank flew over to the US to meet Scottie in person. Numerous TV stations covered their reunion.

The summer of 1952 was a fairly busy time for the Flight, with the Albatrosses being scrambled on 19, 20 and 26 June to search for missing aircraft. The first search was called off when the aircraft landed safely at base, but the final two each resulted in crew rescues. On 1 July 1952, an SA-16 was sent to investigate a ditching 60 miles (97 km) east of Scarborough.

No further details are known. Ten days later, two SA-16s were ordered into the air after the pilot of an RAF Vampire bailed out east of Great Yarmouth. He was picked up by an RAF launch. On 24 July 1952, two SA-16s were involved in a search for occupants of a ditched Meteor east of Cromer, Norfolk. On 29 July 1952, another SA-16 was diverted to the Dengie Flats range to pick up the body of a Manston F-84 pilot. On 18 August 1952, an SA-16 conducted a search for a missing launch just off Walton-on-the-Naze. The next day, another Albatross was involved in the search for a sinking vessel in Thames Estuary. The Southend lifeboat picked up the survivors. Finally, on 20 August 1952, one of Manston's amphibians performed another search mission, this time for a Dutch boat in distress off Clacton.

A quantum leap in rescue capability came on 3 August of 1952 with the arrival of the Sikorsky H-19 'Chickasaw' helicopter. The H-19 did not have to wait long to go into action. On Thursday 4 September, a Manston-based F-84E disappeared in cloud during a letdown to the base. Both helicopters and two SA-16s were scrambled to search for the aircraft. Crash wreckage was later found on Margate Sand, 5 miles (8km) off the Kent coast. Sadly, the pilot, Captain Roscoe Nemer from the 513th Fighter Bomber Squadron had perished in the crash, and Manston's first operational helicopter sortie ended with the return of Nemer's body to the airfield.

1952 was rounded off fairly quietly. On 21 September, an SA-16 crew was despatched to search for a capsized dinghy off Sheerness. The occupants were found alive and well, and were picked up by boat. The Manston SA-16s were committed to Exercise *Ardent* during October, to provide search and rescue facilities in the southeastern region. The two aircraft were assigned call signs 'Playmate 32' and 'Playmate 33' for the duration of the exercise. An SA-16 at Burtonwood and an SB-29 at Sculthorpe were also placed on standby. On Sunday 12 October (the last day of *Ardent*), an Albatross from Manston was scrambled to search for the cause of a 'crash' off Walton-on-Naze, but nothing was found. Finally, on 4 November 1952 an H-19 was scrambled to the Felixstowe area on report of a parachute seven miles (11 km) east of the town. This turned out to be a meteorological balloon. This mission was the last for 'A' Flight of the 9th ARS.

From October 1952, all worldwide USAF Air Rescue Service units were re-organized on a Group - Squadron basis. As a result the 9th ARS was elevated to Group status, with three of its detached flights becoming squadrons within the Group. Thus, on 14 November 1952, 'A' Flight at Manston became the 66th Air Rescue Squadron, which retained the men and machines of the 9th ARS detachment. The 66th ARS had sister squadrons at Sculthorpe (the 67th ARS, moving to Prestwick in Scotland during November 1953), the 68th ARS at Burtonwood (inactivated in

November 1953), with the 69th ARS at Wiesbaden the final of the four converted Flights. Finally, on 10 November 1953, the 53rd ARS at Keflavik in Iceland came under the control of 9th Air Rescue Group (ARG). European-based Air Rescue thereafter generally came under the control of the Bordeaux-based 12th ARG. To the outsider, little had changed in the day-to-day running of Air Rescue operations at Manston.

On 14 November 1952, the 66th ARS began operations at Manston, maintaining two alert crews on operational readiness 24 hours a day, 365 days of the year; one crew for the SA-16, the other assigned to the H-19 helicopter. The 66th ARS took over four SA-16s and two H-19s from the 9th ARS Flight.

The H-19s, which could carry up to 10 personnel including a medical assistant, were well-used during their spell at Manston, being ideally suited to short-range rescue missions off the Kent coast. Alongside the long-range SA-16s, the H-19 Chickasaw represented a versatile rescue force. Powered by a 600 hp Pratt & Whitney R-1340-S1H2 radial engine that drove a 53-foot diameter main rotor, the Chickasaw could travel at speeds of up to 100 knots, with a four-hour endurance.

The first operational mission was flown on the afternoon of 20 November 1952 when 66th ARS paramedic Capt. J. C. Strich was dropped from an H-19 onto the narrow Margate jetty to transfer onto the local pilot boat. The object of Strich's dash was the two-man crew of a 406th FBW T-33 jet, who had bailed out after their aircraft had gone out of control. The H-19 stood by as Strich aided the recovery of the two officers, Capt. Charles B. Gresham and Capt. Herbert Kipp from the Dutch vessel *Mercurius*. Both were pronounced alive and well, and were soon returning to Manston by helicopter. Captain Strich was busy again 10 days later when a 513th FBS Thunderjet crashed into the sea off Deal, and the paramedic was again dispatched via H-19 to offer medical help. The F-84, callsign 'Air Force 103', had caught fire, and its pilot had managed to bail out, very quickly being picked up by a tanker and transferred to the H-19. Another successful mission was accomplished.

The first mission of 1953 was not scrambled until 1 February, when two SA-16s were deployed to Leysdown to assist in the rescue of people marooned by floods on the Isle of Sheppey. On 23 March 1953, the C-82A Packet rescue support aircraft 44-23029 caught fire in its dispersal as a result of engine overpriming. The fire was put out with foam. Sadly, the days were numbered for the C-82, whose unreliability had finally rendered it ineffective. In August of 1953, '029 was retired, along with the 67th ARS's example. The supply role would in future be performed by the redoubtable C-47.

On 4 April 1953, Beech C-45 '6994' was performing practice GCA circuits at Bovingdon. Suddenly, and for no apparent reason, it disappeared from the GCA screen, with simultaneous loss of radio contact. Suspecting the worst, the call went out to 66th ARS,

which scrambled an SA-16 to search the GCA pattern and local area. Before the Albatross could reach the Bovingdon area, however, the C-45 landed at the base to report a complete radio failure. Quite why it had disappeared from radar screens was never discovered. Four days later, the 66th was again in action after the ship *Camel Lima* had reported the crash of 20th FBW F-84G 51-991 north of Foulness Island. A pair of SA-16s were immediately sent to search for what was initially thought to be a Manston-based aircraft. It soon became clear that the Thunderjet had originated from Wethersfield, and an air search found no trace of aircraft or pilot Donald C. Goodwin. His body was later sighted, but sank before it could be retrieved.

During early June 1953, 66th ARS Operations Officer Maj C.S. Lowe unveiled the squadron's latest tool — an H-19 equipped with floats to enable amphibious operation. The aircraft was demonstrated by Capt. Willis R. Kusy, one of two H-19 pilots dispatched to Holland the previous February to help during the floods which had blighted the area. On the first day of the 66th's involvement with that operation, over 185 people were rescued, with a total of well in excess of 200 for the whole period the squadron was in the Netherlands.

Captain Kusy had the opportunity to show off the H-19 to the crowds of people attending the reopening of Ramsgate Airport on 28 June. Among other items in the flying programme was a Gloster Meteor formation flown by 500 (County of Kent) Squadron, Royal Auxiliary Air Force, and a display by the Hawker Hurricane G-AMAU, which is still flying today with the RAF Battle of Britain Memorial Flight. Life was not always so rosy for the 66th's helicopters, though. On 8 July 1953, the pilot of Chickasaw 51-3889, callsign '419', radioed Manston tower that he had crashed three miles (4.8km) from the airfield. The pilot reported control failure, but all aboard were unharmed. The damage to the aircraft was not repairable at Manston, and the unfortunate H-19 was transferred to Burtonwood on 15 July for further action. There it became a 'Christmas Tree', supplying parts for other H-19s in Europe, until, by then a bare shell, it was transferred back to the USA in March 1956.

Late summer of 1953 brought the usual spell of scrambles, beginning on 18 August, when an SA-16 searched the area ten miles (16 km) south of Eastbourne. This turned out to be a false alarm. The next day, an Albatross was diverted to eight miles (13 km) southwest of Beachy Head for a reported ditching. Nothing was found. An SA-16 and a T-33 (the latter from the 406th FBW) were diverted from local flying on 31 August 1953 to an area ten miles (16 km) south of Littlestone. Again, nothing was found. During September, SA-16 51-7165 was airborne 1½ miles (2.4 km) southwest of Knoll Buoy, Dengie Flats for a sunken yacht.

The Mayor of Margate, Alderman H.V. Ward donned his Mae West for a two-hour SA-16 flight on

223: *In the mid-1950s, markings on 66th ARS SA-16s changed slightly; the large 'U.S Air Force' insignia was placed on the forward fuselage and the 'Rescue' titling was placed on a black band across the tail fin. (MAP)*

224: *Two 66th ARS Albatross amphibians await their next sortie, 51-7165 at left and 51-7161 at the right. '161 was damaged at Manston on 12 January 1954 during a JATO takeoff. (Manston History Club)*

225: *The Albatross crew that took part in the epic rescue of Frank Jarrett on 20 May 1952 were (back row, L-R): 2/Lt Ben Howell (co-pilot), Capt Scottie McHenry (pilot), 2/Lt Joseph Glasgow (navigator) and TSgt Jerry Ferragiro (engineer). Front row L-R: Pfc Louis Stamp (radio operator), A/2c John Richardson (medic) and A/2c J.J. Scotty Jr (medic). (Scotty McHenry)*

Saturday 19 September 1953. Flying at 2,000 feet (609 m), he was taken over his home on the North Foreland, then over Canterbury and Dover before making a water landing in Margate Harbour. The pilot of the Albatross, 1st Lt. Victor Ruffer later commented; *"It was his first flight, but he took to it like a real veteran"*. Ruffer had flown his 1,000th SA-16 hour that morning, the initial idea being to fly the Mayor in an H-19, but it was, unusually, unserviceable. The SA-16 was airborne again during 8 October on a search mission. 51-033 initially flew southwest to search for an aircraft that had crashed 15 miles south of Bournemouth. Before the aircraft could make any headway in that direction, however, the crew was advised to proceed to Minnis Bay first, as an aircraft had crashed in the sea there too. On Tuesday 13 October a proposal from the Air Ministry for an Air-Sea Rescue Training Area at sea off Margate came before the town's Council. The idea was rejected, as it was considered to be too close to the town, and might displease holidaymakers.

On 19 October 1953, Vampire NF 10 WP252 from 25 Squadron at West Malling crashed into the sea 10 miles (16 km) south east of South Foreland, near the Goodwin sands. The pilot and navigator bailed out after the aircraft went into a spin at 20,000 feet (6090 m) and could not be recovered. One of 66th ARS's SA-16s was scrambled, but sadly the pilot of the Vampire, Flying Officer Didmon-White was found to be dead at the scene. Flying Officer Breeze, the Vampire's navigator, was recovered alive by a Swedish freighter, however.

The next day, a 29 Squadron Meteor NF 11, WD603, flying from Tangmere (callsign 'Offset Blue 1') made an emergency transmission to say that he was short of fuel and on one engine. The pilot turned his aircraft towards Ford Royal Naval Air Station, but crashed into the sea eight miles (13 km) south south-east of the airfield. SA-16 51-7151 was diverted from local flying to a position 15 miles (24 km) south of Beachy Head where the aircraft was believed to have ditched. The search was called off when the pilot was recovered, alive and well.

As with the 9th ARS, pilots from the 66th ARS often made use of Manston's runway width to take off, as David B. Tharp, a dispatcher with the 3917th Air Base Group remembers:

"I got to know several of the [ARS] pilots quite well, one that comes to mind was Capt. Ruffer. I recall one day when I called Rescue to scramble — an RAF pilot was in trouble over the North Sea. I don't recall just where, but it was not far from Manston. Capt. Ruffer and his crew took off crossways of the runway, and while climbing out saw the RAF pilot bail out of his craft. They set course with him in sight and picked him up just after he landed in the water. When they came back to Base Operations the RAF officer said his under clothes didn't even get wet, he was out of the water that quickly".

David Tharp is probably referring to the 20 October mission referred to above.

The closure of 68th ARS at Burtonwood brought a further H-19 to Manston during November 1953. This Chickasaw, 51-3893 *Hopalong*, had become (along with 51-3894 *Whirl-o-Way*) the first helicopters to cross the Atlantic when they were ferried straight from the Sikorsky factory at Bridgeport, Connecticut to Europe in mid-1952. The flight of the two helicopters to Europe could make a book in itself, and the daring exploits of the crews involved deserves a mention here.

The main reason for the flight was to prove the viability of such long-range helicopter deployments. Secondary to this, the study of flight problems and pilot fatigue, as well as economical constraints made the flight attractive. It had been estimated that the cost of transporting the H-19s as air cargo would have been around $6,000, and the air ferry method was thought to be an attractive and cheaper option, should the first deployment prove successful. Before the two helicopters could depart for England, however, numerous organisational matters needed to be arranged; the rescue aspect receiving most attention. In all, one C-54 transport (callsign: 'Playmate'), one each of SB-17 ('Juke Box Alfa') and SB-29 lifeboat-equipped rescue aircraft, and a Grumman SA-16 amphibian ('Duckbutt Alfa') would accompany the helicopters on their crossing. The cost of this support effort must have been phenomenal, and presumably exceeded the $6,000 air cargo costs. But it was stated that any such future crossings would be made en masse, thus reducing the individual cost per aircraft.

On 15 July 1952, the H-19s and crews were ready for the takeoff. Both helicopters had been fitted with three 100-gallon drums in their cabins, which enabled enough fuel to be carried for the long legs of the crossing. The fuel in these drums had to be manually transferred to the aircraft's fuel system, however. Departing Westover AFB in Massachusetts, the lead H-19 was piloted by experienced 29-year old Capt. Vincent H. McGovern, with 96 Korean War combat rescues under his belt. In the co-pilot's seat was Capt. Harry C. Jeffers, another combat-experienced chopper pilot. In the second aircraft was 1/Lt Harold W. Moore, with co-pilot Capt. George O. Hambrick. Moore was a veteran of 112 combat missions in Korea, and piloted the first helicopter to carry the truce negotiators to Panmunjom. His co-pilot had been stationed at Goose Bay in Labrador, Canada for over a year and a half, so he was a useful crewmember.

Their route took them initially to Presque Isle, Maine, taking 4 hours and 35 minutes. The first of numerous bouts of bad weather then delayed the helicopters in Maine until 17th July, when the next (eight-hour) hop was made into Goose Bay. Bad weather and mechanical problems with *Hopalong* delayed departure to Bluie West 1 until 21 July, and even then, 200 miles (322km) into the leg, 'Playmate'

— 100 miles (160 km) ahead of the main formation — radioed that stiff headwinds were being experienced. Sadly, the aircraft would have to return to Goose Bay; eight hours in the air and no distance covered! Another attempt on 23 July was abandoned, and on 24th, the helicopters again set out, experienced extremely dense fog, and turned back again. This time, however, the headwinds were coming from the west, and upon reaching Cape Harrison, Labrador after 4 hours and 40 minutes of flying, it was decided to land, as the mere 125 miles (201 km) to Goose Bay would have put their remaining fuel from their 12-hour endurance on the limit, so bad were the headwinds. Cape Harrison was the site of a radio station, and the four crewmembers weathered out an overnight storm with the seven Canadian personnel at the base. Next day, the helicopters managed to return to Goose Bay to prepare for their final attempt at Greenland. Leaving on the 27th, bad weather again played its part, and the two H-19s were forced to fly in clear air at 50 feet — dodging icebergs as they did so. The plan to land at Bluie West 1 was also scrapped, and despite worsening weather, beyond their point of no return, the chopper crews had no option but to divert into the small, inhabited island of Simiutak, 42 miles (67 km) short of their intended destination. Spending another night with a radio crew, the H-19s completed their 10-hour leg to Bluie West 1 on 28 July.

The remainder of the trip was, by comparison, uneventful. Leaving for Keflavik, Iceland on the 29th, the leg took 9 hours and 50 minutes, strong tail winds helping to break existing helicopter distance record of 703.6 miles (1134 km) by 137 miles (221 km). Bad weather grounded the flight in Iceland for a day, the final leg into Prestwick, Scotland being completed on 31 July. This 10 hour and 5 minute sector broke the distance record — set only two days earlier — by a further 103 miles (166 km).

After a brief stay in Scotland, the helicopters departed for Burtonwood, and finally on to Ypenburg in Holland on 2 August, where their arrival opened the ILSY (International Luchtvaart Show Ypenburg) air show. The presence of the helicopters had been the result of a last-minute request by KLM, the Dutch national airline. And it was the president of KLM, Dr. Albert Plesman, who welcomed the American aviators and their machines. The two H-19s finally reached the end of their journey at 9th ARS 'D' Flight in Wiesbaden, Germany two days later. The total distance covered was 3,984 miles (6,425 km), for 51 hours and 55 minutes of flying time. From Germany, 'Hopalong' was allotted to the 9th ARS 'C' Flight at Burtonwood, and was assigned to Manston when the former base's ARS unit (by then designated as the 68th ARS) closed down. *Hopalong* became, in many ways, the most public face of the USAF at Manston, and something of a celebrity in its own right.

November 1953 brought two further search/res-cue missions. On the 16th, SA-16 51-040 and H-19 51-3890 were involved in an unspecified search in the Dungeness area. Ten days later, on 26 November, the crew of a USAF C-119 transport, call-sign '2660' reported that their compass was broken and that they had no gyro. SA-16 51-7161 took off to intercept the aircraft and acted as escort. The C-119 later arrived safely at Manston.

The final mission of 1953 was flown on 29 December. An Avro Anson C 12, PH812 from 231 Operational Conversion Unit at Bassingbourn had experienced instrument failure off Canvey Island, followed closely by a double engine failure. The pilot of the aircraft, callsign 'Pinion 23', managed to broadcast a mayday prior to ditching off the Essex coast. The 66th ARS was alerted, and a lone SA-16 took off from Manston to search the area. Fortunately the Anson pilot was rescued, none the worse for his ordeal.

Starting the New Year off literally with a bang, on 12 January 1954, SA-16 51-7161 crashed on runway 29 during a JATO take-off. It is not known how badly damaged the aircraft was, but there were no injuries to the crew. Just over a week later, on 21 January 1954, Meteor NF 11 WM175 of 85 Squadron, based at West Malling crashed into the sea four miles (6.5 km) north west of Whitstable after running short of fuel on approach to Manston in bad weather. The crew, comprising Flying Officers Wilson and Pattison, were on exchange from 87 Squadron at Wahn in West Germany. Pattison's body was recovered from the waters of the Thames Estuary three months later, but of F/O Wilson or his aircraft, there was no trace.

On the evening of Thursday 8 July, a combined exercise was held off Margate between the local section of the Royal Navy Minewatching Service and the 66th ARS. Objects resembling mines were dropped by an SA-16, and these drops were monitored by members of the Navy's Minewatching Team stationed on Margate jetty. Then, using 'secret' instruments, the details of the simulated drops were relayed by Teletype to a central monitoring station for assessment. Maj. Lowe commanded the SA-16. There was then a relatively quiet period until the end of the year. On 23 August 1954, an H-19 was dispatched to a 513th FIS F-86F crash near Sturry. The rescue helicopter circled over wreckage and landed, but the pilot was dead at the scene. On 24 October an SA-16 piloted by Capt. Howard L. Richards searched for a missing 406th FIW C-47 in France. Although the 66th ARS aircraft was not the first to locate the wreckage of the C-47, Manston's rescue crews did discover the crash site of a WWII B-24 Liberator bomber in the mountains near Nice. This find enabled ground recovery teams to retrieve the bodies of the crew for burial in the United States.

At 2 am on the night of Sunday 28 November 1954, Ramsgate Coastguard flashed a message to the 66th ARS that the South Goodwin lightship with eight crew men had broken its moorings and was adrift near to the treacherous Goodwin Sands. With winds reaching 69 mph (111 km/h), however, an immediate scramble would be impossible and it was not until 7.30 am that an SA-16, piloted by Capt. H.L. Richards left Manston and radioed the position of the lightship, which by now had run aground on the sands and keeled over. Other crewmembers on the Albatross were 1st Lt. Raymond Rung, Capt. George Williams, and S/Sgts. Kennison, Hilliard and Proietti. Alas, conditions were still too severe to risk a setdown by the big amphibian, and the plane returned to base, after reporting that there were no signs of life on the wave-battered hulk. At 9 am an H-19, piloted by Capt. Curtis E. Parkins, finally managed to take off in barely abated winds, and flew the short distance out to the search area. 25 minutes later, Winchman A/1c Elmer Vollman lowered the hoist to a pyjama-clad research scientist, Mr. Ronald K. Murton, who was spotted clinging to the ship's superstructure. As Parkins hovered the chopper, Vollman slowly winched in the near-frozen scientist, and within 10 minutes of reaching the scene, the aircraft was back at base. Also on board during the mission were Maj. Paul L. Park, Operations Officer of the 66th, and Capt. Willis R. Kusy. As soon as Ronald Murton was placed in the hands of Manston's medics, the H-19 again took off, bound for Sheerness. It transpired that three of the lightship's crewmembers were thought to be trapped in an air pocket near the galley, and the diversion to Sheerness was necessary to pick up rescue equipment. Landing in the Town Square, diving equipment was placed aboard, and the helicopter was once again aloft for the dash back to the Goodwin Sands. Also placed on alert back at Manston was a team of men led by Warrant Officer Harry J. McGahan of the 406th Motor Vehicle Sqn, who would be ready with oxy-acetylene cutting equipment, if needed.

Arriving at the light ship, Parkins put his H-19 into a hover before lowering the rescue equipment onto a waiting boat. Low on fuel, the helicopter dashed back to Manston on its last drops of gasoline. Sadly, the effort was wasted; the remaining seven crew of the South Goodwin had all perished. Capt. Parkins and his crew later received awards from the RNLI — Parkins a Silver Medal for Gallantry. On Saturday 5 November 1955, Col. Hugh Manson presented Kusy and Vollman with an Oak Leaf cluster to their Air Medals.

Less than a week after the epic South Goodwin rescue, the squadron was in action again. At 10 o'clock on the morning of 5 December 1954, the phone rang in the 66th ARS alert room. SA-16 pilot Capt. Howard Richards answered and was immediately informed of his next mission: to rescue a Royal Auxiliary Air Force pilot from 604 Squadron who had abandoned his Meteor aircraft at sea, four miles (6.5 km) east of Shoeburyness, Essex. Shouting *"scramble!"*, Howard raced to his Albatross, followed closely by co-pilot Lt. Raymond Rung and navigator Capt.

George Williams. Within seven minutes of the alarm being given, Richard's aircraft was airborne with its six-man crew, but unbeknown to those in the SA-16, the RAuxAF pilot was already having a seriously bad day.

Pilot Officer Brian Cross had departed 604 Squadron's home base at North Weald, Essex on a training mission aboard Meteor F 8, WH408. As he reached 30,000 feet (9,146 m), his aircraft suddenly went into a high-speed stall and entered a flat spin. As speed increased, the Meteor began to break up, and Cross realised that ejection was the only way out. Pilot Officer Cross ejected at 20,000 feet (6,097 m), but as his parachute opened a large chunk of Meteor debris slammed into his canopy, which caused the parachute to alternately collapse and open in an alarming fashion. There began a terrifying drop through nearly four miles as Cross prayed that his parachute would withstand the jerks and wrenches of its inflation and deflation. He hit the water less than half a mile from the shore, where the depth was only four feet or so. He immediately got into his dinghy, no doubt expecting a long wait for rescue.

Twenty-two minutes after the rescue call, an Albatross amphibian from Manston arrived in the search area. Three minutes later, pilot Capt. Richards spotted the RAuxAF pilot in his one-man dinghy in the water below. Immediately, Richards brought his aircraft in to land in the three-foot swells, chopping his left engine to avoid hitting Cross as he pulled up close to the Meteor pilot. When Cross was next to the SA-16, Richard cut the other engine, and coasted up to the yellow dinghy. Brian Cross was quickly pulled into the rear door of the big Grumman amphibian. He was in shock and suffering from a bloody nose, but, at 10.33 am, the unfortunate pilot was safe and well and on his way to Manston. The British press soon found out about the heroic but routine rescue of Brian Cross, and in addition to its gushing praise on the front pages of numerous newspapers, hundreds of 'thankyou' letters poured in to the 66th ARS from grateful members of the public. This became a regular occurrence after this type of rescue. In stark contrast to the jet fighters at Manston, which were seen by the local populace as a noisy and unwarranted invasion into their lives, the 66th ARS was truly appreciated for its heroic deeds, and the squadron was also exploited for PR opportunities. On Wednesday 9 February 1955, the Mayor of Ramsgate, Alderman F.G. Butcher was flown by 66th ARS SA-16 up the north Kent coast over Herne Bay by Capt. Gordon F. Priest.

A further RAF Meteor pilot was rescued in the afternoon of Monday 14 February 1955. Flying Officer Alan M. Wright of 111 Squadron contacted Manston tower at 4.55 pm, when he had only six minutes of fuel left. At 4.59, the tower lost contact and at 5.05 pm, with no fuel remaining, Wright bellied the Meteor into a field 300 yards (274m) from the St. Nicholas roundabout just west of Manston. 66th ARS crews were immediately scrambled, and the the H-19 was airborne at 5.11 pm. The helicopter, piloted by Capt Charles E. Van Horn was at the scene of the crash just one minute later and just six minutes after take-off the H-19 had the RAF pilot safely on board.

On 26 May 1955, 160 officers and men from the part-time Territorial Army visited the 66th ARS for training on the evacuation of wounded personnel by air. Instruction was given by Maj. M.J. Kelly of the 66th, followed by a 'live' pick-up by H-19. This training was put to good use on Thursday 9 June, when two SA-16s searched for survivors of the 10,700-ton Swedish oil tanker *Johannishus*, which had collided with another ship 21 miles east of Ramsgate. The amphibians searched from 4.30 am until 12 noon, and eventually rescued 12 survivors of the 43-man crew. From mid-1955, alongside other rescue types, the H-19 helicopter gained an 'S' prefix, denoting Search-Rescue.

SA-16 51-025 got in trouble on Wednesday 17 August while practising sea landings off Margate. Water entered the hull after hitting a submerged object which then prevented a safe take-off. Margate lifeboat took the aircraft in tow and began to bring it ashore at the old Westgate slipway. An SH-19 piloted by Capt. Harold Welch then cleared a space for the aircraft amidst the hundreds of holiday makers. The pilot of SA-16 was Capt. V. Dixon and also on board was Col. Marshall Strickler, Commanding Officer of the 9th ARG, who later reported that: *"I think we hit an obstruction in the sea. We became flooded and it became impossible to take off. There was not much danger of sinking, but the nose of the plane was well down in the water and we had to beach it quickly. No one was hurt"*. The aircraft was repaired and flown away at high tide on the next day.

A Dutch Navy Grumman TBM-3S Avenger anti-submarine aircraft crashed into the sea 10 miles (16 km) off Calais on Saturday, 18 February 1956. The four crew of the aircraft, (serial 1-7/53089), immediately took to their life raft as the Avenger began to sink. The accident happened around midday, and within minutes a 66th ARS Albatross, piloted by Capt. Joyce Aly was airborne en route to the area. Within 15 minutes, all four Dutch crewmen were aboard the Albatross, and a straightforward mission would have ended there but for one thing – the weather was by now so bad, with frequent snowy blizzards reducing visibility to only a few yards, that take-off was impossible. Instead, Capt. Aly elected to taxi into Calais harbour. Accompanied now by an RAF helicopter from Martlesham Heath and an air-sea rescue launch from Newhaven, the Albatross arrived at the French port two hours later, where she was storm-bound for several days. The Dutch airmen were all landed safely, and mention should go to the rest of the Albatross crew; 1st Lt. Odonval Y. Cundiff (co-pilot), 2nd Lt. Joe Twilla (navigator), S/Sgt. Grover H. Hilliard (engineer) and A/1c Louie Maynard (radio operator).

The continued snowfall brought Manston to a standstill when on Sunday 19 and Monday 20 February the area experienced its highest snowfall of the century. During this period, aside from the 'run-of-the-mill' rescues and searches, the 66th ARS was involved in a previously untold chapter, as Lt. Col. Noble Webster, then a Major and 9th ARG Chief of Operations explains:

"The squadron, besides being on constant alert to cover their area of responsibility, was tasked to fly very dangerous ECM [Electronic Counter Measures] coverage missions. These missions were into the North Sea area without a filed flight plan; conducted low-level below radar coverage, day or night regardless of weather conditions".

On 10 October 1956, a US Navy Douglas R-6D transport with 48 enlisted men, two officers and nine crew, took off from Lakenheath, bound for Lajes in the Azores. The transport was bound for the United States, returning personnel who had served out their tours in the UK. The R-6D radioed its position as 180 miles (290 km) west of Land's End — the most southerly point in Great Britain — and that was the last message received from the aircraft. When it failed to arrive in the Azores, a huge air and sea search was immediately put into action. According to the Air Rescue Service, as many as 100 aircraft from half a dozen countries joined the search, as well as an aircraft carrier and dozens of other ships. Three SAC B-47 bombers also combed the area from high altitude to provide radar search facilities. At Manston, the 66th ARS were immediately in the thick of it, recalls Noble Webster:

"The 66th ARS was the first to arrive in the search area for the missing MATS R-6D aircraft, and maintained a maximum effort commitment of all four SA-16s every day throughout the mission. This mission was directed and controlled by the Rescue Control Center 9th ARG, Bushy Park".

In the early stages of the search nothing was found, but strange SOS signals were then received, and this ray of hope provided new impetus for the searchers. Sadly, after seven days of searching the only items found were two wheels, which were confirmed as coming from the R-6D, and an empty, half-inflated life raft. The search was called off, and no other trace of the aircraft or its personnel was ever found.

In January 1957, Manston's famous helicopter *Hopalong* was transferred to Texas. This aircraft had rescued a lone bird-watcher from the South Goodwin Lightship in a gale during November 1954, and taken part in 76 rescues, accumulating 1,300 flying hours during its time at Manston. Another of the SH-19s, '3890' also left, having taken part in 64 rescues and accrued 1,054 flying hours.

A number of rescues took place during June 1957, marking one of the busier periods for the squadron. On Sunday 16 June 1957 an SA-16 on a training mission radioed that a boat was adrift off Margate. It was subsequently found to be empty and the occupants had been rescued near Birchington earlier in the day.

At the end of the month, the SA-16 and an SH-19 were sent to Dumpton Gap, where a yacht had capsized, but neither were required. The following day, on 31 June an SA-16 went to assist in the search for a Yugoslav asylum seeker; he had jumped from a ship in Pegwell Bay, just to the south of the airfield. The aircraft dropped flares, and the coastguard subsequently spotted the man, who was taken to hospital. Later in the day, 66th ARS was alerted to search Rye Harbour for a missing girl, but she was later found alive and well. These were some of the last rescue missions carried out by the squadron.

On Tuesday 14 May 1957, the Central Air Council in Washington D.C. had ordered the inactivation of the 66th ARS *"..within a year"*. At the time, the squadron was equipped with five SA-16s and two SH-19s. The 66th Air Rescue Squadron quietly, and almost unnoticed by the local population, departed Manston by the end of 1957. Al Vette was the Squadron Chief Pilot at this time:

"We moved the 66th lock, stock and barrel up to Prestwick, Scotland in October of 1957. The 66th was then redesignated [absorbed by] the 67th ARS and continued to operate until the Prestwick base closure in 1966. They then moved down to Moron AB in Spain (near Seville)".

But almost as soon as the squadron had departed, its loss was felt. On the evening of Wednesday 13 November 1957, Manston was asked to assist in the search for pilots of two RF-84F Thunderflash aircraft which had crashed off Herne Bay. The two missing aircraft were flown by pilots from the 302nd Tactical Reconnaissance Squadron (TRS), based at Sembach AB in Germany. Their mission had kicked off during the morning from Sembach, and would lead 1st. Lt. James R. Bulger, flying 52-7340 and 1st. Lt. Orville O. Buck in 52-7370, into France for a stop at the big maintenance base of Chateauroux, then on to Manston, where it is thought that they planned to night stop prior to returning to Germany on 14 November.

All went well on the first stage of the photographic sortie, the pair, led by 1st Lt. Bulger, landed at Chateauroux AB around lunch time. After a stop of three hours, the mission then proceeded to Manston, about 1 hour 30 minutes flying time to the north. Weather forecast for arrival at Manston was 1,100 feet broken cloud, with overcast at 3,000 feet and three miles visibility — standard British weather, and not bad at all for mid November. The flight across the Channel progressed smoothly, and at 5.02 pm, four minutes ahead of their ETA, the flight reported over the North Foreland radio beacon, four miles northeast of Manston, for penetration to land.

The RF-84s held for a further eight minutes, until they were cleared for a standard ADF approach with a GCA pickup. The weather at this point had worsened a little, to 2,500 feet (762m) overcast, but with four miles (6.4 km) visibility. The flight was then instructed to complete a communications check with Manston GCA Final on Channel 15, and then return to Channel 13, Approach Control. This was accomplished, and the aircraft were ordered to descend to 3,500 feet (1,067m) and report over the beacon, which was acknowledged, then further instructed to descend a further 1,000 feet (304m), which was also complied with. At 5.15 pm, the flight were told to roll out onto a heading of 340 degrees

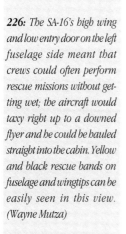

226: *The SA-16's high wing and low entry door on the left fuselage side meant that crews could often perform rescue missions without getting wet; the aircraft would taxy right up to a downed flyer and he could be hauled straight into the cabin. Yellow and black rescue bands on fuselage and wingtips can be easily seen in this view. (Wayne Mutza)*

227: Like a number of other Manston aircraft, SA-16 51-040 was used on an air-to-air photography sortie by the Air Ministry during the early 1950s. The photographs later appeared in the Joint Services Recognition Journal. This aircraft carries the standard 300-gallon Mk.8 external fuel tanks fitted to early SA-16s. (via Bruce Robertson)

and contact GCA Final for landing instructions. As the Thunderflashes contacted GCA, they were flying roughly west, about two miles (3.2km) north of Margate. The GCA controller then advised the aircraft to turn left for the downwind leg to land on runway 11.

Neither pilot acknowledged this turn, and the only transmission heard was *"Speed brakes now"*, and immediately afterwards, at 5.22 pm, the blip on the GCA controller's screen scattered and then disappeared. Controllers dread such an event, which generally can mean only one thing — a catastrophic occurrence of some sort.

Immediately, a large-scale sea and air search was instigated, involving not only the aircraft from Manston, but also the Margate and Ramsgate lifeboats. It was not until the next day that the first and only piece of wreckage — a drop tank — was found washed ashore at Grenham Bay, Birchington. The search was called off soon after. Sadly, the only Manston-based aircraft capable of conducting any sort of meaningful search were the two 406th ABG C-47s, and their input in the mission was limited. Although local newspapers claimed that members of the 66th ARS had taken part in the search, this is now considered unlikely. It was later determined that the RF-84Fs had

collided whilst executing their turn to land and plummeted into the sea off Herne Bay, giving neither pilot the chance to eject. The bodies of the crewmembers were never recovered.

Existing only 'on paper' at Prestwick, the 66th ARS was finally inactivated on 18 January 1958.

Commanding Officers

Flight A, 9th ARS

Maj. Michael F. Ognisty: 12 April 1951 to circa September 1951

Maj. J. Nelson: circa September 1951 to 14 November 1952

66th ARS

Lt. Col. W.P. Gordon: July 1954 to June 1955

Maj. Frank G. Uhring: June 1955 to ?

Lt. Col. Leonard .H. Burgess: ? to May 1957

Lt. Col. Marshall J. Crispen: May 1957 to October 1957 (Squadron inactivated)

228: Sadly, despite USAF interest in preserving the original Hopalong, *Manston's most famous resident was scrapped before it could be saved. Nonetheless, the USAF Museum at Wright Patterson has restored this H-19B into the colours worn by 51-3893 during its stay at Manston. (Richard B Saich).*

Epilogue

The Air Ministry wasted no time in planning for the post-USAF use of Manston. Rumours circulating in early 1958 spoke of the airfield becoming a missile base, but the signing of a joint US-UK agreement on 27 February for the deployment of 60 Thor missiles effectively ruled Manston out; instead the rockets would be based at RAF Feltwell, RAF Driffield and RAF North Luffenham. In any case, the difficulty of securing the airfield and its proximity to population centres would have made the choice highly unlikely.

On the same day that the missile agreement was being signed, and even before the USAF had departed, the Air Ministry stated that the airfield could be used for emergency and commercial use. Many ideas were now considered and dropped in quick succession, and in a letter to Mr. T. J. Bligh at the Treasury, dated 5 May 1958, Mr. L.T.G. Sully of the Air Ministry stated that it had been proposed to base P.1s (English Electric Lightnings) in Kent, probably at Manston. By October, this idea had been dropped, but the airfield had been earmarked instead as one of 30 UK bases to become dispersal airfields for RAF aircraft in time of emergency.

The reality was, however, far less glamorous. On 30 June 1958, Manston was returned to RAF Fighter Command control, and reduced to Care and Maintenance status on 1 August. After a short period of disuse, the airfield was again opened as a Master Diversion Airfield on 28 March 1959, gaining RAF personnel and being parented by RAF West Malling. Civilian operators were also accepted at this time and the first airline, Silver City, arrived less than a month later and took up residence on the eastern side of the airfield. This area became known as the 'Civil Side'. Customs services became available in 1960, and this heralded the way for numerous trooping flights, and later on, tourist operations.

The RAF presence also grew at the base. Arriving in January 1960, the Air Ministry's fire school, the Central Training Establishment would begin training soon after, and remains at Manston to the present day. In addition, during March 1961, the Whirlwind helicopters of No. 22 Squadron 'D' Flight began search and rescue (SAR) operations, hauling holiday-makers from the seas and cliffs of Kent more often than fulfilling its primary task of rescuing military personnel. The squadron remained until March 1969, when Bristow's Helicopters took over these duties. In 1972, RAF SAR helicopters returned to Manston in the shape of the Wessexes of 72 Squadron's 'D' Flight. In June 1976, a dedicated SAR squadron, No. 22, formed 'E' Flight at Manston and took over the Wessex operation until the late 1980s, when the Sea Kings of 202 Squadron moved in.

Control of Manston had been handed over to 3 Group, Bomber Command, on 1 October 1962, and was further transferred to 19 Group, Coastal Command in August 1967. Despite these changes of 'ownership', however, little change was noted initially at Manston. Gradually, though, military aircraft from all nations began to use Manston to clear Customs, as they arrived and departed from the UK. Alas, the rise in civil operations up to the present day has matched the general decrease in military activity, the departure of SAR helicopters in mid-1994 being a particularly sad note. But the 1980s and 1990s have seen the development of a spacious modern civil passenger terminal, and although this has yet to be used to its full extent, the capability is undoubtedly there. Nevertheless, the overhaul of airliners on the eastern side has often given Manston the look of a major airport, and with numerous cargo flights departing the airfield during the 1990s, bound for Rwanda and Bosnia, Manston looks to have carved itself a unique niche in the market. Further expansion of the airfield has taken place on the old 'loop' dispersal where a growing industrial estate is now situated. The next phase of expansion, to include a dedicated rail terminal and expanded aircraft parking areas is also planned. Manston may yet become London's fifth major airport.

229: The ability of Manston's Albatross amphibians to operate from even choppy seas saved many lives; this aircraft, 51-7161 is about to land on a practice mission. The aircraft served with 66th ARS until returned to the United States in February 1955; it later passed to the Spanish Air Force. (via Wayne Mutza)

APPENDIX 1
USAF aircraft based at Manston 1950 to 1958

Boeing SB-29 Superfortress

Serial	Unit	Remarks
44-84030	9th ARS	To 'B' Flight circa June 1951
44-84086	9th ARS	To 'B' Flight circa June 1951

De Havilland Canada L-20A Beaver

Serial	Unit	Remarks
52-6138	92nd FBS	

Douglas C-47

Serial	Unit	Remarks
43-16004	406th ABW	To 47th BW, Sculthorpe
43-16040	406th ABW	
43-16044	406th ABW	Crashed on Mt. Carbono, Italy 24/10/54
43-49158	406th ABW	To 81st TFW, damaged at Bentwaters?, struck off 22/6/64
44-77218	406th ABW	To Colombian AF as FAC 677
4*-**9784	406th ABW	

Fairchild C-82 Packet

Serial	Unit	Remarks
48-0568	9th ARS	To 'B' Flight circa June 1951
44-23029	9th ARS, 66th ARS	Retired August 1953

Grumman SA-16A-GR Albatross

Serial	Squadron	Remarks
50-176	9th ARS, 66th ARS	
50-177	9th ARS, 66th ARS	
51-003	9th ARS	
51-024	66th ARS	To 67th ARS 07Oct57
51-025	66th ARS	Beached St Mildreds Bay 17/8/55, to Grumman 13/12/56
51-033	66th ARS	To Grumman 04Jun56
51-034	66th ARS	To 67th ARS 09Oct57
51-035	66th ARS	To 53rd ARS 09Aug55
51-040	66th ARS	To Grumman 12Sep56
51-042	66th ARS	
51-7151	66th ARS	To Philippine AF
51-7161	66th ARS	To Mobile Air Materiel Area 15/2/55
51-7165	66th ARS	
51-7169	66th ARS	To 67th ARS 10/10/57
51-7185 con-	66th ARS	To Grumman for SA-16B version 16/8/57
52-7218	66th ARS	To 67th ARS 16/10/57

Grumman SA-16B-GR Albatross

Serial	Squadron	Remarks
51-0053	66th ARS	From Grumman 17/9/57, to 67th ARS 14/10/57
51-0059	66th ARS	From Grumman 01/9/57, to 67th ARS 16/10/57

Lockheed T-33
T-33A-LO

Serial	Unit	Remarks
49-885	406th FIW	To 36th FDW ?/8/58
49-923	31st FEW, 12th FEW	To 59th Air Depot, Burtonwood 21/12/51
49-946	31st FEW, 12th FEW, 123rd FBW, 406th FBW/FIW	Crashed near Ash 27/2/51, repaired
49-1000	123rd FBW, 513th FBS	Crashed in sea off Margate 20/11/52
49-1001	92nd FBS	
49-1006	123rd, 406th	To 20th FBW
51-4177	406th FIW	
51-4382	512th FIS	To 86th FIW 19/3/58
51-4469	514th FIS	W/o 31/5/56 Wheelus AB, Libya
51-4473	513th FIS	To 86th FIW 13/4/58
51-4474	514th FIS	Crashed Manston 09/4/58, scrapped 21/4/58
51-4476	92nd FBS, 514th FIS	To 406th FIW 3/56, to 86th FIW 06/5/58
51-4477	513th FIS	To 86th FIW 13Apr58
51-8756	514th FIS	Force landed at Harwell 4/57, repaired. To 20th FBW
51-17415	512th FIS	
51-17428	92nd FBS	
53-5055	514th FIS	
53-5056	406th FIW	
53-5827	92nd FBS	W/o Nouasseur AB

North American F-86D Sabre
F-86D-36, delivered April 1956 – June 1956

Serial	Squadron	Remarks
51-6145	512th FIS	To 3131st ARP Sqn Chateauroux 19/3/58
51-6147	512th FIS	To 86th FIW 19Mar58
51-6150		To 86th FIW 01Feb57
51-6151	513th FIS	To 86th FIW 13Apr58
51-6165	513th FIS	To 86th FIW 13Apr58
51-6167	513th FIS	W/o at Wheelus AB 14/1/58, Capt. John C. Hutson killed

Serial	Squadron	Remarks
51-6168	512th FIS	To 86th FIW 19Mar58
51-6171	512th FIS,	
	513th FIS	To 86th FIW 19Mar58
51-6173	513th FIS	To 86th FIW 13Apr58
51-6179	514th FIS	To 86th FIW 06May58
51-6181	514th FIS	To 86th FIW 21Apr58
51-6183	514th FIS	To 86th FIW 06May58
51-6185	514th FIS	To 86th FIW 21Apr58
51-6188	514th FIS	To 86th FIW 06May58
51-6192	513th FIS	To 86th FIW 13Apr58
51-6205	514th FIS	To 86th FIW 21Apr58
51-6216	512th FIS	To 86th FIW 19Mar58

F-86D-45, delivered October 1954 – January 1955

Serial	Squadron	Remarks
52-4053	513th FIS	To 86th FIW 13/4/58
52-4063	513th FIS	To 86th FIW 14/5/58
52-4075	513th FIS	To 86th FIW 13/4/58
52-4077	513th FIS	To FIAT Turin 08/4/58
52-4082	513th FIS	To 86th FIW 13/4/58
52-4083	514th FIS	To 86th FIW 06/5/58
52-4091	513th FIS	To 86th FIW 13/4/58
52-4092	514th FIS	To 86th FIW 06/5/58
52-4095		To 86th FIW 06/5/58
52-4101	513th FIS	To 86th FIW 13/4/58
52-4113	513th FIS	To 86th FIW 13/4/58
52-4124	513th FIS,	
	514th FIS	To 86th FIW 21/4/58
52-4130	513th FIS	To 86th FIW 13/4/58
52-4131	514th FIS	To 86th FIW 21/4/58
52-4135		To 86th FIW 17/3/55
52-4137	512th FIS	To 86th FIW 19/5/58
52-4138	513th FIS	To 86th FIW 13/5/58
52-4140	513th FIS	To 86th FIW 06/5/58
52-4141	514th FIS	Crashed at Manston 19/11/56, To Burtonwood and scrapped 30/6/59
52-4144		To 86th FIW 16/3/55
52-4145	514th FIS	To 86th FIW 16/3/55
52-4148	514th FIS	To 86th FIW 21/4/58
52-4151	512th FIS	To 86th FIW 19/3/58
52-4162	512th FIS	To 86th FIW 19/3/58
52-4167	514th FIS	To 86th FIW 21/4/58
52-4171	513th FIS	To 86th FIW 13/4/58
52-4185	512th FIS	To 86th FIW 24/4/58

F-86D-50, delivered October 1954 – February 1955

Serial	Squadron	Remarks
52-4200	513th FIS	To 86th FIW 13/4/58
52-4203	512th FIS	To 86th FIW 19/3/58
52-4204	514th FIS	To FIAT Turin 30/4/58
52-4208	512th FIS	To 86th FIW 13/4/58
52-4209	513th FIS	To 86th FIW 13/4/58
52-4210	513th FIS	To 86th FIW 13/4/58
52-4215	513th FIS	W/o 18/8/56
52-4216	513th FIS	W/o Tille, France 01/11/56, pilot 1st. Lt. R L Zbornak ejected OK

Serial	Squadron	Remarks
52-4219	513th FIS	To 86th FIW 13/4/58
52-4222	512th FIS	To 86th FIW 19/4/58
52-4224	513th FIS	To 86th FIW 13/4/58
52-4225	512th FIS	W/o in North Sea 30/10/57, 1st. Lt. David W Johnson presumed dead
52-4226	513th FIS	To 86th FIW 13/4/58
52-4229	513th FIS	To 86th FIW 13/4/58
52-4230	512th FIS	To 86th FIW 19/3/58
52-4245	513th FIS	W/o in Tyrrhenean Sea off Sicily 27/2/57, pilot 1st. Lt. R Platenburg OK
52-4277		To 431st FIS 30/9/56
52-4296	512th FIS	To FIAT Turin 07Jan58
52-4304	514th FIS	To 86th FIW 21/4/58
52-9996		To 86th FIW
52-10012	514th FIS	
52-10019	514th FIS	
52-10028	512th FIS	To 86th FIW
52-10029	512th FIS	
52-10030	512th FIS	
52-10033	514th FIS	To 86th FIW
52-10034	513th FIS,	
	514th FIS	
52-10035	512th FIS	To 86th FIW
52-10037	512th FIS	
52-10039	513th FIS,	
	514th FIS	
52-10041		To 86th FIW
52-10044	512th FIS	To 86th FIW
52-10045	512th FIS	
52-10050	512th FIS	To 86th FIW
52-10053	512th FIS,	
	514th FIS	To 86th FIW
52-10055	512th FIS	
52-10056	513th FIS	W/o near Castellamare, Sicily 27/2/57, pilot John Hutson OK
52-10061	514th FIS	To 86th FIW
52-10065	512th FIS	To 86th FIW
52-10067	514th FIS	To 86th FIW
52-10072		
52-10074		To 86th FIW
52-10082	512th FIS	
52-10086		
52-10110	512th FIS	To 86th FIW
52-10130	514th FIS	To 86th FIW

F-86D-60-NA

Serial	Squadron
53-898	Yuma Rocketry Team /56
53-1041	Yuma Rocketry Team /56
53-1058	Yuma Rocketry Team /56
53-3699	Yuma Rocketry Team /56
53-4051	Yuma Rocketry Team /56
53-4064	Yuma Rocketry Team /56

North American F-86F Sabre

F-86F-25-NH

Serial	Squadron	Remarks
51-13371	514th FBS	To 7559th Maint Gp Burtonwood 22/11/54
51-13410	514th FBS	To 7559th Maint Gp Burtonwood 22/11/54
51-13420		To Scottish Aviation Prestwick 17/12/54
51-13435	514th FBS	To 7559th Maint Gp Burtonwood 22/11/54
51-13449	514th FBS	To Scottish Aviation Prestwick 18/1/55
51-13456	514th FBS	To Scottish Aviation Prestwick 18/1/55
51-13460		To Scottish Aviation Prestwick 15/12/54
51-13464	512th FBS	To 512th FDS Soesterburg 13/12/54
51-13465	514th FBS?	W/o Nouasseur 23/4/54
51-13471		To 7559th Maint Gp Burtonwood 22/11/54
51-13474		To 7559th Maint Gp Burtonwood 21/9/54
51-13475		To Scottish Aviation Prestwick 15/12/54
51-13477	514th FBS	To Scottish Aviation Prestwick 20/12/54
51-13478	514th FBS, 512th FBS	To 512th FDS Soesterburg 14/12/54
51-13479		To Scottish Aviation Prestwick 17/12/54
51-13480	514th FBS	To Scottish Aviation Prestwick 22/12/54
51-13484		W/o 04/12/54
51-13485	514th FBS, 512th FBS	To 512th FDS Soesterburg 13/12/54
51-13488		To 7559th Maint Gp Burtonwood 21Sep54
51 13490	514th FBS	W/o Norfolk, 04/10/54, 2nd. Lt. J D Smith killed
51-13491	514th FBS	To Scottish Aviation Prestwick 17/12/54
51-13495		To Scottish Aviation Prestwick 22/12/54
51-13499		To 7559th Maint Gp Burtonwood 24/9/54
51-13501		To Scottish Aviation Prestwick 20/12/54
51-13502		To Scottish Aviation Prestwick 13/1/55
51-13503	514th FBS	To Scottish Aviation Prestwick 22/12/54
51-13504		To Scottish Aviation Prestwick 15/12/54
51-13505		To Scottish Aviation Prestwick 13/1/55
51-13508	514th FBS	To Scottish Aviation Prestwick 17/12/54
51-13509		W/o Manston 02/12/53, Capt L F Barrows killed
51-13510		To 7280th Maint Gp Nouasseur 23/4/54
52-5272	512th FBS	To 512th FDS Soesterburg 13/12/54
52-5273	512th FBS	To 512th FDS Soesterburg 13/12/54
52-5274		To 512th FDS Soesterburg 13/12/54
52-5275	512th FBS	To 512th FDS Soesterburg 13/12/54
52-5276	512th FBS	To 512th FDS Soesterburg 13/12/54
52-5281	512th FBS	To 512th FDS Soesterburg 13/12/54
52-5284	512th FBS	To 512th FDS Soesterburg 13/12/54
52-5285	512th FBS	To 512th FDS Soesterburg 13/12/54
52-5286	513th FBS	To Scottish Aviation 1954
52-5287	512th FBS	To 512th FDS Soesterburg 13/12/54
52-5291	512th FBS	To 512th FDS Soesterburg 13/12/54
52-5293	512th FBS	To 512th FDS Soesterburg 13/12/54
52-5302	513th FBS, 512th FBS	To 512th FDS Soesterburg 13/12/54
52-5303	513th FBS	To Scottish Aviation 1954
52-5308	512th FBS	To 512th FDS Soesterburg 13/12/54
52-5311	512th FBS	To 512th FDS Soesterburg 13/12/54
52-5312	513th FBS, 512th FBS	To 512th FDS Soesterburg 13/12/54
52-5314	512th FBS	To 512th FDS Soesterburg 13/12/54
52-5315	512th FBS	To 512th FDS Soesterburg 13/12/54
52-5316	512th FBS	To 512th FDS Soesterburg 13/12/54
52-5317	512th FBS	To 512th FDS Soesterburg 13/12/54
52-5318	512th FBS	To 512th FDS Soesterburg 13/12/54
52-5330	512th FBS	To 512th FDS Soesterburg 13/12/54
52-5331	512th FBS	To 512th FDS Soesterburg 13/12/54
52-5332	513th FBS	To Scottish Aviation 1954
52-5334	512th FBS	To 512th FDS Soesterburg 13/12/54
52-5337	513th FBS	To Scottish Aviation 1954

Serial	Squadron	Remarks
52-5350	512th FBS	To 512th FDS Soesterburg 13/12/54
52-5357	512th FBS	To 512th FDS Soesterburg 13/12/54
52-5384	512th FBS	To 512th FDS Soesterburg 13/12/54
52-5407	513th FBS	To Scottish Aviation 1954
52-5418	512th FBS	To 512th FDS Soesterburg 13/12/54

North American RB-45C Tornado

Detached from Barksdale AFB January-May 1951

Serial	Squadron	Remarks
48-019	91st RW	
48-021	91st RW	
48-023	91st RW	
48-026	91st RW	
48-027	91st RW	
48-029	91st RW	
48-038	91st RW	

North American T-6F

Serial	Squadron	Remarks
44-81727	406th FBW	
44-81730	406th FBW	
44-81777	406th FBW	
44-81785	406th FBW	

Republic F-84D Thunderjet

20th FBW: 55th FBS blue, 77th FBS red, 79th FBS yellow

F-84D-5-RE

Serial	Squadron	Remarks
48-696	79th FBS	To Republic
48-699		W/o 07Sep50 over West Germany, pilot killed
48-702	77th FBS	To FEAF
48-704	79th FBS	To Republic
48-708	77th FBS	To instructional airframe, Amarillo, Texas
48-709	77th FBS	To Republic
48-710	77th FBS	Dbr after overshot runway, Waterbeach 05/9/50, Charles A King
48-711	79th FBS	To Republic
48-712	79th FBS	To Republic
48-713	77th FBS	To 2500th ABG, Mitchel Field, NY
48-715	79th FBS	To FEAF
48-716	55th FBS	To Republic
48-717	77th FBS	
48-718	77th FBS	
48-720	79th FBS	To Republic
48-721	79th FBS	To Republic
48-722	79th FBS	To Republic
48-723	79th FBS	W/o 05/8/50, crashed in Channel, Lewis R Striegle killed
48-724	79th FBS	To Republic

Serial	Squadron	Remarks
48-725	77th FBS	To Republic
48-726		W/o 25/7/50, en-route to Bluie West 1, pilot drowned
48-727	55th FBS	To Republic
48-728	77th FBS	To Republic
48-729	77th FBS	
48-731	79th FBS	To Republic
48-732	55th FBS	W/o at Shaw AFB after return to US
48-733	79th FBS	To Republic

F-84D-10-RE

Serial	Squadron	Remarks
48-746	55th FBS	To Republic
48-748	79th FBS	To Republic
48-749	55th FBS, 77th FBS	To Republic
48-751	79th FBS	To Republic
48-753	77th FBS, 79th FBS	To Republic
48-754	77th FBS	W/o 18/9/50 after mid-air with Meteor VW431, Charles E Wilson killed
48-755	79th FBS	To Republic
48-756	77th FBS	To Republic
48-758	55th FBS	To Republic
48-759		W/o 07/9/50 over West Germany, pilot killed
48-760	79th FBS	To Republic
48-762	55th FBS	W/o 20/11/50, crashed in Channel, pilot killed
48-764	55th FBS	To Republic
48-765	79th FBS	To 363rd TRG
48-766	55th FBS	
48-767	55th FBS	To Republic
48-768	55th FBS	To 3200th Wing, Eglin AFB
48-769	55th FBS	
48-770	55th FBS	To 78th FIG
48-771	55th FBS	To 363rd TRG
48-772	55th FBS	To Republic
48-773	55th FBS	To Brookley AMC
48-774	55th FBS	To Republic
48-775	55th FBS	To Republic
48-776	55th FBS	To Republic
48-777		To Republic
48-778	79th FBS	To Republic
48-779	77th FBS	W/o at Shaw AFB 22/12/50
48-781	77th FBS	To 3595th Wing, Nellis AFB
48-782	77th FBS	To Republic
48-783	77th FBS	To Republic
48-784	77th FBS	To Republic
48-785	77th FBS	To Republic
48-787		Undershot at Manston 08/8/50, John J Walsh OK
48-788		W/o on mission from Manston 31/10/50
48-789	77th FBS	To 363rd TRG
48-790	79th FBS	To 363rd TRG

Serial	Squadron	Remarks
48-791	79th FBS	To Republic
48-792	79th FBS	To 363rd TRG
48-793	55th FBS	To 363rd TRG
48-794	79th FBS	To Republic

Republic F-84E Thunderjet

31st FEW: 307th FES red, 308th FES yellow, 309th FES blue

12th FEW: 559th FES red, 560th FES yellow, 561st FES blue

123rd FBW: 156th FBS yellow, 165th FBS red, 167th FBS blue

406th FBW: 512th FBS yellow, 513th FBS red, 514th FBS blue

F-84E-1-RE

Serial	Squadron / Remarks
49-2023	31st FEW, 12th FEW, 123rd FBW, 406th FBW To Burtonwood
49-2032	309th FES, 12th FEW, 123rd FBW, 513th FBS To 3600th PTW, Luke AFB
49-2034	31st FEW, 560th FES. W/o Mildenhall 19/10/51, Wayne R Finch killed
49-2038	31st FEW, 12th FEW, 123rd FBW, 406th FBW To Burtonwood 19/9/53
49-2042	309th FES, 12th FEW, 123rd FBW, 512th FBS To 3645th Wing, Laughlin AFB
49-2043	308th FES, 12th FEW, 123rd FBW, 512th FBS, 513th FBS. To 3595th Wing, Nellis AFB
49-2044	309th FES, 12th FEW, 167th FBS. W/o 27/3/52, Capt Charles E Mack killed
49-2045	31st FEW, 12th FEW, 123rd FBW, 512th FBS To 3645th Wing, Laughlin AFB
49-2047	309th FES, 12th FEW, 123rd FBW, 406th FBW. To 3645th Wing, Laughlin AFB
49-2051	309th FES, 12th FEW, 123rd FBW, 406th FBW. To 3645th Wing, Laughlin AFB
49-2053	307th FES, 12th FEW, 167th FBS. W/o Vianden, Luxembourg 04/12/51
49-2054	307th FES, 12th FEW, 123rd FBW, 512th FBS To 3600th Wing, Luke AFB
49-2055	308th FES. Dbr 26/6/51 after forced landing 5m N of Dover, w/o 29/6/51
49-2056	309th FES, 12th FEW, 123rd FBW, 513th FBS To 3645th Wing, Laughlin AFB
49-2057	309th FES, 12th FEW, 167th FBS W/o after landing accident 12/3/52
49-2059	309th FES, 12th FBW, 123rd FBW. To Burtonwood 59th AD 11/5/52
49-2060	308th FES, 12th FEW, 123rd FBW, 512th FBS To 3600th Wing, Luke AFB
49-2061	309th FES, 12th FEW, 123rd FBW, 512th FBS To 3600th Wing, to Luke AFB
49-2062	31st FEW, 12th FEW, 123rd FBW, 513th FBS W/o 06/2/53, midair with 49-2383 nr Deal. Lt. C Jones killed
49-2063	309th FES, 12th FEW, 123rd FBW, 513th FBS To 3645th Wing, Laughlin AFB

Serial	Squadron / Remarks
49-2064	308th FES, 12th FEW, 123rd FBW, 512th FBS To 3645th Wing, Laughlin AFB
49-2065	308th FES, 12th FEW, 123rd FBW, 406th FBW. To 3645th Wing, Laughlin AFB
49-2066	31st FEW, 12th FEW, 123rd FBW, 512th FBS, 513th FBS. To 3600th Wing, Luke AFB
49-2068	308th FES, 12th FEW, 123rd FBW, 512th FBS. To 3600th Wing, Luke AFB
49-2069	309th FES, 12th FEW, 123rd FBW, 514th FBS. To 3645th Wing, Laughlin AFB
49-2071	307th FES, 309th FES, 12th FEW, 123rd FBW, 513th FBS. Crashed in sea off Dover 30/11/52, Capt. R Denanny rescued
49-2072	307th FES, 12th FEW, 123rd FBW, 406th FBW. To 3600th Wing, Luke AFB
49-2073	309th FES, 561st FES, 123rd FBW, 513th FBS. To 3600th Wing, Luke AFB
49-2074	308th FES, 12th FEW, 156th FBS. W/o 14/5/52, crashed 1 m from Foreness Point. Pilot Capt. C K Walker rescued
49-2075	307th FES, 12th FEW, 123rd FBW, 513th FBS. To 3645th Wing, Laughlin AFB
49-2076	309th FES, 12th FEW, 123rd FBW, 406th FBW. To 3600th Wing, Luke AFB
49-2078	309th FES, 12th FEW, 123rd FBW, 406th FBW. To Brookley AMC 06/7/53
49-2079	307th FES. W/o 21/6/51 after ground collision with 49-2090 and subsequent fire at Manston
49-2081	308th FES, 12th FEW, 123rd FBW, 406th FBW. To 3600th Wing, Luke AFB
49-2082	307th FES, 12th FEW, 123rd FBW, 513th FBS. To 3645th Wing, Laughlin AFB
49-2084	308th FES, 12th FEW, 123rd FBW (406th FBW?). To 3645th Wing, Laughlin AFB
49-2088	308th FES, 12th FEW crashed in sea off North Foreland 13/9/51, George D Lee killed
49-2090	307th FES, 12th FEW, 123rd FBW, 513th FBS
49-2094	309th FES, 12th FEW, 123rd FBW, (514th FBS?). To 3600th Wing, Luke AFB
49-2095	309th FES, 12th FEW, 123rd FBW, 406th FBW. To 3645th Wing, Laughlin AFB
49-2097	308th FES, 12th FEW, 123rd FBW, 406th FBW. To 3645th Wing, Laughlin AFB
49-2099	307th FES, 12th FEW, 123rd FBW, 513th FBS. To 3645th Wing, Laughlin AFB?
49-2101	307th FES, 12th FEW, 123rd FBW, 513th FBS. To 3645th Wing, Laughlin AFB
49-2102	307th FES, 12th FEW, 123rd FBW, 512th FBS. To 3645th Wing, Laughlin AFB
49-2103	309th FES, 12th FEW, 406th FBW. To 3645th Wing, Laughlin AFB
49-2105	308th FES. Crashed Nash Lane, Margate 24/1/51, pilot Cmdr W D Biggers USN, killed

Serial	Squadron / Remarks
49-2109	309th FES, 12th FEW, 123rd FBW, 406th FBW. To 3645th Wing, Laughlin AFB
49-2111	307th FES, 12th FEW, 165th FBS. Crashed at St Peters 27/4/52, pilot Capt. C Fogarty and 3 people on ground killed
49-2112	309th FES, 561st FES, 123rd FBW, 513th FBS. To 3600th Wing, Luke AFB
49-2117	307th FES, 12th FEW, 123rd FBW, 406th FBW. To 3645th Wing, Laughlin AFB
49-2118	307th FES, 12th FEW, 123rd FBW, 406th FBW. To 3600th Wing, Luke AFB
49-2121	31st FEW, 12th FEW, 123rd FBW, 406th FBW. To 3645th Wing, Laughlin AFB

F-84E-5-RE

Serial	Squadron / Remarks
49-2212	406th FBW. To 406th from 86th FBW 08/5/53, to 3645th Wing, Laughlin AFB
49-2214	406th FBW. To 406th from 86th FBW 08/5/53, to 3645th Wing, Laughlin AFB
49-2220	406th FBW. To 406th from 86th FBW 08/5/53, to 3600th Wing, Luke AFB
49-2244	512th FBS. To 406th from 86th FBW 28/5/53, to 3645th Wing, Laughlin AFB

F-84E-15-RE

Serial	Squadron / Remarks
49-2327	31st FEW, 12th FEW, 123rd FBW. Dbr at Manston 31(?)/3/52, to 59th AD Burtonwood 14/7/52, w/o 17/9/52
49-2328	31st FEW, 12th FEW, 123rd FBW, 512th FBS. To 3645th Wing, Laughlin AFB
49-2329	307th FES, 12th FEW, 123rd FBW. To Brookley AMC by 17/9/53
49-2330	31st FEW, 12th FEW, 123rd FBW, 513th FBS, burned out at Manston 20/1/54
49-2332	309th FES, 12th FEW, 167th FBS, 406th FBW (514th FBS?). To 3600th Wing, Luke AFB
49-2342	307th FES, 12th FEW, 123rd FBW, 513th FBS. Crashed on Dengie Flats Range 29/7/52, 1st.Lt. J E Sims killed
49-2344	307th FES, (12th FEW?), 123rd FBW, 406th FBW. To 59th AD, Burtonwood 16/8/53
49-2345	308th FES, 309th FES, 12th FEW, 123rd FBS, 513th FBS. To Bentwaters?
49-2346	31st FEW, 12th FEW. W/o 25(?)/8/51 on deployment to Norway, Capt Bryce Long rescued
49-2347	309th FES, 12th FEW, 123rd FBW, 513th FBS. Crashed in sea off Margate 04/9/52, Capt. R Nemer killed
49-2348	309th FES, 12th FEW, 123rd FBW, 406th FBW. To 3645th Wing, Laughlin AFB, now on display Rickenbacker ANG Base, Ohio
49-2349	308th FES, 12th FEW, 123rd FBW, 406th FBW. W/o after in-flight fire near Deal 20/8/52

Serial	Squadron / Remarks
49-2350	308th FES, 12th FEW, 123rd FBW, 512th FBS. To 3645th Wing, Laughlin AFB
49-2357	309th FES, 12th FEW, 123rd FBW, 514th FBS. To 3645th Wing, Laughlin AFB
49-2362	308th FES, 12th FEW, 123rd FBW. To 3645th Wing, Laughlin AFB
49-2363	309th FES, 12th FEW, 167th FBS. Badly dam aged during engine run-up Manston 25/5/52, to 59th AD Burtonwood 22/6/53
49-2368	307th FES, 12th FEW. W/o 18/9/51
49-2371	307th FES, 12th FEW, 123rd FBW, 512th FBS. To 3645th Wing, Laughlin AFB
49-2372	309th FES, 12th FEW, 123rd FBW, 406th FBW. To 3645th Wing, Laughlin AFB
49-2374	308th FES, 12th FEW, 123rd FBW, 406th FBW. To 3645th Wing, Laughlin AFB
49-2379	307th FES, 123rd FBW, 513th FBS. Badly damaged at Manston 13Mar51 after forced landing, to 3645th Wing, Laughlin AFB
49-2383	308th FES, 12th FEW, 123rd FBW, 514th FBS. W/o 06/2/53 after midair with 49-2062 nr Deal; Capt. P Conserva killed
49-2391	309th FES, 12th FEW, 123rd FBW, 512th FBS. To 3645th Wing, Laughlin AFB

F-84E-25-RE

Serial	Squadron	Remarks
51-569	513th FBS	

F-84E-30-RE

Serial	Squadron	Remarks
51-609	406th FBW	
51-616	512th FBS	
51-639	514th FBS	
51-640	513th FBS	Wing CO's aircraft
51-642	513th FBS	Sqn CO's aircraft
51-645	12th FEW, 123rd FBW, 512th FBS.	Col. Cy Wilson's aircraft

Republic F-84F Thunderstreak
F-84F-35-RE

Serial	Squadron	Remarks
51-17074	92nd FBS	
52-6424	92nd FBS	
52-6445	92nd FBS	
52-6452	92nd FBS	
52-6516	92nd FBS	
52-6521	92nd FBS	Crashed Cliffsend 09/6/55, pilot 1st. Lt. John Caswell OK
52-7018	92nd FBS	
52-7039	92nd FBS	
52-7044	92nd FBS	

F-84F-45-RE

Serial	Squadron	Remarks
52-6648	92nd FBS	To Luftwaffe 58/59 as DE-113
52-6704	92nd FBS	To Luftwaffe 58/59 as DE-374

Serial	Squadron	Remarks
52-6712	92nd FBS	To Luftwaffe 58/59 as DD-255
52-6737	92nd FBS	To Luftwaffe 58/59 as DD-244
52-6743	92nd FBS	To Luftwaffe 58/59 as DD-326
52-6746	92nd FBS	To Luftwaffe 58/59 as DD-239
52-6764	92nd FBS	To Luftwaffe 58/59 as DD-375
52-6778	92nd FBS	To Luftwaffe 58/59 as BF-105
52-6784	92nd FBS	Played 'MiG' in *Iron Petticoat*, noted in burnt condition at Burtonwood 5/58
52-6788	92nd FBS	To Luftwaffe 58/59 as DE-107
52-6794	92nd FBS	To Luftwaffe 58/59 as DD-349
52-6800	92nd FBS	
52-6806	92nd FBS	To Luftwaffe 58/59 as DE-118
52-6808	92nd FBS	To Luftwaffe 58/59 as DD-370
52-6812	92nd FBS	Marked 'USAFE Champs'
52-7090	92nd FBS	To Luftwaffe 58/59 as DE-114
52-7096	92nd FBS	Crashed Cleve Court, Manston 14/6/56, pilot Lt T Adams OK
52-7098	92nd FBS	To Luftwaffe 58/59 as DE-275
52-7101	92nd FBS	To Luftwaffe 58/59 as DD-366
52-7107	92nd FBS	To Luftwaffe 58/59 as DD-338

F-84F-50-RE

Serial	Squadron	Remarks
52-6825	92nd FBS	To Luftwaffe 58/59 as DD-362
52-6877	92nd FBS	

Sikorsky SH-19A Chickasaw

Serial	Squadron	Remarks
51-3878	66th ARS	Arrived 10/54, to 67th ARS 01/9/55
51-3879	66th ARS	Arrived Manston 1/54, to 67th ARS 08/9/55
51-3889	66th ARS	Arrived 03/8/52, crashed near Manston, 7/53, to 59th ADW Burtonwood 15/7/53
51-3890	66th ARS	Arrived 03/8/52, to 3510th CCTW Randolph AFB TX 31/12/56
51-3893	9th, 66th ARS	'Hopalong', to 3510th CCTW Randolph AFB TX 31/12/56

Sikorsky SH-19B Chickasaw

Serial	Squadron	Remarks
53-4458	66th ARS	Arrived 23/9/56, to 67th ARS 09/10/57
53-4459	66th ARS	Arrived 23/9/56, to 67th ARS 13/10/57

Stinson L-5 Sentinel

Serial	Unit	Remarks
*	406th FBW	
*	406th FBW	

APPENDIX 2
Bibliography

Books

Ashworth, Chris, Action Stations 9. *Military Airfields of the Central South and South East*, PSL, Wellingborough, England, 1985, 313pp, ISBN 0-85059-608-4

Bowyer, Michael J.F., *Force for Freedom*, PSL, Sparkford, England, 1994, 232pp, ISBN 1-85260-415-8

406th FIW, *406th Fighter Interceptor Wing, 406th FIW*, Manston, England, 1955, 100pp.

Robert Jackson, *Strike Force - The USAF in Britain Since 1948*, Robson Books, London, England, 1986, 182pp, ISBN 0-86051-303-3

Kevin Keaveney, Aerofax Minigraph 15 *Republic F-84 (Swept-Wing Variants)*, Aerofax Inc., Arlington, USA, 1987, 48pp, ISBN 0-942548-20-5

John C. McLure and Charlotte S. McLure, *Follow Me - The Life and Times of David C. Schilling*, Taylor Publishing Co, Dallas, USA, 1995, 148pp, Library of Congress Catalogue Card No. 94-96715.

RAF Manston History Club, *RAF Manston in Old Photos*, Allan Sutton, Stroud, England, 1993, ISBN 0-7509-0135-7

Jack H. Smith, *The Coonskin Boys Men and Mustangs of the 167th Fighter Squadron West Virginia Air National Guard*, Pictorial Histories Publishing Co., Charleston, USA, 1987, 46pp, ISBN 0-933126-86-7

Rocky Stockman, *The History of RAF Manston*, RAF Manston, England, 1986, 128pp, ISBN 0-9511298-0-5

Office of History, USAFE, *Forty-Five Years of Vigilance for Freedom: USAF in Europe, 1942-1987*, USAF, 1987, 294pp.

Magazines

The Aeroplane
April 8, 1955; 'Dogs' on Watch, Staff
Air Classics
March 1987; Kentucky Air National Guard, Tom Ivie
Air International
November 1995; High Tide, Rene J. Francillon
Flight
? 1955, Exercise *Beware*

29th April 1955, Automatic Interception

General Electric Company Jet Service News

October 1978; GE Jet Engine Plant in Cincinatti Observes Thirtieth Year, Staff

The Saturday Evening Post

November 1, 1952; We Flew the Atlantic in Helicopters, Capt. Vincent H. McGovern

June 4, 1955; Adventures of the Death-Cheaters, Lawrence Earl

Unknown

?, 1956; Playback-NADAR Helps Keep Score During the 1956 Rocketry Meet, James Carey

Newspapers

Air Force Daily

Monday February 22, 1954; 5,828 Hours Without an Accident, Staff

East Kent Times & Broadstairs Mail

15th July, 1950; American Jets for Manston

22nd July, 1950; Official welcome for American Airmen

20th June, 1956; Three Escape in Jet Crash

The Saber (Manston Newspaper, previously *SaCk TaCk*),

Vol.2 No.1, Wednesday, August 25, 1954; 513th Operations Officer Dead in Sabre Crash, Staff

Vol.2 No.15, Thursday December 2, 1954; Manston Aircraft Lead in Sea Rescue Drama,Staff/Saber Salutes Manston Lifesavers, Staff

Vol.4 No.21, Thursday May 24, 1956; Fighter Squadron Sets New Record, Staff/Rescue Ramblings, Staff

Vol.4 No.36, Thursday September 6, 1956; Rocketry Team Departs for Arizona Next Week, Staff

Vol.5 No.13, Thursday March 28, 1957; Will Manston Regain the Rocketry Crown?, Staff

Vol.5 No.14, Thursday April 4, 1957; 513th Smashes Rocketry Records in Tripoli

Vol.5 No.16, Thursday April 18, 1957; 512th to go to Wheelus AFB, Tripoli This Month, Staff

Vol.5 No.29, Thursday July 18, 1957; Manston - Best Base in UK, Staff

Vol.5 No.40, Thursday October 3, 1957; Hughes Trophy Unveiled/Manston Airman in USAFE Roadeo, Staff

SaCk TaCk (Manston Newspaper, re-named *The Saber* from Vol. 2 No. 1)

Vol.1 No. 1, Wednesday 16 December 1953; For the Best in the UK -Use Manston GCA, Staff

Sembach Jet Gazette

Monday, June 16, 1958, 512th, AF's Top Ftr Sq. in '57, Out to Repeat in '58, G. Franklin Fox

?, 86 'Dogs' Growl No More; 512th, Top AF Unit, Retires, Staff

Thanet Advertiser & Echo

14th July 1950; Americans are Coming

8th August 1950; I Hope You Will Like the Americans

26th September 1950; Lunch at Manston, Supper in America

29th September 1950; Americans Help to Fight Big Farm Fire

10th October 1950; Failure Would Have Meant Death — Escaping Czechs Fly to Manston

Thanet Gazette

28th July 1950; Welcome to the Yanks.

4th August 1950; Hush Hush.

25th August 1950; Low Flying Will Go On.

20th October 1950; Flaming Bomber Seen On Waterfront.

26th January 1951; Jet Crashes In Garden.

1st February 1952; American Colonel Wants Clean Up.

2nd May 1952; Jets Dive On St. Peters: 3 Killed.

16th May 1952; US Jets Grounded After Second Crash.

23rd May 1952; No Cause Given For St. Peters Jet Crash.

30th May 1952; Jet 'Sabotage': No Evidence.

11th July 1952; Manston Air Base The Safest.

1st August 1952; Manston US Pilot Killed.

4th September 1952; Pilot Dies In Sands Crash.

17th October 1952; US Commander Leaves.

7th November 1952; New American CO Here.

21st November 1952; Doctor Is Dropped On Jetty From Helicopter.

5th December 1952; They Call Him The Hover Doctor.

27th March 1953; US Fliers Decorated.

12th June 1953;

1. Eyes From The Skies Will Make Thanet Resorts Safest.

2. US Stratojets Here.

4th September 1953; Supersonic Booms May Shake Thanet.

25th September 1953; A Mayor's Eye View.

9th October 1953; Air Sea Rescue Zone Opposed.

4th December 1953; US Pilot Killed.

24th December 1953; Santa Stayed In Mid Air.

15th January 1954; More USAF Jobs For Thanet Men.

7th May 1954; Cambodian Had First Jet Trip.

16th July 1954;

1. Minewatchers And USAF Cooperate.

2. Sabre Jets In Exercise.

27th August 1954; US Major Killed In Jet Crash.

15th October 1954; US Pilot Killed.

29th October 1954; 21 Manston Airmen Missing In Vanished Plane.

5th November 1954; 21 Died In Air Crash.

3rd December 1954; Lightship Disaster - Why?

11th February 1955; Did Not Need His Crossbow!

18th February 1955; Crash Pilot Was Hopped To Base.

1st April 1955; Parachute Makes Landing Safe.

27th May 1955; Manston Open Day Was Over Before It Began.

10th June 1955;

1. Out For The Day When Jet Plane Hit Her House.

2. Saved From Sea On Fire.

22nd July 1955; Steps To Avoid Jet Nuisance.

19th August 1955;

1. Helicopter Gave Warning.

2. A-Bomber Rumour Scotched.

26th August 1955; Negro GI Went Beserk-Killed Three.

16th September 1955; USAF Jets To Stay At Manston.

11th November 1955; Manston The Safest.

20th January 1956; 40 Bungalows For USAF.

15th June 1956; Jet Wrecked Lady Carson's Wall-And Gooseberries.

27th July 1956; Air Secretary Promises MP To Probe Jet Nuisance.

17th August 1956; Crashed In Sea.

7th September 1956; Jets Will Fly On Battle Of Britain Sunday.

5th October 1956; Russian 'Invasion'.

12th October 1956; Some Jets To Leave Thanet.

26th October 1956; The Flying Mayors.

2nd November 1956; Runway May Go Further West Says Minister.

25th November 1956; Pilot Lost Control When Plane's Tyre Burst.

1st February 1957;

1. Manston May Be Debated In Congress.

2. Most Famous Helicopter Leaves.

1st March 1957;

1. Those Jet Noises.

2. Sabre Pilots Baled Out Over Med.

8th March 1957; Jet Kills Airman.

22nd March 1957; Jets May Go To New Site For 'Revving Up'.

29th March 1957; Jet Noise Nuisance On TV.

26th April 1957; Less Jet Noise At Whitsun.

3rd May 1957; Jet Noises Penalty Of Speed Age.

10th May 1957;

1. Jet Noise Probe.

2. New US Air Rescue Chief.

17th May 1957;

1. Famous Air Rescue Squadron To Disband.

2. Practical Test For Jet Noise Committee.

24th May 1957; 'Open Day' At Manston Air Base.

5th July 1957; Sea Search For Political Refugee.

6th September 1957; Americans Off Next April?

20th September 1957; Jets In NATO Exercise.

27th September 1957; 'Jet Noise Is Driving Me Mad' Says Col. Manson.

8th November 1957; Jet Sound Track For Premier.

15th November 1957; Missing Jets: No News.

17th January 1958;

1. Americans Going Home?

2. US Pilot Killed.

24th January 1958;

1. It's Goodbye To The Yanks.

2. Plane Crashed-Caught Fire.

7th February 1958;

1. Plane's Wing Hit Snowbank.

2. What Is The Future Of Manston Airfield?

14th March 1958; Birchington Says 'Au Revoir' To Americans.

21st March 1958; 'Farewell' Parade At Manston.

3rd April 1958; The '406th' Say Farewell To Thanet.

11th April 1958; Four Killed When Jet Hit Car.

18th April 1958; Did Empty Fuel Tank Cause Jet Crash?

Thanet Times, various, 1950-58, microfilmed records Ramsgate Library

UK Eagle

Vol.6 No.31, Friday December 3, 1954; Manston Helicopter Crew in Dramatic Rescue at Sea, T/Sgt Bert Tavender

Vol.10 No.14, Friday April 4, 1958; Kent Takes the 406th's Salute, Staff

Unknown sources

?, ?,November 1950, Jet Pilots Fly Amid Danger, Even When They're Training, William McGaffin, Arkansas Gazette-Chicago News Service

?, Thursday, May 30, 1957, 512th Breaks USAFE Record, Staff

?, Thursday, July 11, 1957, 512th Sq Named Trophy Winner, Staff

?, ?, 512th FIS Members Going to Washington, Staff

? August, 1957, Manston Rocket Aces Training for U.S. Meet, Staff

Miscellaneous

USAF Historical Records Agency, Maxwell AFB:

20th FBW History July 50-September 52, Microfilm roll M0524

12th FEW History December 50-June 52, Microfilm roll M0453

31st FEW History July 50-March 52, Microfilm roll M0597

123rd FBW History October 50-June 52, Microfilm roll N0167

406th FIW History, 1953, Microfilm roll

512th FBS History July 1953, Microfilm roll K0507

81st Fighter Wing History, Stewart S. Stabley, privately published

Press release, Office of Information Services, 406th FIW, 21 August 1956; Europe's Top Jet Rocketry Team.

USAFE,date?, *History of the Skyblazers*

Office of History 20th Fighter Wing, Final Edition-*History of the 20th Fighter Wing and RAF Upper Heyford*, December 1993

3rd AF History Office, *A History of Third Air Force 1940-1988*, August 1989

USAF, *USAF Aircraft Basing in Europe, North Africa, and the Middle East, 1945-1980*, Larry Benson

Records held at the Public Record Office in Kew, London:

USAF Fighter Squadrons in the UK   AIR8 1477

USAF Bases in Europe   AIR8 1478

USAF Range Requirements in UK   AIR 2 10518

RAF Fighter Command Exercise Reports AIR 8 and 16 series

RAF Fighter Command USAF Stations   AIR 8 1662

RAF Manston Station Records:

February 1949 - December 1950   AIR28 1075

January 1951 - December 1955   AIR28 1245

January 1956 - December 1960   AIR28 1397

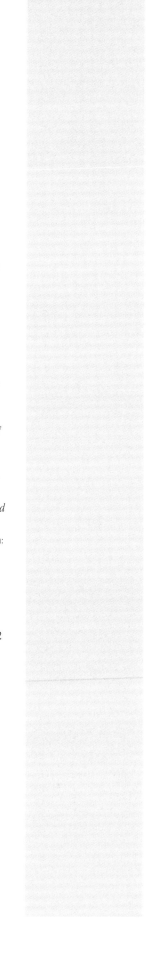

INDEX

230 Above: *This 1955 photo shows 513th FIS aircraft in various markings states. 52-4200 at front has the 'harpoon' design but no 513th badge, 52-4219 to its left has similar markings but with the Wing commander's 406th FIW badge on the fuselage. 52-4113 on the right wing is still showing the early-style slanted tail bands and finally, 52-4082 has the full 513th 'harpoon' colour scheme and also wears a 406th FIW badge. The leading pair are F-86D-50s, those at right being F-86D-45s. At this point, no 1951-fiscal year F-86D-36s had been delivered to the wing. (via Dave Keep)*
231: *A typical publicity shot showing the weapons capable of being carried by the F-84F Thunderstreak. Probably the stores of most interest, and of most importance to Manston's 92nd FBS, are the large black 'objects' either side of the rockets which appear to be nuclear weapons.*
232: *An F-86D engine being loaded onto a C-119, Sabres of the 514th FIS can be seen in the background. Physical distance between the western taxiway and the 514th's eastern dispersal can be appreciated. (Cowles Bristol)*